The Muslim Brotherhood and the Kings of Jordan 1945–1993

South Florida-Rochester-Saint Louis
Studies on Religion and the Social Order

ISLAM AND THE WORLD SUBSERIES
Edited by Tamara Sonn

Volume 18

THE MUSLIM BROTHERHOOD
AND THE KINGS OF JORDAN
1945–1993

by
Marion Boulby

The Muslim Brotherhood and the Kings of Jordan 1945–1993

by

Marion Boulby

With a Foreword by John O. Voll

Scholars Press
Atlanta, Georgia

The Muslim Brotherhood and the Kings of Jordan 1945–1993

by
Marion Boulby

Published by Scholars Press for the University of South Florida, University of Rochester, and Saint Louis University

Funds for the publication of this volume were provided by
The Tyson and Naomi Midkiff Fund for Exellence
of the Department of Religious Studies at the University of South Florida
The Max Richter Foundation of Rhode Island
and
The Tisch Family Foundation of New York City

Library of Congress Cataloging in Publication Data

Boulby, Marion, 1961–
The Muslim Brotherhood and the kings of Jordan, 1945–1993 / by Marion Boulby; with a foreword by John O. Voll.
p. cm. — (South Florida-Rochester-Saint Louis studies on religion and the social order ; v. 18)
Includes bibliographical references and index.
ISBN 0-7885-0553-X (cloth : alk. paper)
1. Jamāʿat al-Ikhwān al-Muslimīn (Jordan)—History. 2. Islam and politics—Jordan. 3. Jordan—Politics and government—20th century. I. Title. II. Series.
BP63.J6B68 1999
322'.1'095695—dc21 99-20109
CIP

Printed in the United States of America
on acid-free paper

For my parents, Jean and Mark Boulby

TABLE OF CONTENTS

Foreword

by John O. Voll

The universal and the particular come together in the movements of religious resurgence in the final decades of the twentieth century. The Islamic Revolution in Iran, the rise of a Hindu party in India, and the emergence of the Christian Right in the United States are only parts of the worldwide resurgence of religion. In most regions of the world and in all major world religious traditions, this revival is an important aspect of national and international affairs. While this is a global phenomenon, it is expressed through many specific individuals and movements. Universal ideals and global networks of relationships find their foundations in particular local groups.

To understand this important part of contemporary world affairs, it is helpful to have a global analytical perspective.[1] However, it is essential to have in-depth studies of specific movements for the generalizations to have validity. Unfortunately, while there are many volumes on the general religious resurgence or religious resurgence in a major region or collections of short case studies, there are too few substantial studies of major movements. Marion Boulby provides such a substantive, in-depth study of a significant movement in her analysis of the Muslim Brotherhood in Jordan.

Boulby's research is specially important in developing a more complete understanding of the religious resurgence in the Muslim world. In many ways, the "Resurgence of Islam" has become the most visible of the major religious revivals. The late twentieth century resurgence is commonly identified as "fundamentalism." Even though that term originally applied to a Protestant Christian movement, in discussions of the current resurgence, "Islamic fundamentalism has become a metaphor for fundamentalism in general."[2] However, there are remarkably few volumes

---

1 See, for a good example of this more global approach, Roland Robertson and JoAnn Chirico, "Humanity, Globalization, and Worldwide Religious Resurgence: A Theoretical Exploration," *Sociological Analysis* 1985, 46:3: 219-242.

2 Bobby S. Sayyid, *A Fundamental Fear: Eurocentrism and the Emergence of Islamism* (London: Zed Books, 1997), p. 8.

on specific movements of Islamic revival.[3] Often country studies substitute for more in-depth analysis of actual movements. There have been many excellent books written, for example, about the Islamic revolution in Iran, the development of the subsequent Islamic republic, and "Islam in Iran." However, there are few book length studies of specific organizations, like the Pasdaran (Islamic Guards) or Mujahidin, which participated in the revolution or subsequent political developments.

Important features of the religious resurgence may be viewed differently sometimes as a result of the concrete study of a group like the Muslim Brotherhood in Jordan. The history presented by Boulby does not require a major revision of the understanding of the dynamics of the Islamic resurgence. However, it does suggest dimensions of the revival which do not receive as much attention as they should. Specifically, Boulby's study is a reminder that some aspects of the resurgence are not simply new features emerging in the late twentieth century, that the turn to Islam is not simply a last resort after all else has failed, and that Islamist movements are not inherently or necessarily movements of violent opposition to existing society.

The longevity and continuity of the modern Islamic revival are perhaps the most important aspects which get a new emphasis in Boulby's study. Most of the major works on the Islamic resurgence emphasize that it is a relatively recent phenomenon. R. Hrair Dekmejian, for example, begins the preface to the second edition (published in 1995) of his major study of "fundamentalism" in the Arab world with the statement: "The last two decades have seen the rise of Islamic activism in Muslim communities throughout the world."[4] Another scholar, even in a book emphasizing the continuity of the Muslim experience in the modern world, similarly begins the chapter on "the Resurgence of Islam" with the statement: "The last quarter of the twentieth century is a time of global transformation and reorientation, and in the early years of its fifteenth century, beginning in

---

[3] Richard Mitchell's study of the Muslim Brotherhood in Egypt, for example, was published originally in 1969 but it remains the standard work on the subject. See Richard P. Mitchell, *The Society of the Muslim Brothers* (New York: Oxford University Press, 1969; reprinted 1993). More recent important studies of major Islamist movements are Seyyed Vali Reza Nasr, *The Vanguard of the Islamic Revolution: The Jamaaʿat-i Islami of Pakistan* (Berkeley: University of California Press, 1994) and Abdelwahab El-Affendi, *Turabi's Revolution: Islam and Power in Sudan* (London: Grey Seal, 1991).

[4] R. Hrair Dekmejian, *Islam in Revolution: Fundamentalism in the Arab World* (2nd ed.; Syracuse: Syracuse University Press, 1995), p. xiii.

1979-1980, Islam was in the midst of a new surge of dynamism."[5] In broader terms, the directors of the Fundamentalism Project, which studied religious resurgence as a global phenomenon, described, in 1992, "fundamentalism" as "a pattern of belief and behavior that has emerged in all the major world religions over the past twenty-five years and is gaining prominence and influence in the 1990s."[6]

In these and many other presentations, the Islamic resurgence is viewed as a phenomenon of the final quarter of the twentieth century. However, from the perspective of the experience of the Muslim Brotherhood in Jordan, the beginnings of the resurgence might be seen in the 1940s.

Observers and participants in the politics of the 1990s need to be reminded that, in the years immediately following World War II, there were many indications of an Islamic resurgence. The establishment of Muslim Brotherhood organizations in Syria, Sudan, and Jordan is part of a broader picture. In a number of its "Current Situation" reports in 1947, for example, the Central Intelligence Agency (CIA) mentioned the importance of Islamic elements. The report for Egypt noted that "nationalism and the pan-Islam movement are expected to increase in Egypt," and specifically mentioned the Muslim Brotherhood as an important new element in the political scene.[7] In North Africa, the CIA noted "the reappearance of influential Moslem leaders"[8] and explicitly noted that in Palestine, should "a 'Jihad,' or Holy War, be declared, the Ikhwan [Brotherhood] would be the spearhead of any 'crusade.'"[9]

There were other important indications of a relatively high level of Islamic activism throughout the Muslim world. When the Dutch attempted to reestablish imperial control in Indonesia after the defeat of the Japanese, they faced not only a resurgent Indonesian nationalism but also

---

[5] John Obert Voll, *Islam: Continuity and Change in the Modern World* (2nd ed.; Syracuse: Syracuse University Press, 1994), p. 289.

[6] Martin E. Marty and R. Scott Appleby, *The Glory and the Power: The Fundamentalist Challenge to the Modern World* (Boston: Beacon Press, 1992), p.3.

[7] Central Intelligence Agency, *The Current Situation in Egypt.* ORE 54 (16 October 1947), pp. 1-2. Secret Document, declassified through the Historical Review Program, 21 July 1992.

[8] Central Intelligence Agency, *The Current Situation in French North Africa.* ORE 63 (18 December 1947), p. 2. Secret document declassified through the Historical Review Program, 21 July 1992.

[9] Central Intelligence Agency, *The Consequences of the Partition of Palestine.* ORE 55 (28 November 1947), p. 4. Secret document declassified through the Historical Review Program, 21 July 1992.

Islamic revolt. After independence, the new nationalist government faced important Islamic revolutionary movements like the Darul Islam revolt in Sumatra and elsewhere.[10] Even in Turkey, probably the most secularized of the independent states in the Muslim world, in the years following World War II, it was possible for a well-informed analyst to write in 1954 about the "revival of Islam in secular Turkey."[11]

Boulby's examination of the development of the Jordanian Brotherhood in the middle of the twentieth century and its continued vitality throughout the second half of the century is an important reminder of the longevity of the impulse for religious affirmation in the context of the modern world and of the appeal of Islam as something more than simply a last resort after all else has failed.

A second aspect of the contemporary resurgence might also be seen in a different light when viewed from the Jordanian perspective. The current Islamic revival is often portrayed as a result of the failure of Western-inspired ideologies and world views of modernization which dominated much of the politics of the Muslim world in the 1960s. In the words of one comprehensive study, "the 1970s marked the end of an era of optimism for these [Middle Eastern] countries, an era in which they sought to achieve modernity by the emulation of Western and socialist models. . . . The 1970s became a repository of failed dialectical processes—ideological, developmental, and political—which came together to create a situation of hopelessness and pessimism among Muslims, from which there appeared to be no exit. Hence the return to Islam as the only remaining medium of identity and authenticity."[12] In the turn away from these more Western-style views, the Iranian Revolution was frequently viewed as a key turning point and inspiration. The changes were dramatic and the "regeneration of the Islamic ethos . . . caught the non-Islamic world [and, in fact, many Muslims as well] by surprise."[13] The new spirit of religious revival ran counter to the expectations of most leaders and scholars, who assumed that modernization would automatically lead to

---

10 See, for example, the major study, Nazaruddin Sjamsuddin, *The Republican Revolt: A Study of the Acehnese Rebellion* (Singapore: Institute of Southeast Asian Studies, 1985).

11 Howard A. Reed, "Revival of Islam in Secular Turkey," *The Middle East Journal* 8, No. 3 (Summer 1954): 267-282.

12 Dekmejian, *Islam in Revolution*, p. 31.

13 E. Hrair Dekmejian, "The Anatomy of Islamic Revival: Legitimacy Crisis, Ethnic Conflict and the Search for Islamic Alternatives," *The Middle East Journal* 34, No. 1 (Winter 1980): 1.

secularization of society and a reduction of the public role of religion in society and politics.

The Muslim Brotherhood in Jordan, however, was not established in response to the failures of Western radical and modernizing ideologies. Those ideologies were, in fact, on the rise in the late 1940s, when the Jordanian Brotherhood was created. It was this, rather than the failure of Western ideologies, which led some people in the Muslim world to establish Islamically-based organizations in the period immediately following World War II. The first Muslim Brotherhood organization had been established in Egypt in 1928. The founder, Ḥasan al-Bannā, worked to create an alternative to Western-style modernization which he saw as dominating Egyptian society. His writings and the work of the Egyptian Brotherhood provided a model for others, especially in the late 1940s.

Muslim Brotherhoods were established in a number of countries in the Arab world. They were inspired by the example of Egypt, which became an important prototype for Islamic revivalist organizations. In contrast to the situation at the end of the twentieth century, in the late 1940s, this "resurgence" was in part a Muslim response to the appeal of communism and other radical Western ideologies, not their failure. In Egypt itself, young members of the organization saw the Communists as a significant challenge.[14] Following the establishment of the Brotherhood in Syria, the "Syrian Communist Party and the Baʿth were the Brotherhood's principal rivals for influence among the middle and lower middle classes."[15] The context is similar in Sudan, where the early Islamic movement that provided a foundation for the Sudanese Muslim Brotherhood was established in the debates and struggles between communists, liberals, and Islamically-oriented students in the late 1940s. It was the success, not the failure of these other movements that impelled some of the students to organize the Islamic Liberation Movement.[16]

Boulby makes it clear that the primary inspiration for the establishment of a Muslim Brotherhood organization in Jordan was the issue of the future of Palestine rather than competition with leftist radicals. Abd al-Latif Abu Qurah, the founder, concentrated on creating support for the

---

14 See, for example, the autobiographical account in Hasan Hanafi, *al-Din wa al-Thawrah fi Masr, 1952-1981*, vol. 6. *al-Usuliyyah al-Islamiyyah* (Cairo: Madbuli, 1989): 219.

15 Umar F. Abd-allah, *The Islamic Struggle in Syria* (Berkeley: Mizan Press, 1983), p. 93.

16 Hasan al-Turabi, *al-Harakah al-Islamiyyah fi al-Sudan* (Cairo: al-Qari' al-Arabi, 1991/1411), p. 23.

jihad in Palestine against the Zionist movement and the establishment of the state of Israel. However, even in this context, the rise of a movement of Islamic resurgence faced the strong rivals of local movements advocating more secular nationalist or leftist ideologies and programs. An important part of the cooperation that developed between King Abdullah and the new Brotherhood is that the King thought that the Brotherhood "recalled the younger generation to their religious duties and obligations and was, therefore, of value in checking the spread of Communism in Transjordan."[17]

This rise of movements of Islamic resurgence in the 1940s was not part of turning to Islam after the failure of Western alternatives. Islam was a viable basis for activist movements even in the time of rising influence of more secular ideologies. This is an important reminder not only that origins of resurgence(s) are complex but also that there was much to indicate an Islamic revival in the *middle* of the twentieth century. The later resurgence is not simply a product of events in the final quarter of the century but has at least some important foundations in earlier movements.

The current portrayal of the Islamic resurgence provides important perspectives for understanding the dynamics of religion and politics in the contemporary Muslim world. There were and are many new forces at work in religious life during the final quarter of the twentieth century and many turned to Islam because of the failure of Western political ideologies of modernization. In general terms, there is no compelling reason to reject the concept of the religious resurgence in the final quarter of the twentieth century. However, Boulby's study shows that important elements in this late twentieth century resurgence have deeper roots than the politics of the 1970s and 1980s, and it also suggests that some of the interpretations of the "causes" of this resurgence need to be expanded.

A third aspect of the experience of the Jordanian Brotherhood as presented by Boulby is the integration of this Islamist movement into the existing political and social dynamics. This is in contrast to much of the description of Islamist movements in the late twentieth century. There has been a significant emphasis on the violence of the movements of Islamic resurgence. The image of a violent Islamic resurgence is emphasized by people who portray relations between the Muslim world and the West as a

---

[17] Mary C. Wilson, *King Abdullah, Britain and the Making of Jordan* (Cambridge: Cambridge University Press, 1987), p. 166. Martin is quoting the British Resident in Jordan in 1947, Kirkbride.

"clash of civilizations."[18] Bruce Lawrence, in a major recent study, argues that the popular image of Islamic movements as violent is so pervasive that it is necessary to "shatter the myth" and see "Islam beyond violence."[19] For those who speak of an Islamic threat, John L. Esposito has posed the issue clearly in a book which has been translated into many languages, *The Islamic Threat: Myth or Reality?*[20] In his analysis, it is clear that while there are movements in the Islamic resurgence which advocate and engage in violent opposition to the existing social and political institutions, violence in not a necessary part of an Islamic resurgence.

Studies like Boulby's provide the necessary balance to the more sensationalist coverage of small terrorist movements. In Jordan, a major Islamic movement has for decades basically worked within the system to Islamize societal and political institutions. While the Jordanian Brotherhood has been an opposition party, it has not been an advocate of violent revolution.

In many ways, the experience of the Muslim Brotherhood in Jordan is important within the broader context of international affairs. Utilizing the analysis of Boulby, it becomes possible to ask whether or not the fears of those who see an Islamic threat are justified in supporting the suppression of movements of Islamic affirmation that are willing to work within the system. Does the often-repeated statement that Islamist participation in the democratic process means "one man, one vote, one time," or fears that Islamists will "highjack" democracy provide adequate basis for overturning the decisive electoral victory of an Islamic party in Algeria or the suppression of a party whose leader became prime minister of Turkey through proper political procedures?

The experience of Jordan as portrayed by Boulby provides an important example of how a movement of Islamic affirmation like the Muslim Brotherhood can work constructively within the political system, even in opposition. The Brotherhood began in Transjordan imbued with a spirit of jihad or holy war, but this was not to be a war against the existing social order of Jordan. In fact, the Muslim Brotherhood in Jordan cooperated with the monarchy and was an important source of support in the early days of the reign of King Hussein in the 1950s. The Brotherhood

---

18 See, for example, Samuel P. Huntington, *The Clash of Civilizations and the Remaking of World Order* (New York: Simon & Schuster, 1996).

19 Bruce B. Lawrence, *Shattering the Myth: Islam Beyond Violence* (Princeton: Princeton University Press, 1998).

20 John L. Esposito, *The Islamic Threat: Myth or Reality* (Revised edition; New York: Oxford University Press, 1995).

in Jordan has for more than a half century provided a refutation for those who would see "Islamic movements" as violent responses to the social changes of the modern era.

In an era of globalization, it is still important to understand the specifics of the local. The Islamic resurgence of the final quarter of the twentieth century is a global phenomenon. Yet, an examination of the experience of a specific "local" movement like the Muslim Brotherhood in Jordan, as presented by Marion Boulby, can provide important reminders that are not always apparent in more general analyses. The final quarter of the twentieth century has witnessed a major religious resurgence, but the experience of the Brotherhood in Jordan reminds us that at least some aspects of this resurgence begin significantly earlier. While much of the incentive for the late twentieth century resurgence was based on the failure of other ideologies, the Muslim Brotherhood experience reminds us that Islam is not simply an ideology of last resort. Finally, the experience in Jordan also is a reminder that Muslim revivalists can constructively work within the system to Islamize society and that violence is not inherent in the programs of Islamic resurgence.

A Note on the Sources and Methodology

There is relatively little literature, in Western or Arabic sources, on the modern history of Jordan in general. Nor have there been any major works published to date on the history of the Jordanian Muslim Brotherhood. The only significant source available in English (translated from Hebrew) is Amnon Cohen's *Political Parties on the West Bank*[1] which is helpful in providing information about the Muslim Brotherhood's activities on the West Bank in the 1947 to 1967 period. Cohen's work is based on a study of the Jordanian Secret Police Files confiscated by the Israeli government in 1967. These files contain information on the organization and membership of the Muslim Brotherhood. Unfortunately, they are not available to researchers as a result of an Israeli government decision. In Arabic, the only major work containing information about the Jordanian Muslim Brotherhood was published by Mūsā Zayd al-Kīlānī, entitled *Al-Ḥarakah al-Islāmiyyah fī al-Urdunn.*[2] However, this work proved to be no more than a translation of the chapter on the Muslim Brotherhood in Cohen's volume.

The bulk of the research for this book was undertaken in Jordan between 1991-1993. In Jordan, the author was somewhat constrained by the sensitivity of the regime towards this research. Nonetheless, it was possible to conduct an extensive series of interviews with members of the Muslim Brotherhood, their supporters and their critics. The material gained from these interviews was supplemented by an analysis of the Brotherhood's few publications, most notably the newspapers *al-Kifāḥ al-Islāmī* and *al-Ribāṭ* (although the latter had only begun to appear in 1992 and there were few issues available). Also useful were Jordanian press sources and data on the election results provided by the Ministry of Information.

The holdings of the National Archives in Washington and the Public Records Office in London were also examined. The National Archives yielded no useful information. But British Foreign Office correspondence

---

[1] Amnon Cohen, *Political Parties in the West Bank under the Jordanian Regime, 1949–1967* (Ithaca: Cornell University Press, 1982).

[2] Mūsā Zayd al-Kīlānī, *al-Ḥarakah al-Islāmiyya fī al-Urdunn* (Amman, 1990).

relating to Jordan in the 1950s provided some commentary on the activities of the Muslim Brotherhood in that period.

Finally, it is necessary to make a clarification with regard to terminology. The term "Islamist" has been selected here to refer in the broadest and least essentialized sense to the diverse spectrum of Islamic political movements and ideologies in the twentieth century.

A Note on Transliteration

Arabic terms, names of individuals and organizations are transliterated according to MESA (*Middle East Studies Association*) guidelines. Place names, and the names Hussein and Nasser are presented in the form of common English usage.

ACKNOWLEDGMENTS

I gratefully acknowledge the financial support provided for my research by the University of Toronto School of Graduate Studies Open Fellowship and Travel Fund and the Department of Middle East and Islamic Studies. I also thank the faculty of the Department of Middle East and Islamic Studies for their contribution to the dissertation on which this book is based.

I am especially indebted to my supervisor, Professor James Reilly, for his guidance, support and critical appraisal of my work over the years.

I am also grateful to Professor John O. Voll for his advice and his comments on this book.

There are many in Jordan I would like to thank who must, for their own safety, remain nameless. Amongst these, I must particularly thank the student members of the Islamic Bloc at the University of Jordan for candid and open discussions. I share with many of them the hope for greater political freedom in Jordan.

Those in Jordan I may acknowledge publicly for their assistance with my research include Dr. ʿIzzāt ʿAzzīzī, Dr. Fatḥī Malkawī, Dr. Mūsā Kīlānī, former M. P. Layth Shubaylāt and his staff, the staff of the University of Jordan library, the staff of the Ministries of Planning, Education and Information and the staff of the Muslim Brotherhood Parliamentary Office in Amman. I am also grateful to the staff of the American Centre for Oriental Research in Amman for their hospitality during the time I spent there in 1992 and 1993.

On a more personal note, I must thank Scott Quaintance, Elena Balzerini, Pascal and Valerie Torrin for their friendship and the many adventures we had together in Jordan. I also thank my friends in Toronto, especially Greg Radwan, Ayla Kiliç and Nancy Smart, whose almost daily encouragement helped me greatly during the last few months of completing this work.

Finally, I am most grateful to my family for the humour, tolerance and unwavering support over the years I have spent on this project.

INTRODUCTION

This book examines the ideology and social base of the Jordanian Muslim Brotherhood from its founding in 1945 to 1993. This work is predicated on the notion that, while there has been considerable discussion of contemporary Islamist organizations in Middle Eastern and Western literature, there has been insufficient attention devoted to the historical specificities of these movements in nation states. As a result, this analysis focuses on the relations between the Brotherhood and the Jordanian state as a determinant of the Brotherhood's ideological and social development. This analysis brings several major characteristics of the Brotherhood to light.

First, the movement has taken a pragmatic, reformist and non-confrontational approach. The Brotherhood had a symbiotic relationship with the regime from 1945 through to the early 1990s. This relationship gave the Brotherhood the benefits of legal status in return for which it avoided open criticism of the regime and maintained a moderate, reformist agenda.

Second, the Brotherhood has demonstrated since the 1950s a willingness to work within a parliamentary system and play by the rules. Analysis of the Brotherhood in the parliament of 1954 to 1957 and 1989 to 1993 shows that the movement worked seriously to effect reform through parliamentary means and to improve its performance with relation to political parties.

Third, the Brotherhood, while accepting to work within a parliamentary system, and publicly upholding the compatibility of Islamic and liberal democratic principles, does not in fact endorse liberal democracy as a final goal but rather aspires towards a sort of "theo-democracy" in which a representative assembly legislates according to the Islamic principle of consultation within the parameters of divine law.

Fourth, symbiotic relations between the Brotherhood and the regime were beginning to disintegrate by the end of the 1989–1993 period. This took place in the general context of the regime's policy of implementing limited, top-down pluralism in which the parliament should have little autonomy. In the final analysis, the Muslim Brotherhood, while still commanding a large and popular constituency, was ineffective in implementing its Islamizing agenda through reformist means, leaving major questions with regard to its future course of action.

Chapter One
Historical Survey of Jordanian State Development

Although the Muslim Brotherhood did not come into existence until 1945, it is necessary to review the development of Transjordan from the time of the establishment of the British Mandate since it is in this formative period that the major characteristics in Jordanian state development were defined. The history of the state of Jordan dates back to 1921 when Britain, having been awarded Mandate control of the territory east of the Jordan river by the League of Nations, agreed to back a government of the area under the rule of ʿAbdallāh, son of Sharīf Ḥusayn ibn ʿAlī of the Hijaz. At the Jerusalem conference of March 27, 1921 Winston Churchill formally proposed that ʿAbdallāh should form a government in the area with British monetary and military aid which would be recognized as independent at some future date.

The British decision to let ʿAbdallāh rule was influenced by a variety of considerations: the desire to limit French expansion in the Fertile Crescent and at the same time be relieved of the burden of local government in Transjordan, the hope that McMahon's broken promise of an independent Arab homeland would have at least the appearance of being partly fulfilled, and the wish that ʿAbdallāh's demands for the Syrian throne be appeased.[1] For the ambitious ʿAbdallāh, Transjordan provided a throne and a base from which he hoped to satisfy his expansionist tendencies so as to rule over the region of Ottoman Greater Syria.[2]

ʿAbdallāh's thirty-year rule left an enduring stamp on the modern Jordanian state, defining many of its major features today. First, his administration was characterized by considerable British military, political and financial control. The independent state of Jordan inherited financial dependency from the Mandate period. The country's limited economic

---

[1] Aqil Hyder Hasan Abidi, *Jordan: A Political Study, 1948–1957* (London: Asia Publishing House, 1965), 5.

[2] See Mary Wilson, *King Abdullah, Britain and the Making of Jordan* (Cambridge: Cambridge University Press, 1987) for a detailed analysis of ʿAbdallāh's rule. Churchill made it clear to ʿAbdallāh that if he succeeded in resisting the French for a six-month period Britain would make every effort to see ʿAbdallāh made emir of Syria.

resources have ensured that its survival has been based over the decades on British, American and Arab Gulf support. For Britain and the United States, economic support for Jordan has been motivated by its strategic position and proximity to the oil-rich Gulf.

Dependence on outside economic assistance has been a constant burden for King Hussein, who has frequently had to juggle the political demands of his creditors with domestic pressures.[3] As Robert Satloff has noted, "The history of Hashemite Jordan is as much coloured by a continual struggle against dependence on outside financial support as it is by an uphill battle for political recognition and legitimacy."[4]

Second, the chief task of the Mandate period was the consolidation of control over Transjordan, a pastoral nomadic region which had not come under any centralized power. The ways in which ʿAbdallāh and the British went about asserting centralized control have had a fundamental impact on the subsequent dynamics of the state. Tribesmen were pacified and integrated into the state through the British-run Arab Legion which for more than half a century was a mainstay of the Hashemite regime.[5] The process of state building also brought the attendant creation of an embryonic professional class which would staff ideological opposition parties and the Muslim Brotherhood.[6] ʿAbdallāh also introduced a style of patrimonial rule that has been a characteristic of the regime to this day and is used to build support through patronage and to balance competing interests.[7]

---

3 For a discussion of some of the economic and political challenges facing the development of the Jordanian state see Valerie Yorke, *Domestic Politics and Regional Security: Jordan, Syria and Israel* (Aldershot: Gower, 1988).

4 Robert Satloff, *From Abdullah to Hussein: Jordan in Transition* (Oxford: Oxford University Press, 1994), 5.

5 P. J. Vatikiotis, *Politics and the Military in Jordan: A Study of the Arab Legion (1921–1957)* (New York: Praeger, 1967), 4–5.

6 The definition of this class is based on the pioneering study of the professional middle class by Manfred Halpern. This is a class which sought to advance itself through education and professional skills rather than through wealth or personal connections. See Manfred Halpern, *The Politics of Social Change in the Middle East and North Africa* (Princeton: Princeton University Press, 1963), 52–63. For a more recent discussion of this class based on Halpern's definition, see Alan Richards and John Waterbury, *A Political Economy of the Middle East: State, Class and Economic Development* (Boulder: Westview, 1990), 49 and James A. Bill and Robert Springborg, *Politics in the Middle East* (New York: Harper and Collins, 1994), 126.

7 Bill and Springborg, *Politics*, 153. They describe patrimonial rule as follows: "In the patrimonial Middle East, the sovereign is located at the center of the political

Third, the Mandate period saw the introduction by the British of a constitutional system of parliament. Although parliamentary life has been circumscribed in Jordan and has experienced periods of disruption with the abolition of political parties and the curtailing of political freedoms, the parliament has played a central role in Jordan's history as an institution which has both strongly challenged the regime and provided it with an instrument for cooptation of opposition and legitimization.[8] While the constitution is based on positivist Western constitutional precepts, it declares Islam to be the state religion. ʿAbdallāh and Hussein after him also sought to derive legitimacy from their Sharifian descent, emphasizing adherence to Islam and Islamic values.

Finally, ʿAbdallāh took probably the most important decision in Jordan's history with the annexation of the West Bank in 1950. The state's absorption of a Palestinian population created a major hurdle in the Hashemite quest for political legitimacy and in the forging of a Jordanian national identity. It also granted the Jordanian state a significant role in Middle East politics by tying it to the Palestinian question, a role which may have ensured its survival due to the strategic interests of Britain, the United States, and Israel.

---

system. He is surrounded by advisors, ministers, military leaders, personal secretaries, and confidants. The one thing that all members of this inner circle share is unquestioned personal loyalty to the leader. This is best indicated by their continued reflection of the will and personality of that leader. These individuals may relate submissively and passively to the leader but they do not relate in this way to their own peers and followers. Here, they are caught up in the most intense manipulations and machinations possible."

[8] See Kamel S. Abu Jaber, "The 1989 Jordanian Parliamentary Elections", *Orient* 31 (1990):67. Abu Jaber argues that the regime's "promise" of a parliamentary system has had a strong influence on the political dynamics of the state. "The promise is unique in itself and the regime was often made accountable against the background of that promise, which was especially important in periods of crisis. When parliament was reduced, political parties banned and certain freedoms curtailed in the 50s, early 70s and later in the 80s the regime never resorted to either abolishing the constitutional framework altogether or the establishment and maintenance of a police state. Though such a prospect was almost always present, and sometimes perhaps very tempting—especially in view of an atmosphere of crisis within the country as well as abroad and in view of the repressive nature of some of the surrounding regimes." For more information on constitutional development in British-mandated Jordan, see Kamel S. Abu Jaber "The Legislature in the Hashemite Kingdom of Jordan: A Study in Political Development," *Muslim World* LIX (July-October 1969): 220–231. For discussions of turbulent parliamentary life in the 1950s see Robert B. Satloff, *From Abdullah to Hussein* and Naseer H. Aruri, *Jordan: A Study in Political Development 1921–1965* (The Hague: Martinus Nijhoff, 1972), 116–173.

The Mandate

In Transjordan the British and ʿAbdallāh faced a major challenge in state and nation building. The country had no natural geographic borders except for the Jordan river and had little to distinguish its inhabitants from their neighbours.[9] The population was predominantly Sunnī Arab (with Sunnī Circassians forming the main ethnic minority of less than five percent of the population), and tribal. In the absence of significant urban centres and state security, tribal identification extended throughout the population. This population was mostly illiterate.[10] There was only one secondary school in the country[11] and primary schools (*katātīb*) were limited to villages where there was an instructor available.[12]

Transjordan's economic development had been limited by the fact that it had been a marginal territory under the Ottoman empire. The country had limited agricultural resources because of a scarcity of water and it possessed a large portion of desert area. Transjordan's economy was primarily agricultural and characterized by a pastoral/peasant split in mode of life and economy. In the north, village life predominated over a nomadic agriculture. Northerners tended to have closer links with urban centres of Palestine and Syria. Historically, the Hashemites have relied on the support of southern tribes while they have faced more political opposition from the north.

The first two decades of Mandate rule were devoted to the expansion and centralization of state control. The British administered the Mandate indirectly through their resident to whom ʿAbdallāh was responsible. ʿAbdallāh was an autocratic and ambitious individual who was frustrated by the extent to which his powers were circumscribed. He was hampered

---

9 Wilson, *Abdullah,* 58.

10 *UNESCO Statistical Yearbook,* 1993, 1.3: Illiterate Population. There are no statistics on literacy for this period. However, it is clear that illiteracy rates were high in the 1920s if we take into account UNESCO statistics which indicate that by 1976, after several decades of rapid educational expansion, 32.4% of the Jordanian population still remained illiterate.

11 Satloff, *From Abdullah to Hussein,* 7.

12 UNESCO, "Jordan: Educational Developments in 1951–52," in *International Yearbook of Education, 1952* (Paris: 1952). The katātīb schools are described as follows: "Prior to the introduction of a State system of education, the kuttāb was the predominant type of school. Any person in a village who happened to know how to read and write, opened a kuttāb to which small boys went to read and memorize the Koran and learn a little arithmetic and writing."

not only by tight British financial and administrative control but also by the fact that he had no base or roots in Transjordanian society.

ʿAbdallāh, as an outsider, could not rely on Transjordanian support. He consolidated his power through cooptation of a heterogenous political elite of Transjordanian shaykhs and sub-national (Palestinian and Circassian) minorities in a network of state patronage. He maintained his power in part by encouraging the segmentation of the tribal elite, undercutting the interests of those who might pose a challenge to the state.[13] He preferred to deal with the tribes through patronage, playing on inter-tribal competition and awarding loyalty with land and tax assessments.[14] With the first elections of 1929, tribal shaykhs were also introduced to the political system.

One of the first difficulties the Mandate government faced was the shortage of local personnel capable of running a rudimentary state bureaucracy. In view of this shortage, the government was staffed with British, Palestinian and Syrian employees. The first cabinet was composed entirely of members of the Syrian Arab Independence Party (*Ḥizb al-Istiqlāl al-ʿArabī*) which had supported Faysal's throne in Syria and who, after he was removed from power, clustered around ʿAbdallāh in Amman.[15] But the nationalists' agenda soon came into conflict with ʿAbdallāh's aspirations. They sought the unification of geographical Syria, did not support Transjordan as a separate state, and opposed ʿAbdallāh's cooperation with the British. As a result of these differences, the nationalists were removed from office.[16] The Syrian nationalists were replaced in the higher levels of government by second-generation Palestinians and Syrians and Circassians rather than by members of the Transjordanian elite. The loyalty of these expatriates could be counted on as they had no local bases and their power was based solely on their allegiance to the state.[17] Delegating power to expatriates without "fiefdoms" served to keep power away from potential tribal opponents. Transjordanian tribal shaykhs were, however, coopted into the govern-

---

13 See Valerie Yorke, *Domestic Politics and Regional Security: Jordan, Syria and Israel.*

14 Wilson, *Abdullah,* 98.

15 See Wilson, *Abdullah,* 62 and Abidi, *Jordan,* 14 for more information about ʿAbdallāh's relations with the Syrian nationalists.

16 See Abidi, 15–16 for a discussion of how ʿAbdallāh discriminated against the Syrian nationalists with the Law of Nationality of 1928.

17 Satloff, *From Abdullah to Hussein,* 7.

ment at lower levels, filling seats on the Legislative Council elected in 1928.

Reliance on the loyalty of sub-nationals has characterized the kingdom throughout its history. A circle of non-Transjordanian "king's men" survived into Hussein's era, with even Jordan's East Bank-born premiers having roots outside Jordan.[18]

The British policy for eliminating inter-tribal rivalries and directing loyalty towards the state had two main components: the rationalization of land ownership and the pacification and absorption of tribes by the Arab Legion. The Arab Legion was the primary vehicle for the pacification and integration of a tribal society into the state.[19] Glubb Pasha succeeded to the command of the Arab Legion in 1930 and, after completing a similar assignment in Iraq, ruthlessly stamped out tribal insurrections and rivalries. His most successful achievement was the incorporation of tribesmen into the military itself. Vatikiotis has argued that this incorporation favoured the diversion of tribal loyalty to a sense of allegiance to the monarch.[20] The incorporation of tribesmen into the military brought a profound alteration in the tribe as a political unit. Sons of sheikhly families no longer mobilized their tribesmen against each other. Instead they took on leadership roles in the army where they developed more of a communal identity with members of other tribes in the same brigades and regiments.[21]

The British also set about the breaking up and settlement of land in the 1930s. Some quasi-communal land was transformed into individual plots while in other cases tribes got some agricultural lands in individual

---

18 Satloff, *From Abdullah to Hussein,* 7.

19 Vatikiotis, *Politics,* 5.

20 Ibid.

21 Linda Layne, *Home and Homeland: The Dialogics of Tribal and National Identities in Jordan* (Princeton: Princeton University Press, 1994), 40. As stated earlier, the bedouin dominated military has been a mainstay of the Hashemite regime to this day. But it must be emphasized that the military bedouin have not been the only mainstay of the Jordanian state. As Linda Layne argues, there has been a tendency to overdetermine the role of tribalism as the mainstay of the monarchy and to over identify the monarchy with tribalism because tribalism was a formative feature in the composition of the state. Layne has questioned assumptions that up until the present the bedouin constitute the majority of the armed forces, saying that data to support such assertions are rarely given. Layne argues against the frequent assertion that tribes uphold the monarchy, pointing rather to the tendency of the Hashemite regime to buttress itself by relying on a strategic political minority characterized by multiple definitions, a position adhered to by this study.

holdings and some grazing lands in common. Land privatization favoured sedentarization of tribes and the decline of the pastoral economy. Numerous bedouin, motivated by the deteriorating nomadic community, became settled farmers.[22] From the point of view of the British, regulation of land and the establishment of a reliable land registry not only served the purpose of submitting the tribal population to further state control. It also curtailed ʿAbdallāh's efforts to extend his own patronage networks amongst the tribal shaykhs.[23]

Britain's aim was to create through land settlement a class of small and medium-sized landowners, rather than large landowners who might pose a challenge to the state. However, some large landowners did emerge amongst tribal leaders.[24] The existence of a landowning rural nobility would lead gradually to the creation of new class interests in Transjordan after World War II.[25]

In the late 1930s Transjordan remained primarily an agricultural society. The manufacturing industry was undeveloped, which is not surprising given that "only a century earlier Transjordan had been little more than a large pasture."[26] The total population of Transjordan in 1938 was estimated at 300,000 and its largest towns were Amman and Salt with populations of roughly 20,000 each.[27] Communications were limited, education remained rudimentary. There was as yet no native intelligentsia or bureaucracy and as a result no basis for local political organization.

Political life up to 1948 was "stale and desultory" in the hands of a triumvirate of ʿAbdallāh, the British (operating primarily through the military), and the prime minister, representing the non-Transjordanian political elite.[28] Mandate rule was autocratic in nature, reflecting not only the protection of Britain's strategic needs in an unstable political environment, but also the personality of ʿAbdallāh. ʿAbdallāh's aspirations for an independent Transjordan did not involve the encouragement of

---

22 Layne, *Home and Homeland*, 42 and Michael P. Mazur, *Economic Growth and Development in Jordan* (Westview Special Studies on the Middle East: Westview, 1979).

23 Wilson, *Abdullah*, 98.

24 Ibid.

25 For a discussion of the major achievements of colonial states in "consolidating the position of landowners and in midwiving the birth of the middle class" see Richards and Waterbury, *A Political Economy*, 49.

26 Mazur, *Economic Growth*, 7.

27 Wilson, *Abdullah*, 129.

28 Satloff, *From Abdullah to Hussein*, 7.

popular political participation. He preferred to build and maintain a power base through informal consultations at the elite level. He was hostile to the introduction of constitutional parliamentary rule by the British in 1928.

Transjordan was ruled without a constitution until February 1928 when the Anglo-Jordanian agreement formalized Britain's control of the Mandate's domestic and foreign affairs through its High Commissioner.[29] The agreement incorporated Western constitutional precepts, providing for the establishment of a legislative assembly in an effort to bestow an element of legitimacy on Mandate rule.

The British were also unenthusiastic about any development that might corrode their authority. As a result, the twenty-one man Legislative Council which emerged was powerless. No law could be implemented without the emir's approval and the resident's consent. Indeed the electoral law governing the first elections of 1929 was designed so that the Legislative Council could pose little trouble to the government. A system of indirect balloting enabled the government to control elections, and provided for a disproportionate representation of sub-national minorities, in keeping with the government's policy of cooptating these within the bureaucratic elite. In general, the electoral law advanced the government's policy of divide and rule, ensuring that council seats were awarded to regime loyalists with a variety of different interests.[30]

In spite of the lack of popular political organization, demonstrations broke out against the Anglo-Jordanian agreement.[31] These were organized by Syrian nationalists in coalition with tribal shaykhs. The opposition organized its first congress at Amman on July 25, 1928 and drew up a document of their demands known as the National Pact (*al-mithāq al-waṭanī*). This reflected an incoherent expression of political opposition and did not indicate any clear course for the achievement of the country's independence.[32] Leaders of the National Congress threatened to boycott the elections but did not pursue the boycott wholeheartedly since they did not wish to give up their chance to participate in the legislature. In

---

29 For a detailed analysis of the Anglo-Jordanian agreement see Aruri, *Jordan*, 75–78, and Wilson, *Abdullah*, 96–98.

30 The members of the executive and legislature were from a small oligarchy of tribal shaykhs, Palestinian, Syrian, Circassian and Christian representatives.

31 Wilson, *Abdullah*, 99.

32 Abidi, *Jordan*, 17.

general, the legislature functioned as a rubber stamp for British policies until independence in 1946.

The 1930s saw the initial development of political party life. The majority of the parties were cliques based on family and tribal affiliation. Individuals could move freely among these parties which were not ideologically differentiated and served merely as units for inter-tribal organization and negotiation. The Nationalists and the nascent Communist Party were the only ideological parties, organized on a non-family, non-tribal basis in the 1930s. Their membership was limited to a tiny political elite and they were branches of more radical organizations based in Syria and elsewhere in the Arab world.

Independent Transjordan and Jordan

In the period from World War II to 1948, ʿAbdallāh realized the apex of his influence and power, and faced little organized opposition. The granting of independence and declaration of ʿAbdallāh as king in 1946 brought no significant changes to political organization. By the Treaty of London (March 1946) Jordan's independence was still considerably circumscribed. It depended heavily on Britain for financial survival. British control of military and financial affairs was maintained by the continued presence of the resident (now transformed into a minister) and the commander of the Arab Legion, which had evolved during the war from a gendarmerie into an effective fighting force.[33] After independence, as before, Jordan was ruled by the worldly trinity of the king, the prime minister, and the British minister.

On the domestic political front, ʿAbdallāh now had considerably more leverage. He had been looking forward to the reduction in British influence to aggrandize his personal power. The Jordanian constitution assured that the legislature did not gain any independence or influence, overtly revealing the paternalistic tendencies of the regime. The legislature was enlarged by twenty members and the number of electoral districts increased from four to nine, giving the impression of a fairer system of representation. In fact, however, this legislature shifted weight away from the towns, which were growing in population and political sophistication, to the rural areas where ʿAbdallāh had his most loyal tribal supporters. The first council elected after independence was composed

[33] Wilson, *Abdullah,* 164.

predominantly of landowners and tribal shaykhs.[34] Although the legislature was now to be selected by one direct election, the king was to choose the speaker of the house and the cabinet remained responsible only to the monarch. The ten-member Council of Notables was appointed by the king for an eight-year term.[35]

The growing political sophistication of the towns reflected slow but significant evolution in the class structure of Jordanian society. The development of private property which could be used by landowners as collateral against loans encouraged the development of commercial activity.[36] Supply patterns during World War II, war profits, and inflation introduced a class of merchant-moneylenders to Transjordan's towns who financed land purchases. The money merchants were Palestinian rather than Transjordanian, reflecting Palestine's significantly more urbanized economy. Land had become a valuable asset during the war. Cultivation had been extended because of high prices for cereals. As an exporter of cereals to Palestine, Transjordan benefitted greatly from the very high level of grain prices during the war. Also, import restrictions were less severe in Transjordan than in nearby countries and Amman became a sort of commercial centre, re-exporting imported goods to neighbouring countries. Amman's population grew tremendously during the war from about 20,000 in 1938 to 60,000 in 1945.[37]

During World War II a new generation of politically active men grew up in the urban centres of Transjordan. This generation opposed ʿAbdallāh's authoritarianism and reliance on Britain.[38] It constituted an embryonic professional class which would develop further with the expansion of the state. Its political inclinations would be channelled in several directions with the flourishing of party life in the 1950s. But in the 1940s this generation was drawn to two growing political movements, the

---

[34] This tendency to weight the legislature in favour of rural areas has been a consistent characteristic of Hashemite policy up to the present day.

[35] Wilson, *Abdullah,* 165. See also Philip J. Robins, "Politics and the 1986 Electoral Law in Jordan," *Politics and the Economy in Jordan,* Rodney Wilson ed., (London: SOAS, 1991), 184–297.

[36] See Wilson, *Abdullah,* 91, where it is indicated that the only significant commercial activity before World War II was carried out in Amman by a group of Syrian merchants who had fled Syria after the French bombing of Damascus in 1925. They traded mostly in cloth and foodstuffs.

[37] Mazur, *Economic Growth,* 8.

[38] Wilson, *Abdullah,* 165.

Muslim Brotherhood (founded in 1945) and the National Socialist Party of Sulaymān al-Nābulsī.

The gradual politicization of Jordan's youth posed no immediate threat to ʿAbdallāh's rule at this time. But, this would change after the war of 1948 when ʿAbdallāh's annexation of the West Bank dramatically altered the social fabric and political dynamics of the Jordanian state.

For ʿAbdallāh the annexation of the West Bank achieved several purposes. It fit with his objective to extend his control beyond Transjordan to Palestine and Syria and helped to compensate for the Hashemites' loss of influence when they were driven out of the Hijaz by ʿAbd al-ʿAziz ibn Saʿūd in 1925 and from Damascus by the French in 1920. Annexation of East Jerusalem also appealed to the Hashemite sense of responsibility as a Sharifian family which had formerly been guardian of Mecca and Medina.

ʿAbdallāh did not demonstrate his interest in the Palestine question until the 1930s, after he had consolidated his power base in Transjordan. There were two distinct currents in the struggle for Palestine: the Ḥusaynī faction who called for the establishment of a Palestinian state, and the Syrian nationalists who envisaged Palestine as part of a reunified Greater Syria. ʿAbdallāh, who still coveted the throne of Greater Syria, made a special point of courting the Syrian nationalists after independence.[39] When partition of Palestine was first suggested in 1937, ʿAbdallāh was in favor of the move, seeing it as a way of decreasing British power in favor of Arab control. His position alienated other Arab leaders, however, who saw his support as an effort to expand his personal power.

When the Arabs lost the war upon Israel's declaration of statehood, ʿAbdallāh annexed the West Bank, transforming Jordan into Transjordan. This caused regional and international perceptions of the country to change. Jordan was initially isolated in the Arab world. The Arab states condemned annexation for a variety of reasons including their perception of ʿAbdallāh as expansionist, opposition to his cooperation with the British and Israel, their own domestic political pressures and, in the case of Egypt, its own territorial interest in Palestine.[40] But over time, as Wilson points out, the Arab states "came to appreciate the utility of Jordan's new role, for Jordan saved them either from having to champion the Palestinian cause directly or from having absolutely to admit their inability

---

[39] *Ibid.*, 160–161.

[40] *Ibid.*, 178.

to do so."[41] The United States and Britain supported an independent Jordan. They had decided not to support an independent Palestine but still wished to contain Israeli expansion in the region in order to limit the damage the creation of Israel had done to their relations with Arab states. Meanwhile Israel hoped that the Jordanian state could "soak up the identity of Palestine."[42] The net result of annexation was that Jordan could rely on a variety of sources of political and financial aid.

Annexation also had profound socioeconomic effects. It superimposed a society with a comparatively well-developed middle class and a significant degree of urbanization on one which was predominantly rural-nomadic. Jordan's population expanded to three times its previous size to include 460,000 residents of the West Bank and 350,000 refugees from Israel.[43] The refugees formed a disparate group. Town dwellers including the educated professionals, merchants, artisans and shopkeepers concentrated in the growing urban centres of Amman and Zarqa. Few of the urban refugees ended up in camps. Many of the Palestinian villagers and peasants, on the other hand, found themselves in refugee camps in Amman, Zarqa, or Irbid.[44]

A survey of Irbid camp refugees found that their single largest occupation was farming and the second largest, government service. The Jordanian economy offered little to the refugees in either area. Annexation of the West Bank had enlarged the country's territory by about 2,000 miles, increasing arable land by only one third.[45] The country was short of water and land for agricultural development. The Jordanian government bureaucracy was too small to incorporate many new employees.

Jordan was strained economically not only by its population increase but also by the changes in its physical geography. With the creation of the state of Israel Jordan was now virtually landlocked, cut off from the Mediterranean, with its only remaining port in Aqaba (having enjoyed good access to the Haifa port before 1948). It had lost the primary coastal

---

41 *Ibid.*, 214.

42 Wilson, *Abdullah*, 214.

43 According to International Bank for Reconstruction and Development statistics cited by Mazur, *Economic Development*, p. 8, the population of Transjordan before annexation was 375,000. After annexation it increased to 1,185,060.

44 For a detailed study of the refugees, see Avi Plascov, *The Palestinian Refugees in Jordan: 1948–1957* (London: Frank Cass and Co., 1981).

45 Mazur, *Economic Development*, 8.

market for its agricultural products. The direction of Jordanian trade had been east-west and now it was north-south. Jerusalem and the West Bank were now at one end of a "circuitous supply route starting in Beirut and circling around via Amman."[46]

From the beginning the Transjordanian government had supplied destitute refugees with food. This put a strain on its limited budget which was barely alleviated by United Nations aid. Britain opted to loan the state one million pounds for development aimed at settling refugees on a more permanent basis. But instead the majority of these funds were used for development of Transjordan's infrastructure, such as road building, to the neglect of the West Bank.[47]

Economic frustrations naturally fuelled Palestinian political dissatisfactions, which would ultimately challenge the monarchy. Palestinians were not all opposed to annexation. But they were not accustomed to subservience to a monarch and were hostile to ʿAbdallāh's dealings with the British and Israelis. Theirs was a nationalist agenda, inherently opposed to traditional elites whom many held responsible for the loss of Palestine.[48] Palestinian frustrations fuelled the emergence of ideological opposition parties demanding a voice in the political process and criticizing the regime's discriminatory policies.[49] These were mostly under the leadership of Palestinian professionals and intelligentsia. These parties—the Communists, the National Socialists and the Baʿth—did not play a major role until the reign of King Hussein.[50] But their emergence at the end of

46 Wilson, *Abdullah,* 198.

47 Ibid.

48 Ibid., 198.

49 ʿAbdallāh's administration favoured Transjordanians over Palestinians for government service. The Arab Legion remained the preserve of Transjordanian tribes.

50 See Abidi, *Jordan,* 198–205 for details on the founding, early organization and agendas of these parties. The Communists became active in Transjordan in the early 1930s, making several unsuccessful attempts at unionizing workers. The Communists' agenda was to overthrow the regime, drive the British out and establish a Republican Arab union including Syria. The Party reemerged in 1946 with demands for termination of the Anglo-Jordanian Treaty, abolition of the monarchy and free elections. The Baʿth Party was established by a small group of Palestinians and Transjordanians in 1947, initially independent of the Arab Resurrection Party of Syria with which it subsequently merged in 1950. The Baʿth advocated the establishment of a pan-Arab state and an Arab cultural and political renaissance. The National Socialist Party was not officially licensed until 1954. Its programme envisaged the preservation of the monarchy with emancipation from British rule. The party advocated moderate reforms to improve social and economic conditions. The National Socialists believed

ʿAbdallāh's reign is significant in signalling the gradual radicalization of Transjordanian politics.

Opposition to ʿAbdallāh's dealings with the British and Israelis, coupled with Palestinian demands for greater political participation upset the political dynamics inherited from the Mandate period. At the highest level, annexation "drove a wedge between the king and his government." For the first time ʿAbdallāh's senior ministers refused to support his policies. Prime Minister Tawfiq Abū al-Hudā resigned rather than support ʿAbdallāh's efforts to save the Jordanian economy through a commercial treaty with Israel.[51] ʿAbdallāh was forced to give up on the treaty when he could not persuade anyone to take Abū al-Hudā's place.

After annexation the parliament was dissolved and elections were held for a new legislature which would incorporate twenty representatives from each of the East and West Banks. Fearing that Palestinians might boycott the elections, ʿAbdallāh promised that he would introduce the principle of executive responsibility to the legislature.[52] The election results indicated the changing dynamics of Jordanian political life. The majority of the West Bank representatives were educated professionals while from Transjordan the landowning contingent was highest.[53]

The new parliament did ʿAbdallāh the favour of confirming the union of the two banks on April 24, 1950. One analyst has referred to this piece of legislation as "the one high-water mark of ʿAbdallāh's diplomacy and also a point where political smooth sailing ended."[54] For this was virtually the last piece of legislation passed by the parliament. It quickly became obvious that ʿAbdallāh had no intention of handing over power to the legislature.

ʿAbdallāh summarily dissolved the parliament in May 1951 after it had criticized foreign control of the Arab Legion, the high salaries paid to foreigners, and the creation of his own bodyguard, the Royal Hashemite Regiment. ʿAbdallāh's attempt to reassert his own authority was cut short by his assassination three months later.

---

in a general Arab union and called on Jordan to unite with Iraq as the first step in this endeavour. The party advocated union with Iraq on several grounds including the strong ties both countries shared with the British and the fact that both were ruled by Hashemites.

[51] Satloff, *From Abdullah to Hussein*, 9.

[52] Abidi, *Jordan*, 68.

[53] Ibid., 197.

[54] Abidi, *Jordan*, 70.

Annexation had set in motion profound political forces with which ʿAbdallāh's successors would have to contend. ʿAbdallāh's rule had gone far in consolidating state control and in fostering allegiance to the state. But it had achieved little in terms of national integration. As discussed earlier, Jordan's population had no natural geographical or economic cohesion. By 1950 communications were still limited. The education system was undeveloped. The massive expansion of the state's population to include Palestinians had the effect of slowing the development of a national entity. ʿAbdallāh, in an effort at integration, had adopted a policy of deemphasizing Palestinian nationalism and erasing any sense of separate Palestinian identification. Palestinian refugees were granted Jordanian citizenship before annexation. This policy was carried on by Hussein, but with limited success.[55] In the 1950s, Palestinian political culture, more highly developed than that of the Transjordanians, overpowered Transjordanian political discourse. In the longer run, the growth of Palestinian nationalism would become a key component in the development of Jordanian Islamist cohesion and political consciousness.

The Interregnum and Political Crisis: 1951–1967

The brief reign of ʿAbdallāh's son Ṭalāl (1951–1953) saw significant liberalization of the political system, setting the stage for Jordan's first experiment with democracy in the 1950s. Ṭalāl's reign also saw the increased prominence of the "king's men" in the palace, senior courtiers and ministers who were happy to encourage democratization as it guaranteed them more power in relation to the monarch.[56]

The constitution of 1952 outlined the fundamental rights of the people, including equality before the law, individual liberty, right to property, freedom of conscience and religious ceremonies, freedom of opinion, the right to hold public meetings and to form political parties.[57] The constitution enhanced the role of the legislature by making the ministers responsible to the Chamber of Deputies, and by granting the Chamber authority over financial and foreign affairs and the power to impeach ministers. Administrations were required to seek a vote of confidence from the Chamber and a two-thirds majority of the house

---

55 Plascov, *The Palestinian Refugees*, 29.

56 Satloff, *From Abdullah to Hussein*, 40.

57 Aruri, *Jordan*, 96–98, provides a detailed description of the constitution. This constitution is still in place today and has been little altered.

could bring down a government. Overall, the provisions of the new constitution limited the ways in which the throne could stymie the role of parliament.[58] However, this constitution also provided for imposition of martial law and the indefinite suppression of parliament.

The era of liberalization was short-lived. After King Hussein's accession to the throne, his regime faced significant challenges from Palestinian nationalist parties which culminated in a coup attempt in 1957 and the imposition of martial law. The Palestinian leadership of these parties was joined by members of a new generation of more urbanized and politicized Transjordanians. The most prominent of these parties, as noted above, were the Baᶜthists, the National Socialists and the Communists. Although the ideologies of these parties differed, they shared a commitment to the creation of a pan-Arab state comprising Egypt, Syria (and sometimes Iraq) as a sure means of defying the Israelis.[59] Establishment of a pan-Arab entity, of course, necessitated the collapse of the Hashemite regime. The new Palestinian leadership was ill-disposed to the Hashemites in any case, since they regarded ᶜAbdallāh as a traitor to their cause for his dealings with the British and Israelis. An important item on the Palestinian nationalists' agenda was to thwart Jordanian attempts to come to terms with Israel's existence. They exposed attempts at negotiating peace treaties with Israel and constantly criticized the government for signing the Rhodes Armistice Agreement with Israel.[60]

The nationalists strongly opposed British influence in the region as well. In this case their views were shared by the Islamist political groups: the Muslim Brotherhood and the more radical Liberation Party (*Ḥizb al-Taḥrīr*).[61]

The nationalist challenges to King Hussein's regime must be viewed in the larger and complex context of political developments in the Middle East region as a whole. Gamel Abdul Nasser rose to power in Egypt in

58 Robins, "Politics and the 1986 Electoral Law," 188.

59 See Aruri, *Jordan*, 98.

60 Clinton Bailey, *Jordan's Palestinian Challenge: 1948–1983* (Boulder and London: Westview, 1984), 10. The Rhodes Armistice Agreement required the Jordanian government to cede 400 square kilometers of Arab-held land to Israel and to maintain quiet along the border.

61 But, as discussed in Chapter Two, the Muslim Brotherhood's cooperative relations with the regime which gave it legal status ensured that the movement remained loyal to the monarchy in the face of the nationalist challenge. The Islamic Liberation Party was denied legal status by the regime on account of its opposition to the monarchy.

1952 and his nationalization of the Suez Canal sent ripples of Arab nationalism across the region, making him a popular hero. Nasser's pan-Arabism provided the ideological framework for Palestinian nationalism in this period. Throughout the 1950s Egyptian funds and propaganda fuelled anti-regime activity in Jordan.

Nasser's rise to power coincided with the intense Cold War period in the Fertile Crescent, marked by the rising influence of the United States and Soviet dealings with Egypt and Syria. There was a widening rift between the radical Arab states of Egypt and Syria and the more conservative, Western-dominated monarchies of Iraq and Jordan.

Early in his career the young King Hussein faced significant challenges to the Jordanian state: juggling the need for external funding with domestic interests, balancing Palestinian nationalist opposition with the need to coexist with Israel. In the mid-1950s Hussein found himself walking a precipice between British and American support needed for the survival of his throne and fervent nationalist opposition to it. Hussein also struggled to reconcile his own commitment to Arab nationalism (which would preserve existing borders) with pan-Arabism, which endangered Jordan's independence.[62] Finally, he faced the challenge of establishing a modus vivendi with Israel to mitigate the danger of Israel destroying Jordan. At the same time he had to pursue a policy sufficiently hostile towards Israel to ensure that he would not be overthrown by the Palestinian opposition.

King Hussein's first reaction to the rising nationalist threat was to oppress it. Radical political parties were stymied by government interference in the elections of 1954. The government, in the hands of the experienced (and conservative) Prime Minister Abū al-Hudā, intimidated opposition candidates and used the army as a vote bank to try to defeat undesirable candidates.[63] As a result of government interference, the elections returned a parliament of government loyalists.[64] Opposition parties were muzzled and their publications banned.

---

62 Yorke, *Domestic Politics,* 11.

63 Satloff, *From Abdullah to Hussein,* 90–91. Abū al-Hudā had been prime minister ten times and had fought to exert control after the death of ʿAbdallāh. For Hussein he filled the role of "strong man" in a dangerous political situation. His cabinet displayed the classic pattern of previous ones: two Circassians, two Christians, one minister from every region, an even split between the East and West banks.

64 Aruri, *Jordan,* 112. The loyalists were members of the Arab Constitutional Community who acquired 27 out of 40 seats.

But repressive measures could not contain opposition for long. The years 1954–1956 saw mounting civil strife in Jordan. The government's plans to join the Baghdad Pact[65] sparked widespread riots, supported by Nasserist propaganda, in December of 1955. Violent demonstrations broke out in Amman and the major towns of the West Bank.

The regime was forced to back down. Hussein withdrew from the Baghdad Pact. He then took the further step of dismissing General John Bagot Glubb, the British commander of the Arab Legion. The army had played a critical role in stamping out riots and was viewed by Hussein as the only strong institution capable of safeguarding the regime. It was not lost on Hussein that the state's strongest and most loyal institution was viewed by many as a foreign occupying power. He had to transform the Arab Legion into a national army.[66] After Glubb's departure, leadership of the military fell to a group of young pro-Nasserist officers led by ʿAlī ʿAbū al-Nuwwār, an East Banker drawn to the Palestinian nationalist cause.

Next, Hussein acceded to nationalist demands for free elections. The elections of 1956 returned an Arab nationalist, anti-monarchical majority and brought in Sulaymān al-Nābulsī, the leader of the National Socialist Party, as prime minister. One of the new government's first acts was to abrogate the Anglo-Jordanian Treaty in March 1957. Jordan's financial support was assumed by Saudi Arabia, Syria and Egypt. Arab nationalist fervour was aroused by the Suez attack by Britain, France and Israel. The government began to move towards diplomatic relations with the Soviet Union and released convicted communists from prison.

Hussein, encouraged by the United States, whose support he felt he needed for survival, launched an attack on Nābulsī for his "communist views." In opposing communist activity, Hussein was able to enlist the support of the Muslim Brotherhood, thus cementing a tacit alliance with it which would endure through the 1980s. When al-Nābulsī refused to back down on his policies, Hussein dismissed the cabinet. The king's confrontation with the National Socialists culminated at that very moment when he discovered a plot hatched by the commander of the Legion, ʿAli Abū al-Nuwwār, to overthrow the monarchy by a military coup.[67] It is

---

65 The Baghdad Pact, formed in February of that year, was a military alliance comprising Britain, Turkey, Iran, Pakistan and Iraq.

66 Satloff, *From Abdullah to Hussein,* 138.

67 See Satloff, *From Abdullah to Hussein,* 168, where he points out that this was a highly complex situation involving a multiplicity of conspiracies.

important to note that the bedouin proved their loyalty to the monarchy at this time; they let it be known that most of them were willing to mutiny against their commanding officers. Such loyalty made a powerful impression on Hussein who has appreciated ever since the role of the bedouin military as a mainstay of his regime.[68]

After the dismissal of the National Socialist government and the suppression of the coup plans, Hussein adopted draconian measures. He enforced a curfew, introduced martial law, dissolved political parties, imposed strict censorship and purged the bureaucracy of Palestinian anti-regime forces. Parliament was allowed to serve its full term, but only after seventeen nationalist and leftist deputies were forced to resign.[69]

The brief experiment with democracy was over. As Robins has pointed out, "This successful iron-fisted action was a potent illustration of the weak institutional position of the legislature in Jordanian politics and the unstoppable power of the executive."[70]

Martial law was lifted from 1963 to 1967 and parliamentary life resumed. But the regime still interfered in elections. The ability of the parliament to bring down a government was undermined. When the Chamber of Deputies returned a vote of no confidence in April 1963 the king dissolved it. The last elections were held in April 1967. The Mandate of the national assembly expired in 1971, but further elections were deemed impossible due to the occupation of the West Bank. The parliament reconvened for an emergency session in the wake of the 1974 Arab summit in Rabat which designated the Palestine Liberation Organization (PLO) as the representative of Palestinians. The king reasoned that if the PLO was to represent the Palestinians there was no place in the Jordanian assembly for their delegates. In light of difficulties posed at that time by the composition of the assembly, it was called upon to pass a constitutional amendment empowering the monarch to postpone the elections under exceptional circumstances. Apart from the extraordinary session of 1974, parliamentary life did not revive until Hussein recalled the Chamber of Deputies in 1984. Martial law was reimposed at the time of the 1967 war and remained in place until 1989.[71]

---

68 Satloff, *From Abdullah to Hussein*, 168.

69 Robins, "Politics and the 1986 Electoral Law", 189.

70 Ibid.

71 Rex Brynen, "Economic Crisis and Post-Rentier Democratization in the Arab World: The Case of Jordan," *Canadian Journal of Political Science*, 25 (1992): 78.

Hussein's reassertion of control in 1957 meant the reconsolidation of the triumvirate of monarchy, non-native dominated bureaucracy, and Transjordan-dominated military which had ruled the country before 1948. In the crisis years of 1954–1957 elements of both the military and the government had begun to pose a threat to the monarchy. But in the years after 1957 neither would be permitted to slide into opposition again. Hussein continued to follow ʿAbdallāh's pattern of maintaining stability by balancing the interests of leading Transjordanian families and minorities through coopting them into influential military and government positions, often on a rotational basis.

The regime made a particular effort to assimilate Palestinians in the post-1957 period in order to defuse the threat to the monarchy of Palestinian nationalism. Steps were taken to appease former oppositionists. Some were granted cabinet posts. Prime ministers popular with Palestinians were appointed in the early 1960s.[72]

Up until 1964 the policy of assimilation seemed successful. Palestinians seemed more willing to abandon radical nationalist programs and work with the Jordanian regime, at least for the time being. The collapse of the United Arab Republic (UAR) and the failure of pan-Arabism had left many nationalists disillusioned.[73] With such divisiveness in the Arab world, Palestinians began to have second thoughts about their future and to worry that they would not regain Palestine in the near term. In this context it made sense to cooperate with the Jordanian regime and secure a place for themselves in the country's future. An improvement in economic conditions also provided an incentive for Palestinians to envisage a future in Jordan. In 1948 it had seemed questionable whether the state would survive at all. Indeed, it is unlikely it would have survived without the benefit of British and then American aid. In 1957, in the context of the Cold War, the United States assumed financial responsibility for Jordan to protect its own strategic interests in the area. Yet while American financial support guaranteed Jordan's survival, it also ensured its political and economic dependency. Hazzāʾ al-Majālī, appointed prime minister in 1954, tried to address the issue of economic dependency by initiating measures for the development of Jordan's own economic

---

72 Bailey, *Jordan's Palestinian Challenge*, 17.

73 The UAR (United Arab Republic) was formed by Syria and Egypt in 1958 and collapsed in 1961.

infrastructure.[74] Jordan was also able to initiate some modest industrial development, such as the phosphates and potash industries, a cement factory (1951), and a factory for manufacturing batteries (1961). Some industrial achievements were accomplished by private initiative and the Law for Encouragement and Guidance of Industries granted many privileges to new industries. The industrial development policy encouraged the emergence of an industrial East Bank elite that included landlords who acquired their wealth under the emirate and who had gradually transferred their wealth into industry. Financiers, wealthy merchants, and real estate owners concentrated in Amman. This group also included some "Jordanized" Palestinians. They were accorded considerable influence by the regime and granted numerous regulatory loopholes and tax exemptions.[75]

These measures were effective in fostering a degree of industrial development which brought promise of a brighter future. A construction boom in urban centres, especially the city of Amman, provided employment for thousands. Amman had developed at a rapid rate, expanding from a population of 60,000 in 1945 to 300,000 in 1966.[76] By the early 1960s the Jordanian population was relatively advanced in the urbanization process compared with other less developed countries. Urbanization, coupled with the spread of education, created a more politicized population. Even in rural areas which were relatively unintegrated with the nation as a whole, villagers were able to learn about national and regional development through the radio which in the 1950s became a feature in almost every home.[77]

Overall, Jordan's promising economic performance contributed to the country's relative political stability in the late 1950s and early 1960s.[78] But after 1964 King Hussein encountered anew the challenge of Palestinian nationalism—this time in the context of a specifically Palestinian rather than pan-Arab identity. Hussein adopted a two-pronged policy, initially

---

74 Infrastructural development included expansion of agricultural production, development of natural resources, road construction, development of the tourist industry, expansion of the port of Aqaba, and encouragement of domestic industry.

75 Aruri, *Jordan*, 58–60.

76 Bailey, *Jordan's Palestinian Challenge*, 20.

77 Aruri, *Jordan*, 69. See for statistics on the distribution of radios.

78 See Bailey, *Jordan's Palestinian Challenge*, 20, where he notes that in the period between 1954 and 1966, Jordan could boast an average annual growth of 8% in GNP, an increase higher than that of any of the neighbouring non-oil-producing Arab states.

catering to the Arab League-supported PLO and also (after 1967) encouraging more radical groups which came under the PLO umbrella, such as Yāsir ʿArafāt's *al-Fatḥ* (Fatah).

Jordan had become increasingly isolated in the Arab world as a result of both keeping its distance from pan-Arab union and maintaining a modus vivendi with Israel. Wanting to keep in line with Arab sympathies towards the PLO and also to monitor the organization's activities, the Jordanian regime hosted the first meeting of the Palestine National Council in Jerusalem in 1964. In 1965 the regime also tolerated the activities of Fatah, which included commando attacks from Jordan on Israeli territory. In 1966, however, the activities of Palestinian commandos led to large-scale Israeli reprisals in the West Bank and to civil unrest. On November 3, 1966, the Israeli army staged a heavy reprisal raid on the West Bank village of Samua in which 18 people were killed and 134 wounded. This incident was followed by widespread rioting against the king. The rioters demanded better arms and accused the king of being unable to defend them.

Jordan was now dangerously isolated in the Arab world—threatened externally by Israel and by Palestinian agitation from within. In this context, against the advice of his aides, Hussein joined Syria and Egypt in the disastrous war of 1967.

The Palestinian Nationalist Challenge: 1967–1973

The 1967 war had dramatic effects on Jordan. The country lost the West Bank to Israel, and while its territory decreased, its population increased significantly with the influx of approximately 300,000 additional refugees from the West Bank and Gaza Strip.[79] The loss of the West Bank benefitted Jordan in one way; it improved its relations with other Arab states. Jordanian annexation of the West Bank had always been a contentious issue and other Arab states were suspicious of Hashemite motives.[80] Now, in the aftermath of the war, oil-rich Arab states provided Jordan with financial donations.

A major effect of the Arab defeat in 1967 was further disillusionment with pan-Arabism and the rise of Palestinian nationalism under a radicalized and more independent Palestine Liberation Organization. In Jordan Palestinian nationalism was accompanied by antagonism towards

---

[79] Mazur, *Economic Growth*, 84.

[80] Yorke, *Domestic Politics*, 38.

the king after the loss of the West Bank and Jerusalem. Palestinian commando organizations grew in popularity. King Hussein wavered between a policy of accommodating the Palestinian commandos—allowing them to undertake some raids against Israel—and a policy of restraining them. At the same time he called for a unified Arab front against Israel which might have subordinated Palestinian commando activities. But no such front emerged, and in this context Palestinian commandos operated more and more freely in Jordan, benefitting from the material support provided by other Arab states. Some Palestinian army officers transferred their loyalty from the king to the nationalist cause. The king, facing a PLO military force which posed a serious challenge to his monarchy, accepted the advice of East Bank tribal advisors and used the military to crush the commandos.[81] In 1970 the monarchy launched its anti-PLO campaign, culminating in a showdown with Palestinian commandos commonly referred to as Black September. By 1971 at least two thousand Palestinians had been killed and several thousand more had fled the country, mostly for Lebanon. The military and political threats of the PLO to the regime's stability were removed, but at considerable cost.[82]

Jordan once again found itself isolated, as Hussein's actions against the PLO offended other Arab leaders. Financial donations pledged by Libya and Kuwait were suspended. Aid from the United States was now stepped up to compensate for the difference. But the two years following the civil war represented hard times for Jordan economically. Apart from physical damage caused to the country, economic activity was reduced sharply.[83] Gradual recovery began in 1973, assisted by an increase in Jordan's foreign aid receipts in 1972. The October 1973 war had only a small and temporary adverse effect on economic development, and in fact indirectly helped the economy. As a result of the Jordanian commitment of an armored brigade to the Syrian front, Kuwaiti aid was restored.[84]

Although the king had saved his throne by crushing the PLO in Jordan, Palestinian nationalism remained a serious threat to his regime's

---

[81] The king was further antagonized by guerrilla activities of the Popular Front for the Liberation of Palestine (PFLP) during this period, including the highjacking of a western airliner to Jordan.

[82] See Yorke, *Domestic Politics,* 14–15, for a summary of these events.

[83] Mazur, *Economic Growth,* 83.

[84] Ibid., 84.

stability.[85] Jordanian society was deeply affected after the civil war as Palestinian nationalist identification with the PLO grew. At the same time, the civil war favoured the emergence of a stronger Transjordanian nationalism, based in part on suspicions of Palestinian intentions which many felt were confirmed in 1970–71.[86] Conflicts between Transjordanian and Palestinian nationalism were subdued in the context of the economic prosperity which came to Jordan in the decade after 1973, but they would resurface in the context of economic recession and pressures for democratization in the 1980s.

Decade of Prosperity: 1973–1983

The decade after 1973 was the most stable and prosperous in Jordan's history. In this period Jordan benefitted from the economic boom in oil producing Arab states brought about by the oil price revolution. The new wealth of neighbouring Arab states reached Jordan in a number of ways. Most important was the expansion of opportunities for Jordanians (of both Palestinian and East Bank origin) to work in oil-rich countries. Workers' remittances grew dramatically in the decade after 1973, accounting for a quarter of the GDP by 1984.[87] At the same time rising Arab oil wealth facilitated an increase in aid payments from Arab sources. According to official government statistics, transfer payments to the Jordanian central government from Arab sources quadrupled between 1973 and 1975, and between 1973 and 1980 foreign assistance accounted for almost 55% of government revenue, while government revenue represented more than 68% of the GDP.[88] Jordan's service sector expanded to meet the needs of rapidly expanding Gulf markets. Jordan's phosphate industry was boosted in the early 1970s by a huge price increase initiated by Morocco, the world's largest supplier.[89] The reopening of the Suez Canal (1975) restored Jordan's direct transport link with Europe through the port of Aqaba. The civil war in Lebanon also

---

[85] Since 1967 Palestinians have represented between 40 and 60% of the Jordanian (East Bank) population. The exact figure is open to question. For a discussion of the factors surrounding this issue see Yorke, *Domestic Politics,* 33–35.

[86] Yorke, *Domestic Stability,* 39.

[87] See Brynen, "Economic Crisis," 79, for a detailed discussion of how in Jordan petrodollar foreign aid and workers' remittances served as crucial aspects of regime stability during the period under discussion.

[88] Mazur, *Economic Growth,* 85.

[89] Ibid., 85.

diverted economic activity towards Jordan. The net effect of all these developments was a construction boom mostly concentrated in Amman.[90] Jordan's reliance on funding from external sources[91] was of key importance to the internal political dynamics of the state. The state's recourse to such externally-generated largesse meant that it was much less restrained by domestic factors and allowed it to maintain political stability through cooptation and extensive use of patronage.[92] In effect, oil wealth served to inhibit demands for democratization in Jordan during this period, as all sectors of society reaped the economic benefits of the status quo.

Political life was circumscribed in this decade. The regime discouraged all formal political activity and a 1973 Press and Publications Law provided for censorship by the security services (*mukhābārāt*). Political power remained in the hands of the king, the senior bureaucratic/business elite, and the military.[93] Tribal leaders received direct material rewards from the crown while mediating allocation and provision of local services in home areas. East Bank landowners were encouraged by state agricultural investment programs. The upper echelons of Jordan's business class (composed of Jordanian and Palestinian elements) enjoyed an atmosphere of free trade and benefitted from the state's encouragement of private sector development.[94]

East Bankers undoubtedly gained more than Palestinians from the state's largesse. But Palestinians also profited significantly and were willing to shelve political differences to benefit from the status quo. The economic boom sharply reduced prospects of unemployment for refugees. Many Palestinians found employment in the oil-rich Arab states and were among the first emigrants.[95] A predominantly Palestinian entrepreneurial

---

90 Ibid., 86.

91 See Brynen, "Economic Crisis," 79, where he states that domestic taxation typically financed only 10–20% of state expenditures and import duties only another 20–30%.

92 See Yorke, *Domestic Politics*, 24, and Brynen, "Economic Crisis," 74, for a discussion of this phenomenon.

93 See Brynen, "Economic Crisis," 82, where he notes that by the late 1980s the police and armed forces totalled 90,000 employees or about 18% of the country's labour force.

94 Mazur, *Economic Growth*, 235.

95 Allan Findlay and Musa Samha, "Return Migration and Urban Change: A Jordanian Case Study," in *Return Migration and Regional Economic Problems*, ed. Russell King (London: Croom Helm, 1986), 178.

class flourished in the trade, service, and small and medium-scale manufacturing sectors.[96] Even Palestinians in the camps became less of a political liability for the regime as they benefitted from increased government spending.[97]

Palestinians' acquiescence to Hashemite rule due to their having acquired a greater economic stake in the kingdom was a great blessing to King Hussein in the later 1970s. After the civil war he struggled to balance Palestinian and Transjordanian with regional and international considerations. The PLO's increased regional recognition and pressure from Jordan's Arab creditors prompted him to endorse the Rabat 1974 resolution. This paved the way for Jordan's reconciliation with other Arab states and their willingness to aid the revival of the state's economy. But King Hussein perceived the formal arrival of the PLO on the international stage as a setback in his attempts at the integration of Palestinians and Jordanians into a single society. He responded to the Palestinian nationalist challenge by cutting back Palestinian membership in the armed forces and reducing Palestinian cabinet ministers from ten to five. He also withdrew financial subsidies for the West Bank. Although he did not withdraw his claim to the West Bank and sought to retain as much influence as possible there through patronage, the king's endorsement of the PLO in 1978 led to an improved climate of political relations between Palestinians and Transjordanians. Most Palestinians realized they were better off in Jordan than in other Arab states.[98]

The economic prosperity of the 1970s brought with it tremendous expansion and modernization of the state. An extensive program of education accompanied by urbanization and industrialization brought significant changes to the structure of Jordanian society. The expansion of education, a priority of the Jordanian government since 1950, was accelerated in the 1970s, particularly in view of its young population.[99] A ten-year education programme launched in 1968 had as its goal the achievement of close to 100% enrollment of children in primary schools and a major adult literacy drive.[100] Both goals were achieved. From 1960

---

96 Brynen, "Economic Crisis," 81.

97 Yorke, *Domestic Politics*, 42.

98 Ibid., 42.

99 The youthfulness of the population is attested to by the fact that in 1979, 43.1% was between the ages of 5 and 20.

100 UNESCO, *International Yearbook of Education* (Paris, UNESCO: 1968), 275–276.

to 1980 the rate of the population enrolled in primary schools in the East Bank rose from 77% to 100%. Enrollment of students in secondary schools increased from 39% in 1960 to 70% in 1983.[101] Adult literacy rates rose from 32% to 70% in the same time period.[102] The education programme also included the expansion of technical schools and teacher training colleges.[103] The University of Jordan was founded in 1970 and Yarmūk University in 1977.

It should be noted that the statistics above obscure the differences in education rates of males and females. Statistics on overall literacy show women at a clear disadvantage[104] but making significant gains on men according to 1990 estimates.[105] This trend, of course, reflects the higher education level of younger generations of women. Since 1980 women have comprised just under 50% of the university population.[106]

The 1970s and early 1980s saw the expansion of state services beyond education. A modern state infrastructure was established with a network of roads, an international airport and excellent port facilities at Aqaba.[107] Health and social services were expanded, particularly affecting conditions in villages.[108]

The economic life of villagers was affected too by the expansion of the state bureaucracy and light industrial development.[109] Formerly, the

---

101 Adnan Badran and Barbara Khader, eds., *The Economic Development of Jordan* (London, Croom Helm, 1987), 77.

102 Ibid.

103 Peter Gubser, *Jordan: Crossroads of Middle Eastern Events* (Boulder: Westview, 1983), 44. Before 1970, Jordan had only two technical schools, one run by UNWRA and the other by a foreign charity. By 1978 there were an additional eighteen government-run institutes (twelve for boys, six for girls).

104 UNESCO, *UNESCO Statistical Yearbook 1993* (Paris, UNESCO: 1993), Illiterate population statistics show that in 1976 32.4% of the total population was illiterate, comprising 19% of males and 45.6% of females.

105 Ibid. Estimates for 1990 were a total illiterate population of 19.9%, comprising 10.7% of males and 29.7% of females.

106 Ibid.

107 Wilson, *Abdullah,* 2.

108 See Gubser, *Jordan: Crossroads,* 31–32, for information regarding provision of rural facilities and services in Jordan in the 1974–1981 period. According to Gubser, by the early 1980s 70% of the villages had schools, almost all villages had clinics, and a major project was underway to provide power to most villages by the end of the decade.

109 See Mazur, *Economic Growth,* 277. This was not a period of major industrialization. According to Mazur the greater part of the growth in Jordan's industrial sector occurred between 1959 and 1966.

economies of villages had been based in agriculture. But during the 1970s the percentage of the Jordanian labour force employed in agriculture declined considerably.[110] Corresponding to this decline was increased employment in the expanding government bureaucracy, especially in the armed forces. Villages also developed new economic bases, concentrating on phosphate and potash extraction, cement factories and light manufacturing and construction.[111] One result of such local economic changes, combined with the expansion of the state's infrastructure and increased education, was a change in the socioeconomic structure of the village. Traditional bases of leadership were replaced with new ones based on modern education and ability to relate to the government and the private sector.[112]

Life was changing in Jordan's urban centres too. During this decade they swelled in size as a result of internal migration and the influx of Palestinian refugees. By the end of the 1970s, 60% of Jordanians lived in urban areas. By 1983 Amman's population had grown to 744,000 and Irbid had expanded to 131,200.[113] Internal migration was motivated primarily by the search for work and higher living standards in the capital.[114] Unemployment was virtually nonexistent as a result of the extensive out-migration of Jordan's labour force to the oil rich states. The physical appearance of Amman changed dramatically during this decade. Remittances from migrant capital funded a construction boom and the city experienced an outbreak of Western-style villas and four- or five-storey apartment blocs. As the city struggled with the provision of housing, municipal services, and sanitation for rural and Palestinian immigrants, it turned to Western planning advisors. The result was the decongestion of Amman's old downtown and the transformation of the city into a sprawling urban mass which had few traces of its Arab heritage.[115]

---

110 *Ibid.*, 111. Labour was redirected to the armed forces and also to the rapidly expanding service sector.

111 Gubser, *Jordan: Crossroads*, 30.

112 Ibid., 31.

113 Arthur Day, *East Bank/West Bank: Jordan and the Prospects for Peace* (USA Council on Foreign Relations, 1986), 69.

114 For a discussion of this, see L. W. Jones, "Demographic Review, Rapid Population Growth in Baghdad and Amman," *Middle East Journal* 23 (1969): 209–215.

115 Eugene Rogan, "Physical Islamization of Amman," *Muslim World* 76 (January 1986): 29.

By the end of this decade of rapid development there were significant changes in Jordanian society. The population was more educated and more urbanized. The state's expanded role combined with socioeconomic development had the effect of altering citizen-citizen and citizen-state relations. Jordanians experienced a decline in tribal and clan cohesiveness as vehicles for social and political action, and individuals identified more directly with the state.[116] Government employment of a large percentage of Jordan's labour force along with its regulation of the private sector served to increase the interdependence between the citizen and state. Both Palestinians and East Bankers were coopted by the state through its economic largesse, overlooking their differences in favour of the status quo. The decade of 1973–1982 can therefore be viewed as one of great political stability in Jordan combined with dramatic socioeconomic change. Stability was ensured by prosperity, but a downturn in Jordan's good economic fortune in the early 1980s would unleash demands for greater political liberalization from an increasingly sophisticated population.

Pressures for Democratization: 1982–1989

After 1982 the prosperity Jordan had enjoyed for a decade came to an end. World oil prices entered a sustained period of decline.[117] The drop in oil prices adversely affected the two major pillars of Jordan's economy: workers' remittances and petrodollar foreign aid. Jordan faced increasing balance of payments problems as the current account balance dipped into the red and economic growth slowed. With the return of migrant workers from the Gulf, unemployment began to rise. A succession of governments in the 1980s, those of Muḍar Badrān (1980–1984), Aḥmad ʿUbaydī (1984–1988), and Zayd al-Rifāʿī (1985–1989) were reluctant to reduce the government spending on which the state's cooptation of the population relied. Instead, they sought to balance the budget through domestic and

116 Linda Layne, *Elections in the Middle East: Implications of Recent Trends* (Boulder: Colorado, 1987), 128. Layne argues that it is a mistake to assume that the weakening of tribal solidarity threatens the Jordanian regime. Such assumptions are based on the idea that tribes provide the bedrock of support for the Hashemite regime. Layne suggests that this approach overlooks the role of other groups in sustaining the monarchy. Further, she points to the greater identification of tribes with the king as a "shaykh of shaykhs" and the ultimate source of authority in the context of less tribal cohesiveness.

117 Brynen, "Economic Crisis", 84. They declined from a peak at US $36 a barrel in 1981 to below US $15 a barrel by 1986.

European loans, driving Jordan's declared external debt up almost three times in the 1980–1987 period.[118] The economic downturn gave rise to political dissatisfaction. Differences between East Bankers and Palestinians resurfaced in the context of both perceptions of the state's unequal distribution of resources in the previous decade and the reinvigoration of Palestinian nationalism after the 1982 Israeli invasion of Lebanon.

Inequalities which had been overlooked in the period of prosperity were now brought to the surface. Palestinians objected to the favouritism shown East Bankers by state patronage and the preponderance of Transjordanians holding senior political and administrative positions.[119] The Israeli invasion of Lebanon and the dispersal of Palestinian guerrillas throughout the Arab world increased Palestinian restlessness, weakened the PLO, and brought to the fore the question of what Jordanian policy toward the West Bank and Palestinians in general should be.[120] The Israeli-Jordanian modus vivendi which had characterized the 1970s had collapsed in the context of repeated Israeli claims to the West Bank. Hussein was concerned that tensions might be further escalated by Palestinian use of Jordan as a base for operations against Israel in the West Bank. He required a formula that would enable Jordan to maintain its claim to the West Bank and illustrate Jordan's indispensability in a peace process by drawing the PLO to the bargaining table. The untenability of the king's position was clear in the 1980s. He could not hope to fulfil Hashemite expansionist ambitions and at the same time retain the loyalty of his Palestinian constituents. Attempts to draw the PLO into a peace process failed in 1983 and 1985, so in 1988 the king announced his decision to sever legal and administrative ties with the West Bank.[121]

Transjordanians were also politically restive. Tribal leaders' identification with the Hashemites was beginning to change. Some were dissatisfied with their share of the economic pie and wanted more say in policy making. In a sense, as Yorke has pointed out, the frustrations of these tribal leaders reflected the gradual erosion of the old informal

---

118 Statistics cited by Brynen, "Economic Growth," 84–93.

119 Yorke, *Domestic Politics*, 75.

120 See Yorke, *Domestic Politics*, 82, and Ziyad Abu Amr, *Islamic Fundamentalism in the West Bank and Gaza: Muslim Brotherhood and Islamic Jihad* (Bloomington: Indiana University Press, 1994), 56.

121 See Yorke, *Domestic Politics*, 43–45, for a detailed discussion of King Hussein's policies towards the Palestinians.

political system as a result of the encroachment of the state.[122] Socioeconomic changes in the previous decades had profound effects on the East Bank population. There was a new, educated and technically skilled generation. This generation of would-be professionals was frustrated by the prospect of unemployment. There also evolved, as one scholar has put it, "a new trans-tribal East Bank political personality" with a strong nationalist, anti-Palestinian element. In the view of some members of this generation, the Palestinians were interlopers who had benefitted unfairly from the economic prosperity of the 1970s. This view was held in particular by bedouin migrants to urban centres who found in the early 1980s that Palestinian entrepreneurs fared better than they did.[123] Of course, not all East Bankers shared such views. But the educated among them, young and old, represented the aspirations of a "new, well-educated and growing middle class to have a greater role in running the country."[124] Members of the political elite, many educated in the West, demanded change in the state's economic and political policies. They called for increased political participation, a fairer system of taxation and control of conspicuous consumption.[125] In the early 1980s the king had responded to pressures for political liberalization by the creation of a National Consultative Council. But the Council had no real power and the political system remained unchanged. The king was unchallenged at the pinnacle of power, ruling with the East Bank-controlled army and security forces and the business-government oligarchy which contained East Bank and Palestinian elements.[126]

Pressures for democratization played a role, but not the only one, in King Hussein's decision to reconvene parliament in 1984. The recall of parliament also reflected the end of political coordination between the PLO and Jordan and was followed by a campaign to reassert Jordan's domination in the West Bank. Hussein was indirectly challenging the PLO monopoly over Palestinian representation which had been granted at the

---

122 Ibid., 26.

123 Adam Garfinkle, "The Nine Lives of Hashemite Jordan" in *The Politics of Change in the Middle East*, Robert Satloff, ed. (Oxford: Westview, 1993), 94.

124 Ibid.

125 Yorke, *Domestic Politics*, 26.

126 Garfinkle, "Nine Lives", 92.

Rabat 1974 summit, a monopoly which had yielded little in light of the PLO's unimpressive track record.[127]

The first act of the newly called parliament was to pass a constitutional amendment allowing elections to take place on the East Bank only. Eight members who had died were replaced in by-elections. The government held free elections in order to gauge public opinion. Political parties remained outlawed and candidates ran as individuals. The regime was taken aback by the election results which returned two members of the Muslim Brotherhood and one Islamist independent to the parliament. This was the first indication of the rising popularity of Islamists.[128] Equally alarming to the government was the fact that Layth Shubaylāt, an independent Islamist, had succeeded in winning an Amman seat which had throughout Jordan's history been the province of the influential Ḥadīd family.

The recall of parliament in 1984 did not herald significant liberalization of Jordanian political life. In addition to maintaining the ban on political parties, the press continued to be censored and the security services harassed regime opponents, in particular members of the Muslim Brotherhood.[129] The parliament was dominated by East Bank notables who were politically quiescent. The newly elected deputies attacked the government on human rights issues and political corruption but achieved little except their own unpopularity with the secret police.

In the meantime Jordan's economic crisis intensified in the context of the ongoing regional oil slump. In 1988 the GDP was reduced by approximately 3.5% and showed no growth the following year. In 1987 alone, 35,000 expatriates returned to Jordan, fuelling high unemployment rates. Economic problems, worsened by the growing size of Jordan's debt, fuelled political discontent.[130]

The outbreak of the *intifāḍah* heightened Palestinian nationalism and opposition to Hussein's policies. The intifāḍah raised the worry for the regime "that a romantic and more violent form of nationalism might

---

127 See Day, *East Bank/West Bank*, 41, where he analyses King Hussein's political motives in recalling parliament.

128 The Muslim Brotherhood's role in these elections is analyzed in detail in Chapter Three. Likewise, the particular appeal of the Muslim Brotherhood in the context of other political and economic developments in the 1980s is taken up in this chapter.

129 This will be discussed in Chapter Three.

130 Brynen, "Economic Crisis," 88.

spread to the East Bank."[131] In fact, no real spread of the intifāḍah took place in Jordan because of two factors: the disinclination of Palestinians to give up their lifestyles in the East Bank and the repressive measures undertaken by the authorities.[132] The government of Prime Minister al-Rifāʿī showed an increasingly autocratic style of rule. Parliament was disbanded in 1988 before King Hussein announced Jordan's disengagement from the West Bank. The disengagement reflected the king's realization, as mentioned earlier, that he could not reconcile the stability of his regime with his ambitions in the West Bank. Hussein sought to amputate Palestinian nationalist threats to his regime and to bolster it with East Bank support. The disengagement was Hussein's way of rejecting some Israeli assertions that "Jordan is Palestine" and of telling the Palestinians "You can take the West Bank (if you can) but you have to leave me alone in the East Bank."[133]

He had underestimated, however, the extent of Transjordanian political and economic frustrations.[134] The disengagement had a negative effect on the economy, contributing to the collapse of the Jordanian dinar and increased dissatisfaction of East Bankers.[135] As economic conditions worsened, the government was forced in the spring of 1989 to seek credits from the International Monetary Fund. The deal involved the government's agreement to a five year economic stabilization programme. This program necessitated austerity measures, and on April 16 the government raised the prices of fuel, beverages and cigarettes.[136] Two days later riots broke out in the southern part of the country, near Maan, an area traditionally loyal to the monarchy. It is significant that no Palestinians were involved in this rioting; it reflected Transjordanian economic discontent. The riots spread to other areas of the kingdom and raised the political awareness of Jordanians.[137]

The riots made Hussein realize that he must undertake economic and political reforms if he wished to maintain the stability of his regime. In the months after the food riots he took steps to reassure Jordanians that a

---

131 Garfinkle, "Nine Lives," 94.

132 Ibid., 95.

133 Ibid., 96.

134 Ibid.

135 Abu Amr, *Islamic Fundamentalism*, 91.

136 Brynen, "Economic Crisis," 90.

137 Abu Jaber, "The 1989 Parliamentary Elections," 70.

liberalization process was underway. The unpopular al-Rifāʿī government was asked to resign and an interim government focussed on economic adjustment and the planning of elections. The king held meetings with tribal delegations, professional associations and provinces. He raised the idea of a National Charter as a new basis for relations between the people and the state, complementing the constitution and warranting the establishment of political parties.[138] In July 1989, the king announced the decision to hold full parliamentary elections later that year. These elections marked a significant turning point in the regime's history, heralding Jordan's second experiment with parliamentary life and the rise to power of the Muslim Brotherhood. The story of this rise to power is the subject of the remaining chapters.

---

138 Ibid., 71.

Chapter Two
Reformism and Pragmatism in the Formative Years, 1945–1957

This chapter discusses the circumstances of the founding of the Muslim Brotherhood in Jordan in 1945 and the formative period of its development up to 1957. The Brotherhood in this period came under the leadership of professionals and developed a reformist ideology which, combined with its pragmatic interest in retaining legal status, paved the way for its establishment of symbiotic relations with the regime.

This formative period is analyzed in three phases. During the first phase, from 1946 to 1948, the Brotherhood was founded by a wealthy merchant with the aid of missionaries from the Egyptian Muslim Brotherhood. It evolved as a loose-knit coalition of merchants whose primary goal was to support the *jihād* in Palestine. The Brotherhood had no further political agenda at this time. It officially adopted principles similar to those of the Egyptian Muslim Brotherhood embodying a strong critique of Western influences on Jordanian society and calling for the education of a generation in Islamic principles to pave the way for Islamic rule. But in reality the Muslim Brotherhood under Abū Qūrah did not seek to implement this agenda. There were two main reasons for this: the unpoliticized nature of Jordanian society and Abū Qūrah's loyalty to the regime. Although it opposed ʿAbdallāh's policies in Palestine, the Brotherhood was willing to overlook any differences to ensure the emir's blessing. Such pragmatism has characterized the movement ever since. ʿAbdallāh granted the Brotherhood legal status as a welfare organization, hoping to secure its support against secularist opposition. These early days set a long-term trend of symbiotic relations between the Brotherhood and the regime which endured through the 1980s. The dynamics of this relationship were simple: for the regime it was safer to coopt the Brotherhood than to risk forcing it into opposition. For the Brotherhood, legal status advanced its reformist agenda.

In the second phase under consideration, 1948 to 1952, the Palestine war marked a significant turning point in the Brotherhood's history. The movement came increasingly under the influence of a new professional membership which had come of age in the towns of Transjordan after

World War II. The new members assumed full leadership of the movement by 1952.

Annexation of the West Bank brought dramatic changes to Jordan. Chief among them was the vitalization of political life under the leadership of Palestinian nationalists. In this context and under the direction of more politicized leadership, the Brotherhood was transformed from a loose-knit charitable association into a political organization which could compete with secularist parties. Its program extended beyond the jihād in Palestine and became more comprehensive, calling for the implementation of sharīʿah and the establishment of an Islamic order (*niẓām*). The Brotherhood's ideology continued to be reformist in nature, stressing non-violence as Ḥasan al-Bannā had done. It emphasized gradual Islamization of society, and consonant with its professional class perspective, it stressed education as a means by which a more Islamically-oriented generation would come to power. Education was viewed as a primary conduit for reform as well as recruitment. The new leadership initiated the development of an *usrah* (family) cell network for grass-roots organization and mobilization of membership.

The third phase examined here, covering the years 1954–1957, is one of the most critical periods in the Brotherhood's history. These years were significant in crystallizing the Brotherhood's ideological traits (which have changed little over the decades). The movement's ideology remained moderate and reformist, defending the legitimacy of Hashemite rule and advocating gradual implementation of *sharīʿah* (Islamic Law) through education. The Brotherhood downplayed the creation of an Islamic state as a serious goal. The liberation of Palestine remained a mainstay of the Brotherhood's agenda but was subsumed in the general context of the liberation of Muslim peoples from imperialist, and by extension, Zionist control. Palestinian political frustrations were for the most part championed in this period by pan-Arabists to whose nationalism the Brotherhood was bitterly opposed.

The most distinctive feature of the Brotherhood's ideology, apart from its moderation, was its imprecision. Concepts of the future Islamic order or state were ill-defined and the implications of the implementation of sharīʿah were not stated. This imprecision betrayed the movement's desire not to challenge the Hashemite regime and the movement's relative lack of intellectual vigour as well as the limited Islamic theoretical legacy on the formation of the state. The movement produced no significant publications in this period except *al-Kifāḥ al-Islāmī* ("The Islamic Struggle"), a fiery political sheet. A brief survey of *al-Kifāḥ al-Islāmī* demonstrates both a superficiality of political analysis and a tendency to resort to bombastic rhetoric which have characterized the movement's few publications.

The years 1954–1957 also marked one of the most significant periods in the political history of the Muslim Brotherhood. In these turbulent years, King Hussein fought to defend his monarchy against Palestinian pan-Arab nationalist opposition. Compared to the nationalists, the Brotherhood was not a significant player in the political drama. But it made two significant decisions during this period. First, it demonstrated its willingness to work within a parliamentary system, participating in the elections of 1954 and 1956. Second, it resolved to support the Hashemite throne against nationalist challenges. The Brotherhood's decision to stand by the king cemented symbiotic relations with Hussein whereby, as in the case of his grandfather ʿAbdallāh, he allowed the Brotherhood to function legally, and to participate in parliament in return for its tacit support. For Hussein, as for ʿAbdallāh, a liaison with the Muslim Brotherhood helped to support his Islamic legitimacy. However, there was a certain uneasiness underlying this liaison, as the king and the Brotherhood often had diametrically opposing views, especially on the issues of alliances with Western powers and Western influences in Jordanian society. At times when the Brotherhood was overbold in criticizing the government, it was subject to repression by the security forces. But, in general, the unspoken agreement between the king and the Brotherhood was that although the movement might express its opposition to the regime's pro-West policies, it would not openly challenge the throne.

Overall, the Brotherhood's strategy reaped good rewards. When the king overcame the National Socialists in 1957 and introduced martial law, all political parties were banned. The Brotherhood was the only political organization to retain legal status under the cover of a charitable organization. This status would serve the movement well in enabling it to develop a grass-roots social base in ensuing decades.

Ḥājj ʿAbdullaṭif Abū Qūrah and the Founding of the Jordanian Muslim Brotherhood

The first branch of the Muslim Brotherhood in Jordan was opened by Ḥājj ʿAbdullaṭif Abū Qūrah in Amman in 1945 with the primary goal of supporting the jihād in Palestine. A "wealthy merchant well known for his charitable works and great religious zeal," Abū Qūrah was born in Salt around 1909. He attended the Islamic elementary school where he "displayed a keen awareness of Islamic subjects."[1] He went on to establish a trading business in Amman. Commercial activity was limited in Transjordan in this period and was dominated in Amman by a group of Syrian merchants trading largely in cloths and foodstuffs. Abū Qūrah was closely affiliated with this group of Syrians who later supported his fund-raising activities on behalf of the Palestinians.[2] The Syrians were the most significant and prosperous merchant community in Amman in the late 1920s and 1930s. They were also among the most urbanized and politicized. They supported Palestinian resistance to British rule, and opposed ᶜAbdallāh's position on Palestine.

ᶜAbdallāh first turned his attention to Palestine in the 1930s, after consolidating his rule over Transjordan.[3] He had both long and short-term goals. In the long term he hoped to satisfy his expansionist ambitions with the merger of Transjordan and Palestine, with adequate safeguards for the Jewish population, under his monarchical rule.[4] ᶜAbdallāh was concerned that the emergence of a Palestinian identity could threaten his regime. He was eager to negotiate a deal with the British and the Zionists. ᶜAbdallāh's position put him on a collision course with the Palestinian nationalists under the leadership of Ḥājj Amīn al-Ḥusaynī, *muftī* of Jerusalem and president of the Supreme Muslim Council. In the short term, ᶜAbdallāh pursued land lease options with the Jewish Agency which served his economic interest and those of other Transjordanian large landowners.[5]

Rumours of ᶜAbdallāh's dealings with the Jewish Agency sparked opposition in Transjordan in 1933, headed by a disparate coalition of

---

[1] ᶜAwnī al-ᶜUbaydī, *Jamāᶜat al-Ikhwān al-Muslimīn fī al-Urdunn wa Filasṭīn, 1945-1970* (Amman: 1991), 34. Abū Qūrah did not go on to achieve a further level of education. As mentioned earlier, Transjordan before 1948 had a rudimentary education system characterized primarily by the village kuttāb.

[2] One of the wealthy merchants who supported Abū Qūrah's endeavors for the Palestinians was Ḥājj Ibrāhīm Manjū. He was a member of a wealthy Syrian commercial family which had settled in Transjordan in the 1920s, fleeing French Mandate rule in Syria.

[3] For general background on this see Chapter One.

[4] Abidi, *Jordan, 19.*

[5] See Wilson, *Abdullah,* 110–114, for a detailed discussion of this period. This emergent group of landowning tribal shaykhs were eager to convert some of their land into capital.

Syrian pan-nationalists, Palestinian government bureaucrats and local leaders.[6]

The first indication of Abū Qūrah's interest in the Palestinian cause came in 1936 when he raised funds from the Amman merchant community to aid the Palestinians in the strike of 1936.[7] Between 1936 and 1939 he visited Palestine where he came into contact with members of the Egyptian Muslim Brotherhood.[8] But Abū Qūrah did not move to establish a branch of the Muslim Brotherhood in Jordan until nearly a decade later in 1944. Then he was impressed by an article in the Egyptian Brotherhood's publication, *al-Ikhwān al-Muslīmūn*[9] (The Muslim Brotherhood) calling for the preparation of the Muslim *ummah* (community) for the jihād against colonialism and Zionism. He wrote to Ḥasan al-Bannā[10] saying that he would like to establish a branch of the Brotherhood in Jordan. That year he went to visit al-Bannā in Cairo,[11] inviting members of

---

[6] Wilson, *Abudllah, 110.*

[7] Dr. ʿIzzāt ʿAzzīzī, interview by author, tape recording, Amman, Jordan, October 30, 1991. Dr. ʿAzzīzī is the son-in-law of Abū Qūrah, and his recollections, along with those of other Muslim Brotherhood members, form the basis of this account. They are substantiated, where possible, by references from al-ʿUbaydī, who bases his material on interviews conducted with the Abū Qūrah family.

[8] There is no hard evidence that Abū Qūrah came into contact with the Muslim Brotherhood in Transjordan before travelling to Palestine. The Egyptian Brothers did not send emissaries to Transjordan before the 1940s. The Muslim Brotherhood's first active involvement outside of Egypt was with Palestinian affairs. After the initial disturbances of 1936 they sent emissaries there and also raised funds to support the Palestinian strike. Despite the shortage of evidence, it seems suspiciously coincidental that Abū Qūrah was engaged in fundraising activities at the same time. While in Jerusalem he did make contact with Khalīfah (the leader of the Jordanian Muslim Brotherhood since 1952), who was studying agriculture at the Khaddūrī College in Jerusalem in the late 1930s. Khalīfah came into contact with the Muslim Brotherhood in Jerusalem. For more information on the activities of the Egyptian Muslim Brotherhood at this period see Richard. P. Mitchell, *The Society of the Muslim Brothers* (Oxford: Oxford University Press, 1969), 15–16; and Ishak Musa Husaini, *The Moslem Brethren* (Beirut: 1955), 75.

[9] The main organ of the Egyptian Brotherhood between 1942 and 1946.

[10] Ḥasan al-Bannā was founder and leader of the Egyptian Muslim Brotherhood until his death in 1949.

[11] There is no specific mention in Egyptian Muslim Brotherhood sources of this meeting, but this is not surprising as Ḥasan al-Bannā was at the time inundated with visitors. See Mitchell, *The Society,* 172, where he notes that "scarcely a week passed without witnessing the appearance at the headquarters of one or more dignitaries and lesser personages from all parts of the Muslim world, as official speakers or merely as listeners at the meetings."

the Egyptian Brotherhood to Transjordan to help spread the *daʿwah* (Islamic propagation) throughout the country. Ḥasan al-Bannā sent him two emissaries, Saʿīd Ramaḍān and ʿAbd al-Ḥakīm ʿAbidīn.[12] These men both played a significant role in Jordan, Syria and Palestine in the 1940s and 1950s as ambassadors of the Egyptian Muslim Brotherhood. They travelled extensively around Jordan in 1945, visiting the major towns of Salt, Karak, Irbid and Amman. Following the pattern of the Egyptian Brotherhood's early recruitment activities in Ismāʿīliyya in the 1920s and 1930s, they organized meetings in mosques in urban centres.[13] In the absence of any other significant institutions, mosques provided the major educational and cultural venues in Transjordanian towns.

The emissaries, of course, brought with them the message of Ḥasan al-Bannā, and so from the beginning the Jordanian Brotherhood was heavily influenced by the ideology of the Egyptians. The Egyptian movement had evolved an agenda highly critical of British imperial influence and national rule of the country's leading political party, the Wafd. Its critique of conditions in Egypt was inspired by the thinking of the late 19th-century Muslim reformist school, in particular the early contributions made to it by Muḥammad ʿAbduh (d. 1905). ʿAbduh sought to counter the influence of Western imperialism on Islamic society by opposing Muslim adoption of foreign laws and asserting the compatibility of Islam with the complexities of modern life.[14] ʿAbduh asserted that such compatibility would be achieved by a regeneration of Islam, abandoning much of the corpus of legal exegesis created by the *ʿulamāʾ* (religious scholars) which he deemed inadequate for the needs of the time, and returning to the two fundamental sources of the Qurʾān and the *sunnah* (Prophetic tradition).

According to ʿAbduh, Muslim history had been in decline since the period of the first four caliphs. This was the last period in which the Islamic state had been governed by a pious ruler, chosen by and responsible to his people for enacting divine law. Since then the Islamic state had undergone a long process of moral decay, extending through the corrupt rule of the Ummayad, Abassid, and Ottoman dynastic

---

12 al-ʿUbaydī, *Jamāʿat al-Ikhwān*, 36.

13 Mitchell, *The Society*, 9.

14 Hamid Enayat, *Modern Islamic Political Thought* (University of Texas Press: Austin, 1982), 77. For a detailed review of ʿAbduh's life and thought, see also Albert Hourani, *Arabic Thought in the Liberal Age, 1798–1939* (Cambridge University Press: 1962), 130–160.

caliphates. Following along the lines of ʿAbduh's thought, Ḥasan al-Bannā and Muḥammad Ghazzālī (a significant theoretician of the Muslim Brotherhood) argued that in the twentieth century, Egypt and the rest of the Islamic world were now threatened by the onslaught of communist and nationalist ideologies which denied the supremacy of sharīʿah in society.[15] Al-Bannā's declared goal was that "the Islamic fatherland be freed from all foreign domination, for this is a natural right belonging to every human being which only the unjust oppressor or the conquering exploiter will deny."[16]

Also following on the thinking of ʿAbduh, Ḥasan al-Bannā believed that the ʿulāmāʾ and their *fiqh* (legal thought) must be deprived of their popularly-attributed sacredness to give the contemporary Muslims freedom from tradition and facilitate the opening of the doors of *ijtihād* (fresh interpretation).[17] A revitalized Islam based on a new, more timely interpretation of the Qurʾān and expurgation of falsehoods from the sunnah would provide the basis for the renaissance of society.[18] Sharīʿah would be implemented to provide the framework of an Islamic order (*al-niẓām*).[19] And, in al-Bannā's words, "a free Islamic state may arise in this free fatherland acting according to the precepts of Islam, applying its social regulations, proclaiming its sound principles and broadcasting its sage message to all mankind."[20]

The first line of approach of the Egyptian Brotherhood was to focus primarily on education rather than political action. Al-Bannā's objective was to create a new generation of believers who would provide the basis for a rejuvenated Islamic society free from foreign domination. The movement therefore turned its attention to the enlightenment of its audience regarding the dangers posed by the decay of Islamic societies. While Ḥasan al-Bannā insisted that Muslims must stand up to the West, his

---

15 Mitchell, *The Society*, 210. Ghazzālī's first work, *Min Hunā Naʿlam* (From Here We Learn), appeared in 1948.

16 Ḥasan al-Bannā, *Five Tracts of Hasan al-Banna* (1906–1949), trans. Charles Wendell (Berkeley: University of California Press, 1978), 21.

17 Mitchell, *The Society*, 236–239.

18 Ibid., 238.

19 Ibid., 235. The meaning of an Islamic order as advocated by the Muslim Brotherhood was ambiguous. In practice the term may refer to some sort of Islamic state (*dawlah*). But, mostly, as Mitchell argues, the term refers to a set of guiding principles for rule, rather than a specific model of government. This issue is discussed in further detail in Chapter Four.

20 Ḥasan al-Bannā, *Five Tracts*, 31.

discourse on the whole had a moderate tone, advocating non-violent means of jihād. He noted, "One of the loftiest forms of jihād is to utter a word of truth in the presence of a tyrannical ruler."[21] Al-Bannā avoided direct attacks on the Egyptian monarchy (to which he seems to have felt some loyalty) but was openly critical from the first of the British-imposed parliamentary system.[22] He and Muḥammad Ghazzālī saw political parties as agents of division and disunity.[23]

But as the Brotherhood spread, it moved towards a position of greater militancy and political action in the context of Egypt's struggle with British imperialism. The perceived Zionist threat was of particular significance in influencing the movement to adopt more militant strategies. With the Palestinian Arab General Strike of 1936–1939, the Egyptian Muslim Brotherhood was transformed into a potent political force which engaged in violence against the regime.[24]

In 1946, at the time of founding of the Jordanian branch of the Muslim Brotherhood, the Egyptian Brotherhood declared its goals to be the following:

1. scientific goal of education
2. practical goal of unification of Islamic countries
3. economic goal of development of the Islamic world
4. sociophilanthropic goal of providing charity
5. patriotic and nationalistic goal of the liberation of the Arab and Islamic worlds from foreigners and the establishment of an Islamic state
6. world peace through the principles of Islam[25]

In comparison with these principles, the Jordanian Muslim Brotherhood had a considerably less comprehensive agenda. The only overtly political goal espoused by the Brothers was the liberation of Palestine. And the early emissaries of Ḥasan al-Bannā in Jordan avoided political topics, confining themselves to the general discussion of Islamic theological themes.[26] The Jordanian movement published the following principles in 1946:[27]

---

21 Ibid., 48.

22 Mitchell, *The Society, 220.*

23 Ibid., 219. It is important to note, however, that Ḥasan al-Bannā would later condone participation in parliament as a means of influencing society.

24 Enayat, *Modern Islamic,* 84.

25 Husaini, *The Moslem Brethren,* 41–42.

26 Muḥammad al-Bannā, interview by author, tape recording, Irbid, Jordan, 25 June 1992. Al-Bannā recalled Saʿīd Ramaḍān's visits to Irbid where he lectured to secondary

> . . . to work towards a new generation which understands Islam in the right and virtuous way, to spread the word supporting Islamic rule based on the revival of the Arab lands, to join forces with Islamic associations in Arab countries for a unified holy war, to encourage the study of true Islam amongst youth and students, to contribute to development of a new Arab culture (based on Islamic principles) and to defend Islamic ideology.[28]

The founding principles of the Jordanian Muslim Brotherhood were heavily influenced by Ḥasan al-Bannā's emphasis on education and did not reflect the Egyptian Muslim Brotherhood's agenda during the period in the 1940s, when the Egyptians were adopting more violent means of action.

There were several reasons for the Jordanian Brotherhood's limited agenda at this time. First, it reflected Abū Qūrah's only real aim in establishing the movement in Jordan, which was to support the jihād in Palestine. He had no interest in broader goals of establishing Islamic rule or challenging ʿAbdallāh's regime or British interests in Jordan. Abū Qūrah's lack of interest in such broader political issues can perhaps be partly explained by his limited education. His attitude also points to Jordan's political culture in the mid 1940s, a culture which was not primed for revolutionary action. This factor cannot have escaped the observation of Ḥasan al-Bannā's emissaries and may well have played into their decision not to encourage a more radical agenda for the Jordanian wing.

Transjordanians were relatively unpoliticized at this point. In the period through World War II to 1948, ʿAbdallāh witnessed the apex of his power.[29] Jordan's population was predominantly rural. Low levels of education and poor communications favoured limited political consciousness. As a result, in the 1940s students comprised the Brotherhood's main audience. The Brotherhood made a point of visiting the secondary schools to give public lectures. They organized boy scouts clubs for primary and secondary school students. These clubs involved social and

---

students and after the lectures formed "a study group of men who met every day studying, inviting everyone." (Muḥammad al-Bannā wished it to be known for the record that he never joined the Muslim Brotherhood and his only contact with the movement was during his high school days.) It should also be noted that he bore no relation to Ḥasan, leader of the Egyptian Muslim Brotherhood.

27 The full extent of ʿAbdallāh's dealings with the Jewish Agency and the British over the future of Palestine was not known at this time.

28 al-ʿUbaydī, *Jamāʿat al-Ikhwān*, 43.

29 For background information on this period, see Chapter One.

athletic activities as well as theological study but, again, they had no political agenda. They proved to be the most effective source of recruitment to the Brotherhood.[30] Because future members of the Muslim Brotherhood were attracted to the movement in high school or preparatory school in the mid-1940s,[31] the Brotherhood would benefit greatly from the rapid expansion of education in Jordan after 1950.

Foundation of the Movement

Before the headquarters of the Muslim Brotherhood was officially established, a delegation of the movement visited King ʿAbdallāh to ask for his blessing.[32] ʿAbdallāh extended his favour to the movement with the understanding that it would function as a purely religious organization:

> He asked the delegate of the brethren to convey his greetings to the Muslim Brethren in the hope that the movement would have no aim but utter devotion to God, to His work, for His sake and for the benefit of the Muslim Brethren.[33]

The Muslim Brotherhood was licensed under the Ottoman Law of Associations, consistent with its status as a purely religious organization.[34]

ʿAbdallāh had several possible motivations for allowing the establishment of the Muslim Brotherhood in Jordan. He likely presumed that by approving the movement he could avoid the development of the Muslim Brotherhood into an active Islamist opposition as had been the case in Egypt. In the post-war era ʿAbdallāh also hoped that supporting the movement would buttress his claim to Islamic legitimacy based on his Sharifian descent. In this regard he was eager to encourage the Muslim Brotherhood in an effort to offset the rise of nationalism. After 1948, pan-Arab nationalism would pose a deadly threat to ʿAbdallāh. This was a nationalism which "contained elements of social and political reform and pinned the loss of Palestine to the robes and frock coats of the old nationalist elites."[35] ʿAbdallāh approved of the Brotherhood as an antidote

---

30 The youth clubs are discussed in detail in Chapter Three.

31 This is based on information obtained by the author in interviews with ʿIzzāt Azzīzī, tape recording, Amman, Jordan, 12 November, 1991; Ziyād Abū Ghanīmah (Muslim Brotherhood spokesman in 1992), tape recording, Amman, Jordan, 13 April, 1992; and Yūsuf al-ʿAẓm (Muslim Brotherhood member of parliament since 1954 and editor of *al-Kifāḥ al-Islāmī*), tape recording, Amman, Jordan, 17 June, 1992.

32 Husaini, *The Moslem Brethren, 81.*

33 Ibid.

34 Al-ʿUbaydī, *Jamāʿat al-Ikhwān*, 38.

35 Wilson, *Abdullah, 199.*

to nationalist-secularist trends, counselling his subjects to "avoid the imitation of false habits (by which he meant both communism and democracy) and keep your old traditions and customs and . . . keep your Islam."[36]

Although he blessed the Muslim Brotherhood, ʿAbdallāh regarded the movement with some suspicion. He knew that the Brotherhood was opposed to his policies in Palestine and he was suspicious of the Egyptian movement's liaison with Ḥājj Amīn al-Ḥusaynī.[37] As a result he kept a close eye on the Brotherhood. He required it to apply to the authorities for permission to set up all new branches and even with regard to purely technical matters such as permission to construct a building. Abū Qūrah was watched by the authorities and was even arrested several times in the early 1950s.[38] But for the most part the regime did not interfere with the organization, and relations were amicable. ʿAbdallāh undoubtedly realized that the movement did not have the support to pose a threat to his plans.

The Brotherhood's decision to seek ʿAbdallāh's approval reflected both its limited political agenda and an element of pragmatism. The Brotherhood sought no confrontation with the regime. During the pre-1948 period the Brotherhood largely ignored its founding principles. Although education was given high priority in theory, in reality the movement engaged in limited recruitment activity, primarily through the boy scouts clubs, and produced no publications. The organizational development of the movement was also limited. Branches were established in the cities of Salt, Irbid, and Karak, where study groups and youth club meetings were held. Abū Qūrah functioned as the secretary general and official leader of the movement but retained little centralized control of

---

36 Ibid.

37 The Egyptian Muslim Brotherhood was firmly allied with al-Ḥusaynī. Although there is no specific evidence that the Jordanians ever met with him, supporting his demands for an independent Palestine was a mainstay of their agenda. Al-Ḥusseinī first met with Ḥasan al-Bannā in Cairo in the late 1920s. In 1935 Ḥasan al-Bannā's brother, ʿAbd al-Raḥmān al-Bannā, visited al-Ḥusaynī in Palestine and shortly afterwards the Brotherhood pledged to help support the general Arab strikes of 1936–1939. Contacts with al-Ḥusaynī were maintained during World War II and after the war relations with the Egyptian movement were resumed through its missionaries to Palestine. When the muftī arrived in Cairo in 1946, the Muslim Brotherhood led a successful plea to grant him asylum. For details, see Mitchell, *The Society*, 55–56.

38 Cohen, *Political Parties*, 145. This is information the writer has been unable to corroborate with Jordanian sources.

activities in other branches. The Jordanian movement remained officially a branch of the Egyptian Muslim Brotherhood, with Abū Qūrah responsible to Ḥasan al-Bannā, the Supreme Guide.

The movement at the time was a loose-knit association of wealthy merchants whose common cause was collection of funds for the jihād in Palestine.[39] The Brotherhood's opposition to ʿAbdallāh's expansionist policies and his dealings with the Zionists did not discourage them from seeking his approval.[40] This willingness to overlook ideological differences with the Hashemites as the price for survival has been an enduring characteristic of the movement up to the 1990s.

Thus, ʿAbdallāh's granting of legal recognition to the Muslim Brotherhood as a charitable association established the framework for a symbiotic relationship which would evolve further between the palace and the Brotherhood when Hussein faced nationalist opposition to his rule in the 1950s.

The Jihād

In October 1947 Ḥasan al-Bannā ordered branches of the Muslim Brotherhood to prepare for jihād in Palestine.[41] This was in response to the recommendation in August 1947 by the United Nations Special Committee on Palestine (UNSCOP) to partition Palestine. The Arab leaders had unanimously rejected partition except for ʿAbdallāh, who privately favoured the UNSCOP recommendation. Nevertheless, on 29 November 1947, the United Nations General Assembly passed a resolution to partition Palestine on the basis of the UNSCOP report.[42]

In Cairo, Ḥasan al-Bannā worked in close association with the Arab League to support the struggle of Palestinians against partition. He felt that governments should not be involved in the Palestine question beyond providing diplomatic and political support and that the Palestinian fighters should be aided by volunteers. The Arab League organized an

---

[39] Ibid.

[40] It should be noted that the full extent of ʿAbdallāh's policies regarding Palestine was not made public at the time. ʿAbdallāh was publicly reticent on the subject of partition but privately advocated it to both the United States and Britain. See Wilson, *Abdullah*, 160–161.

[41] Mitchell, *The Society*, 57.

[42] Wilson, *Abdullah*, 163.

international volunteer movement to fight in Palestine, and members of the Egyptian, Jordanian and Syrian Brotherhoods joined.[43]

In Amman, Abū Qūrah mobilized a small brigade of volunteers to fight in Palestine. A series of meetings took place amongst wealthy merchants in order to raise money and arms. A group of more than fifteen merchants willing to donate funds was organized.[44] The identities of these merchants are not known except for that of Ḥājj Ibrāhīm Manjū, "a very rich merchant very much devoted to the Palestinian cause,"[45] who apparently contributed more funds than anybody else.[46]

Abū Qūrah took around one hundred volunteers to Palestine where they worked in cooperation with Syrian and Egyptian Brothers.[47] A detailed account of the activities of the Muslim Brotherhood in the war is not available.[48] But it seems that the Syrians fought mainly to the north, the Egyptians to the south, and the Jordanians between Jerusalem and Hebron.[49] In 1948 members of the Brotherhood fighting with the Egyptian expeditionary force in Palestine reached Hebron, and this led to the establishment there of a branch by 1949. The majority of the Brotherhood volunteers ended up at the Jordanian sector of the frontier, where they were immobilized as a result of differences with the Jordanian military.[50] Although only a small number of Jordanian Brothers died in the fighting, after the war Abū Qūrah returned to Amman "very frustrated and trying to recover from the misery of that defeat."[51]

---

43 Mitchell, *The Society,* 57.

44 ʿAzzīzī, interview.

45 Ibid.

46 Manjū was from a big commercial and banking family which had moved to Jordan decades before.

47 ʿAzzīzī, interview.

48 Mitchell, *The Society,* 57.

49 ʿAzzīzī, interview.

50 Mitchell, *The Society,* 58, refers in general to "differences" with Jordanian authorities. In view of ʿAbdallāh's secret support of partition and his desire to reach an amicable settlement with the Zionists, he was not eager to involve the Arab Legion in fighting during the 1948 war. But, considering his delicate position with regard to other Arab states, ʿAbdallāh could not refrain from involving the Legion. See Abidi, *Jordan,* 41, for illustrations of the Arab League's policy.

51 ʿAzzīzī, interview.

The Post-War Era and New Leadership: 1948–1952

The Palestine war marked a significant turning point for the Muslim Brotherhood. The movement underwent political radicalization and organizational development in the post-war period. During these years it was transformed from a loose-knit charitable association into a political organization under a new, professional leadership.

Annexation of the West Bank brought profound changes to Jordan's social structure and political culture.[52] Transjordan's population expanded to three times its size to include 460,000 residents of the West Bank and 350,000 refugees.[53] Annexation superimposed on Jordan's predominantly rural-nomadic society a Palestinian society which was significantly more urbanized and politicized; Palestinian concerns therefore came to dominate Jordan's political discourse. A generation of young Palestinian professionals and intellectuals came forward after the war as leaders of nationalist-secularist parties sharing a common commitment to the creation of a pan-Arab state comprising Egypt, Syria, Jordan (and sometimes Iraq) as the basis for defeating Israel.

The Palestinian opposition galvanized into action a new generation of Jordanians. This was, as Wilson has argued, "a generation of politically active young men" who had "matured in the towns of Transjordan" during World War II.[54] World War II supply patterns and land privatization encouraged the emergence of merchant moneylenders and the commercial development and expansion of urban centres, particularly Amman.[55] Many from this generation were attracted to the Palestinian nationalist-secularist parties. Others were drawn to the Muslim Brotherhood, forming the nucleus of its future leadership.

The new generation was the first of the professional class in Jordan, the first generation which would, as Bill and Springborg have observed, "seek to advance itself through their professional skills and talents rather than through the use of wealth and personal connections," and which would

---

52 See the general discussion of these in Chapter One.

53 These are International Bank for Reconstruction and Development statistics cited by Mazur, *Economic Growth*, 8.

54 Wilson, *Abdullah, 165.*

55 See Mazur, *Economic Growth*, 8. See also Wilson, *Abdullah*, 165, regarding urbanization. For general background on changes occurring in this period see Chapter One.

seek its livelihood through salaries, technical fees, scholarships, and professional activities.[56] As Manfred Halpern described this generation:

> These are new men. They are often the very first in the history of the family to be literate. They often discover their best friends at school or in a political movement, not among kin. They are the first to trust strangers on grounds of competence or shared ideology.[57]

The small group of men who formed the nucleus of the Muslim Brotherhood had certain features in common. They were young (in their twenties), they had all attained some degree of post-secondary education, and they were professionals or professionals-in-the-making. They generally came from established East Bank landowning families who may have profited from the expansion of commercial activity. Their families were able to support their post-secondary education outside of Jordan. They had met at school in Jordan or studying abroad.[58]

Annexation had brought the West Bank Brotherhood under the official control of the Amman headquarters. But in this period the Amman leadership had little control over the West Bank branches.[59] It also seems that the West Bank movement up to this time had attracted few Palestinian professionals. Amnon Cohen noted that Palestinian professionals were more attracted to the radical pan-Arabist parties. "The bulk of the movement's members were from conservative religious backgrounds, which would account for the dearth of professionals in its ranks, as professionals tended to have a more Westernized or even radical world view."[60]

Most prominent amongst the new generation who joined Jordan's Brotherhood was Muḥammad ʿAbd al-Raḥmān Khalīfah, who became the secretary general of the movement in 1952 and has held that position to this day. Khalīfah joined the Muslim Brotherhood as a young man in 1945. Born in Salt in 1919, Khalīfah studied agriculture at the Khaddūrī

---

56 Bill and Springborg, *Politics, 127.*

57 Halpern, *Politics of Social Change, 56.*

58 As noted above, many of the Brotherhood's new membership became aware of the movement at school. Yūsuf al-ʿAẓm (later editor of *al-Kifāḥ al-Islāmī*), and ʿIzzāt ʿAzzīzī both completed doctoral studies in Cairo while ʿAbd al-Raḥmān Khalīfah, secretary general of the movement from 1952 to the present, did his legal training in Jerusalem. In the 1990s the Brotherhood continued to be dominated by professionals. More information about them is provided in Chapter Three.

59 Cohen, *Political Parties, 157.*

60 Ibid.

College in Jerusalem before studying law there. After completing his legal diploma he set up a practice in Amman. Although Khalīfah was exposed to the Brotherhood's ideas when he attended the Khaddūrī College, he did not become actively involved with the movement until he moved to Amman. There, his legal office, overlooking the al-Ḥusseinī Mosque, became a gathering place after evening prayers for young professionals in the Muslim Brotherhood as well as for other Palestinian and Jordanian intellectuals and religious functionaries. This group included Taqī al-Dīn al-Nabahānī, a sharīʿah court judge from Jerusalem who later went on to form the breakaway Liberation Party (*Ḥizb al-Taḥrīr*).

This group discussed the need to make the Muslim Brotherhood organization competitive with secular parties. The annexation of the West Bank and the influx of refugees had created new Palestinian urban constituencies to which the Brotherhood should attempt to appeal. In the light of the Arab defeat of 1948, it was necessary for the Muslim Brotherhood to mobilize against imperialist and secular nationalist forces. In this context, Khalīfah and his associates became increasingly critical of Abū Qūrah's leadership, which "was not up to their expectations in terms of education, culture and political issues. . . . The leadership was not dealing with the issues. They started talking about the need to change the leadership."[61] The main criticism of the old leadership was that it was not intellectual and had not placed enough emphasis on educational recruitment.[62]

Events in early 1952 finally jolted the Brotherhood into making the leadership change. Arguments about the political future of the Brotherhood became more heated following the assassination of ʿAbdallāh and Ṭālāl's accession to the throne. Ṭālāl's brief reign brought significant political liberalization and the constitution of 1952 enhanced the role of the legislature.[63] As the secularist parties became more active and influential, the need for the Brotherhood to revamp its political program became more pressing.

---

61 ʿAzzīzī, interview.

62 ʿAzzīzī, interview; al-ʿAẓm, interview; and Dr. Fatḥī Malkāwī, interview by author, tape recording, Irbid, Jordan, 22 March, 1992. According to ʿAzzīzī, Abū Qūrah agreed with the need to change the leadership. ʿIzzāt ʿAzzīzī recalled that he proclaimed at an Amman meeting, "I have started this movement. I am not educated and I cannot do more. Now you need someone more educated."

63 For a more detailed discussion see Chapter One.

At this time, ideological disagreements within the movement resulted in the formation of the breakaway Ḥizb al-Taḥrīr under the leadership of al-Nabahānī. Al-Nabahānī had complained that the Brotherhood lacked Islamist political objectives and that there was a need to work towards a strategy for an Islamic state.[64] Khalīfah was sympathetic to his point of view.

On November 17, 1952, al-Nabahānī submitted a formal application to the Jordanian Interior Ministry to establish a new political party. In spite of the changing ideological mood amongst the Brotherhood, he was unable to find support for his more radical approach. The more confrontational attitude of the Ḥizb al-Taḥrīr towards the regime explains the ministry's refusal to allow the application to proceed.[65]

Meanwhile Khalīfah had disassociated himself from the al-Nabahānī group and accepted an invitation to take over the leadership of the Brotherhood. The circumstances surrounding Khalīfah's decision in this regard are not clear. When asked about his attitude towards the party he replied:

> Ḥizb al-Taḥrīr differs from us in this way. They want to impose with strength and force and we build schools. We use dialogue and kindness. We do not reject those who have changing views, we tell our opinion and then we shut up.[66]

---

[64] ʿAzzīzī, interview.

[65] See Cohen, *Political Parties,* 210, where he states, "The applicants were told that the basic tenets of the proposed platform were contrary not only to the spirit but also to the very terms of the Jordanian constitution. For example, it was pointed out, the proposed platform did not accept the principle of succession as laid down in the constitution; instead, the platform called for an elected ruler. Furthermore, the platform did not recognize nationalism as the overwhelming political norm underlying the basis of the state, but rather the Islamic religion. In other words, the proposed party challenged the very legitimacy of the Jordanian regime and sought to drive a wedge between its citizens."

[66] Muḥammad ʿAbd al-Raḥmān Khalīfah, interview, tape recording, Amman, Jordan, April 4, 1992. The Liberation Party reject the suggestion that they have had recourse to violence in order to achieve their aims, and it is true that there is no record of such activity on their part. Dr. Iḥsān Samāra, a senior official of the party, stated in an interview (tape recording, Amman, Jordan, August 11, 1992), "We do not believe in using force to change society. We believe in building up the mentality in a practical way." The party has functioned underground with no legal status because of its insistence on the construction of an Islamic state. Although the Liberation Party and the Muslim Brotherhood have developed a competitive relationship based on mutual accusations of deviations from the acceptable Islamic path, there is, in fact, little ideological difference between them today.

The program developed by Khalīfah and his colleagues was more ambitious than its predecessor. In 1954 the Muslim Brotherhood's goals were stated as follows:

> 1. Jordan is a part which cannot be divided from the Islamic world; 2. the Muslim Brotherhood refuses to accept any system which does not support Islamic principles; 3. the Muslim Brotherhood will not support any government until it implements the sharīʿah of God in Jordan; 4. the Muslim Brotherhood in Jordan is part of the Egyptian movement; 5. the Muslim Brotherhood considers the Palestinian problem an Islamic problem and will mobilize all material and spiritual forces for the liberation of Palestine from world Jewry and the international crusaders.[67]

These principles were more radical than those espoused by the movement in 1946. As noted above, the founding principles called in vague terms for support of an Islamic order. The Brotherhood now stated its refusal to support any government which would not implement sharīʿah. However, it must be emphasized that this refusal in principle should not be construed as implying the Brotherhood was moving towards a revolutionary agenda. The Brotherhood remained reformist in nature. Its determination to coexist with the regime influenced its tendency to downplay the discrepancies between its agenda and that of the king. Hashemite rule was held by the Brotherhood to be legitimate but could be improved by more stringent attention to the implementation of the sharīʿah.

The Brotherhood has thus sought since the 1950s to justify its loyalty to the king in Islamic terms, which imply that the king should take the counsel of his people in implementing sharīʿah. As the people are the source of the ruler's authority, he should seek the advice of a consultative body (*ahl al-shūrā*). It is the Brotherhood's role to provide the king with counsel.[68]

Yūsuf al-ʿAẓm recently described the Brotherhood's position in the 1950s:

> We wanted the king to be the leader if he agreed with our ideas. . . . The king was entitled and is still entitled to understand Islam comprehensively and he is

---

[67] Al-ʿUbaydī, *Jamāʿat al-Ikhwān*, 129.

[68] This point is further elaborated in the discussion on the Brotherhood's ideology in the 1980s and 1990s in Chapter Four.

entitled also to establish the state, in this case there is no conflict at all. . . . Dialogue, dialogue, we have nothing but dialogue until he will be persuaded.[69]

While supporting the idea of the implementation of the sharīᶜah, the Brotherhood also downplayed its commitment to the creation of an actual Islamic state. This was again, no doubt, partly due to the Brotherhood's desire to facilitate relations with the regime. One Muslim Brotherhood sympathizer has denied that the Brotherhood ever had any intention of establishing an Islamic state. He said:

> The movement was not at any time politically oriented in terms of establishing an Islamic state. . . . [It] was always trying to improve on what was going on and trying to minimize corruption in the state.[70]

Even in cases where Brotherhood members have endorsed the goal of creating an Islamic state, they did not elucidate a clear blueprint of such an entity.[71] Such ideological imprecision is characteristic of the Jordanian Muslim Brotherhood and can be attributed partly to the Brotherhood's lack of intellectual rigour. More significantly, it can be attributed to the Brotherhood's desire not to pose a challenge to the state but rather to coexist with it. The ambiguous nature of the Brotherhood's political ideology can also be attributed to the limited legacy of Islam with regard to state formation, classical political theory having been formulated in the context of an imperial caliphate. This factor has contributed to the ambiguous nature of most Islamist agendas.[72]

The Brotherhood's commitment to Palestine's liberation did not at this time constitute a challenge to Hashemite rule. The Brotherhood viewed the liberation of Palestine in the general context of the delivery of all Muslims from imperialist domination. In this period, Palestinian dissatisfaction with the Hashemite regime was championed by pan-Arabist leaders whose ideology the Brotherhood opposed. On the whole, the Palestinian issue was secondary to a battle between pan-Arabists (who assumed that Arab unification was a precursor to Palestinian liberation) and their opponents, among them the Muslim Brotherhood. The

---

69 Yūsuf al-ᶜAẓm, interview.

70 Fatḥī Malkāwi, interview by author, tape recording, 22 March 1992, Amman, Jordan.

71 For example, Yūsuf al-ᶜAẓm stated in an interview, "It is our faith to establish an Islamic state." But he would not provide details as to the characteristics of this state.

72 The Brotherhood's conception of Islamic rule is discussed in detail in Chapter Four. See also Mitchell, *The Society*, 145.

Brotherhood's political agenda, rather than focusing exclusively on Palestine, reflected the reformist interests of the professional leadership. Their interests lay in the promotion of political reform through education rather than revolution.[73] Accordingly, the new leadership initiated a generalized development and expansion of the Brotherhood's organization and recruitment activities.[74] The basic usrah cells functioned from the late 1940s as the primary agents of recruitment to the Brotherhood, initially through educational institutions.[75] In the early 1950s the Brotherhood began to construct a network of schools.

A lack of data makes it difficult to evaluate the Muslim Brotherhood's support base in the 1950s.[76] In the East Bank its support came primarily from students and professionals (such as lawyers and teachers). Students were easily the most politicized group in society and played a key role in all political parties. Regarding the impact of annexation on the Muslim Brotherhood's membership, it has already been observed that Palestinian professionals did not play a significant role in the movement.[77] But annexation added some new social groups to the movement. These included village elders, large property owners, and religious functionaries, who all played a significant role at local levels in the West Bank. None of these groups had been prominent in the East Bank movement. This can perhaps be explained by two related factors: first, that the Jordanian movement had been confined to urban centres; second, that the West Bank was a more highly politicized society where religious functionaries and landowners were more politically active.[78] Religious functionaries on

---

73 Khalīfah, interview. He stated that when he assumed the leadership in 1952 one of his most important goals was "education for the future."

74 These are discussed in detail in Chapter Three.

75 The role of the usrah cells up to this day will be discussed in Chapter Three.

76 The best sources uncovered so far are the Jordanian intelligence party membership lists cited by Cohen, who extrapolates from them some data on the support base of parties on the West Bank. This data clearly has limitations for an analysis of East Bank party membership, considering the very different populations of the two banks. See Chapter Four below for an analysis of the Brotherhood's current support base.

77 Cohen, *Political Parties*, 164–166.

78 The religious establishment of the West Bank had considerable administrative power with the establishment of the Supreme Muslim Council in 1921. Ḥājj Amīn al-Ḥusseinī was elected the council's chairman in 1922. Mosques and other institutions were used by the Ḥusseinī family for political propaganda purposes. Uri Kupferschmidt, in *The Supreme Muslim Council: Islam Under the British Mandate for Palestine* (New York: Brill, 1987), 196, argues that at the end of the Mandate

the West Bank were a small group but, according to Amnon Cohen, "most of them were in some way or another involved with the Brothers."[79] By contrast, some East Bank religious functionaries attended the discussion meetings in Amman with Khalīfah but they did not play a prominent role in the movement's leadership.[80]

Palestinian refugees provided a significant new constituency for the Muslim Brotherhood after 1948. But the movement's popularity with refugees was associated with its charitable work rather than with its political agenda. According to information from the Jordanian lists, refugees were more likely to be associated with the Muslim Brotherhood than with any other party.[81] The Brotherhood was active in charity work in the camps and was the only political organization to assist the refugees in this way.[82] They distributed food, blankets, clothing and money to families of those killed in the National Guard and many members of the National Guard joined the Muslim Brotherhood.[83] After the war they established branches in camps in Aqbat Jabr, Irbid, Arrub, and Askar.[84] In some camps they established schools and social clubs for children.[85]

Thus, in the years between the founding of the Brotherhood in 1945 and the assumption of its leadership by ʿAbd al-Raḥmān Khalīfah, the movement evolved from a loose-knit coalition of merchants supporting the jihād in Palestine into an organized political party with a broader socioeconomic and political agenda under the leadership of professionals. The movement's primary political goal was to deflect the challenge of the

"clericalism merged into pan-Islamism," although he does not indicate exactly what he means by this in terms of the role of religious functionaries. He does note that the emergence of some branches of the Muslim Brotherhood in the West Bank in the 1940s was supported by the Ḥusseinīs (although there were never any formal links with the Supreme Muslim Council). This is not surprising considering the links between Ḥasan al-Bannā and Ḥājj Amīn al-Ḥusāynī discussed earlier.

79 Cohen, *Political Parties, 165.*

80 It is not clear if they were Jordanian or Palestinian.

81 Plascov, *The Palestinian Refugees,* 135. Plascov worked from the Jordanian intelligence party membership lists cited by Cohen. He states that three lists from Balbus in 1954, 1956 and 1957 show that 25% of the 80 members listed were from refugee camps.

82 ʿAzzīzī, interview.

83 Plascov, 57.

84 Ibid., 136.

85 Ibid. In Askar camp a group of younger refugees requested a Muslim Brotherhood club license. The Muslim Brotherhood established a school in Aqbat Jabr in 1955.

pan-Arabist opposition and to pursue a gradualist Islamist reform program. A distinctive element in the movement's non-confrontational posture was its pragmatic nature and its desire to retain the legal sanction of the regime. This desire, coupled with ʿAbdallāh's need to coopt the movement, crystallized symbiotic relations between the Brotherhood and the monarchy.

1953–1957: King Hussein and the Muslim Brotherhood

The future of the Brotherhood's political agenda became an issue of dissension in the summer of 1954 with Nasser's brutal repression of its Egyptian colleagues.[86] The Brotherhood had so far endorsed Nasser, praising him for his anti-Western posture. Immediately after the Free Officers revolution in Egypt, the Jordanian Brothers had announced full support of the regime which they described as "the Moslem Brothers' regime" having the aims of ousting the British from Egypt, eliminating corruption, and assuring a genuine Islamic form of government.[87]

But now heated debate broke out within the Jordanian Brotherhood over the extent to which they should demonstrate their solidarity with the Egyptian movement and abandon solidarity with Nasser. Khalīfah joined with other senior members of the movement in arguing for downplaying the link with the Egyptian Brotherhood.[88] He was concerned that open alliance with the Egyptians might threaten good relations with the Jordanian government. He worried about the consequences of his organization being associated by Hashemite authorities with the politically militant Egyptian cousins. The Jordanian government's mounting suspicions of (at least) the Egyptian wing of the movement were confirmed by its refusal of entry to Ḥasan al-Bannā's successor as supreme guide of the Brotherhood, Ḥasan al-Hudāybī and Brotherhood emissary Saʿīd Ramaḍān in June of that year.[89]

The Jordanian Brotherhood finally threw caution aside several months later with the news of the arrest of al-Hudāybī in Cairo and the accusation

---

[86] See Mitchell, *The Society*, 103–162. From April to December 1954 the Muslim Brotherhood was subjected to repression by Nasser's regime. The assassination attempt on Nasser on October 26 provided him with an opportunity to crush the Brotherhood completely. By December half a dozen Brothers were hanged, thousands imprisoned, and the organization dissolved.

[87] Cohen, *Political Parties*, 192.

[88] Ibid.

[89] United Kingdom Foreign Office, FOR 371 110874.

that the Muslim Brotherhood was involved in an October assassination plot against the life of Nasser.[90] Khalīfah sent a letter to Nasser, voicing his criticism in extreme language: "It has become clear to all the world just how much you hate Islam and the Muslims."[91]

As Nasser moved against the Brotherhood, its Jordanian members who had been studying in Cairo were obliged to leave.[92] The issue of the Egyptian Brotherhood became a greater source of contention upon the return of these members. The problem now was not whether or not to come out in strong support of the Egyptian Brotherhood, but how to do this. The question of how to respond to Nasser raised broader issues of how the Brotherhood would respond to Nasserist and Palestinian opposition to the Hashemite monarchy. In hindsight, this would be a major decision for the Brotherhood in defining its future relations with King Hussein.

During the summer of 1954 the Brotherhood had become increasingly politically active, declaring its candidacy for the October parliamentary elections and siding with nationalists in criticizing the British imperial presence in Jordan and in attacking the repressive measures undertaken by the government of Prime Minister Tawfīq Abū al-Hudā.[93] On the occasion of the visit of King Saʿūd,[94] the Muslim Brotherhood organized an anti-West demonstration in Amman, described in some detail by a diplomatic observer:

> It appears that the members of the Brotherhood had gathered at the airport to welcome King Saud, but were firmly refused admittance by the police. Whether in their disappointment at this or following their original purpose, they then proceeded through Amman, shouting anti-Western slogans, to the Prime Minister's office, where they delivered a protest against the consumption of

---

90 See Mitchell, *The Society*, 151–152, for details.

91 Cohen, *Political Parties, 192.*

92 ʿAzzīzī was a graduate student in Egypt at the time and was forced to flee after the clash between Nasser and the Brotherhood. He was one of the members of the Brotherhood who was sentenced in absentia by an Egyptian People's Tribunal. Yūsuf al-ʿAẓm had been completing a doctorate in Cairo and he also left Egypt in 1954.

93 For more details on this period see Chapter One.

94 The Saudis were associated with support for Arab nationalist interests as a means for supporting the status quo and delimiting further Western encroachment in the region. For more details see Abidi, *Jordan*, 122–123.

alcoholic drinks by, amongst others, the American ambassador at a party in Jubeiha, at the Government Agricultural School, days previously.[95]

The Brotherhood's first publication, the weekly *al-Kifāḥ al-Islāmī,* was closed down for attacking the government after the publication of only its third issue on August 26.[96] The third number was banned by the government before it went to press. The headline article attacked the prime minister, accusing him of corruption and exploitation.[97] In defiance of the regime the Brotherhood distributed the newspaper secretly with a blank first page that read only "Banned by the tyrants before its publication."[98] The offending article appeared on page two, instead.

The banning of *al-Kifāḥ al-Islāmī* and other political publications was followed by further government repression in the period leading up to the October 1954 elections. Members of the opposition and candidates who were considered a threat to the government were rounded up and jailed.[99] An order was issued for the arrest of Khalīfah, but apparently "supporters intervened on his behalf" and he was allowed to escape to Damascus.[100]

But Khalīfah was clearly not viewed as a significant threat to the regime as he was allowed to return to Jordan and participate in the elections of October 1954. There is a good reason why Khalīfah may not have been regarded with great suspicion by the government at this point in time. Khalīfah's return to Amman coincided with the Brotherhood's

---

95 United Kingdom Foreign Office, FOR 371 110876. "Report on a demonstration staged by the Muslim Brotherhood on June 13, in Amman." June 15, 1954. Chancery, Amman to Levant Dept.

96 At this time Prime Minister Abū al-Hudā, clamping down on opposition in the run up to the October elections, issued Defense Regulations empowering the government to cancel newspaper licenses without the necessity of showing a cause, to dissolve political parties and to prohibit political assemblies. For more details see Aruri, *Jordan,* 111 and Satloff, *From Abdullah to Hussein,* 95.

97 *Al-Kifāḥ al-Islāmī,* 26 August, 1954.

98 Ibid.

99 For more information on this round of government repression see Satloff, *From Abdullah to Hussein,* 96–97, and Aruri, *Jordan,* 111–112.

100 See Aruri, *Jordan,* 112, and Cohen, *Political Parties,* 15. None of my information indicates that Khalīfah was ever actually arrested but Cohen's sources suggest that Khalīfah was jailed later in 1955. Yūsuf al-ʿAẓm, editor in chief of *al-Kifāḥ al-Islāmī* for most of its period of publication, was arrested and jailed twelve times between 1954 and 1957 for distribution of publications and taking an "anti-corruption" stance towards the government.

condemnation of Nasser and its ensuing debate over future policies towards the nationalists and the Hashemite regime. At this juncture the leadership advocated a policy of opposing Nasser by supporting King Hussein against the nationalists. This decision was partly influenced by the Brotherhood's enmity towards secularist-nationalist trends. But it was also undoubtedly influenced by the Brotherhood's recent experience of government repression and its desire to maintain good relations with the government. This decision was of great importance to the future relations between the Brotherhood and King Hussein. The movement made at this point a fundamental commitment to continue to support the monarchy. The Brotherhood would challenge the regime again and at times be rebuked for so doing. But from this point on there existed an unwritten understanding of coexistence between King Hussein and the Brotherhood, echoing the relations between the movement and his grandfather in the 1940s.

Some of the younger membership disagreed with the policy of supporting the king, especially in light of his pro-British stance. And some, including ʿAzīzzī, left the movement at this time, arguing that the Brotherhood should "fight standing on its feet and not ally itself with the Hashemite monarchy or any monarchy." ʿAzzīzī recalled how he felt on leaving the movement in 1954:

> The animosity between the Muslim Brotherhood and Nasser forced [the Brothers] to put their hand behind anyone who would fight Nasser. I thought we should fight Nasser by our own power. All those small regimes were the same, all products of colonization, not the product of the people and none of these governments was elected.[101]

The remaining members, however, decided to participate in the parliamentary elections of 1954. Participation in parliament would give the Brotherhood a louder voice and more influence in political life. Besides, the Syrian Brotherhood had set an example by following a similar course, participating in elections in the 1940s and 1950s.[102]

The Brotherhood made a modest showing in the elections, returning four members to the forty-seat parliament. Two of the Muslim

---

101 ʿAzzīzī, interview.

102 See discussion in Umar Abd Allah, *The Islamic Struggle for Syria* (Berkeley: Mizan, 1989).

Brotherhood seats were occupied by Khalīfah and al-ʿAẓm.[103] These elections were subject to considerable government interference with a majority of government loyalists returned to the parliament, but electoral results of the Muslim Brotherhood were manipulated.[104] Regardless, the movement commanded little popular support at this time compared with the Arab nationalists and therefore posed little threat to the regime.[105] It stressed its status as a charitable organization as opposed to a political party and referred only vaguely to the need for the return to the principles of the Qurʾān and the sunnah.[106]

In spite of the Brotherhood's caution in dealing with the regime, it was still the occasional victim of security crackdowns. These occurred when the movement was more outspoken than usual in condemning government policy. The government tightened its surveillance of the movement in the increasingly inflamed political atmosphere of 1955, amidst nationalist demands that the king explicitly denounce the Baghdad Pact and make a commitment to a neutralist policy.[107] In this case the Brotherhood joined the nationalists in denouncing the pro-West pact. In November, Turkish President Celal Bayar and Foreign Minister Gatin Zorlu visited Jordan to encourage the regime to join the Pact. They received a sullen and uneasy reception. Anti-Turkish leaflets had been distributed in the streets of Amman by the Brotherhood, Communists, and "a shadowy organization calling itself the League of the Officers' Struggle." The Brotherhood leaflet proclaimed:

---

[103] The names of the two remaining Muslim Brotherhood representatives are unavailable.

[104] See Aruri, *Jordan*, 112, for a breakdown of election results. Out of 40 members, 32 government loyalists were elected. See also Satloff, *From Abdullah to Hussein*, 97–98, for a description of the government's interference in the elections. For general background, see Chapter One.

[105] In the free elections of 1956 the Brotherhood was still only able to return four members to the parliament.

[106] See Plascov, *Palestinian Refugees*, 113, where he notes that the Palestinian refugee issue was not important in the election campaigns of 1954. Priority was given to the pan-Arab unity issue which superseded all others. He also notes that the Muslim Brotherhood did not deal with the plight of refugees in publications or Friday sermons.

[107] See Chapter One for general background. For an excellent and detailed analysis of these events, see Satloff, *From Abdullah to Hussein*, 137–138.

> Return to your country, O Jelal Bayar, You will not find in Jordan a single man who agrees to put his hand in yours or to link his fate with yours.[108]

The Jordanian chief of staff issued a report which called for information on various "destructive organizations" operating in the country. He excluded the Brotherhood from this category, being more concerned with Communist activity at this time. However, "he stressed that the movement should be closely watched to make certain that the ideas it was disseminating did not, in fact, run counter to the interests and policies of the state."[109]

The regime's suspicions of the movement were also demonstrated in 1955 with the passing of a decree to monitor the content of Friday sermons.[110] The authorities followed preachers to see if they were connected with the movement, "even kept çertain members of the movement under surveillance," and placed a temporary ban on the Brotherhood's weekly lectures.[111] Regardless of the regime's suspicions, the Brotherhood remained essentially loyal to the crown. It joined with the nationalists in condemning Western imperialism but stood behind Hussein in his final confrontation with them in February 1957.

In 1956 Hussein took various steps to acquiesce to nationalist pressure. First, he ousted British Arab Legion commander Glubb Pasha,[112] an act which brought him considerable praise from the Brotherhood. The Brotherhood lauded him for "advancing the causes of Islamic and Arab unity and for [helping to] free the Arab world from the yoke of imperialism."[113] Secondly, Hussein agreed to free elections which returned an Arab nationalist, anti-monarchical majority, and brought in Sulaymān al-Nābulsī, leader of the National Socialist party, as prime

---

[108] United Kingdom Foreign Office, FOR 371.115684. Duke to FOR, November 4, 1955.

[109] Cohen, *Political Parties, 149.*

[110] Monitoring of mosque preachers was a policy encouraged by the British. A confidential memo from Mr. Wikeley in Jerusalem to Foreign Office, OF 371 121464, January 3, 1956 (No. 494) stated: "A strike has been declared for tomorrow and the Governor of Jerusalem is nervous of more trouble. I have suggested to him that as it is obligatory day of prayer for Muslims he should do what he can to ensure that preachers in the Mosques do not inflame reactionary Moslem feeling."

[111] Cohen, *Political Parties, 149–150.*

[112] For more information on the circumstances surrounding Glubb's dismissal see Chapter One, p. 30. Also see Satloff, *From Abdullah to Hussein*, 138.

[113] Cohen, *Political Parties, 150.*

minister.[114] The Brotherhood again participated in the elections, keeping a low profile. As in 1954 it returned four representatives to the parliament.[115]

The elections ushered in a period of renewed liberalization and anti-Western fervour in which the Brotherhood joined. The new parliament abrogated the Anglo-Jordanian treaty, rejecting alliances with the West.[116] The Brotherhood resumed publication of *al-Kifāḥ al-Islāmī* on January 11, 1957 with an issue which strongly condemned the Eisenhower Doctrine and the American Point Four program for technical assistance to Jordan.

Hussein was increasingly opposed to National Socialist policies which threatened his partnership with the West. The National Socialist government courted Soviet backing and released Communist sympathizers from prison. In February, the king depicted to the public his mounting confrontation with the National Socialists as a battle against Communism.[117] In this context he was able to enlist the support of the Muslim Brotherhood. The Brotherhood abhorred Communist expansionism as much as the Western kind. Yūsuf al-ᶜAẓm wrote in *al-Kifāḥ al-Islāmī:*

> Soviet attempts to extend their influence and establish control in the name of equality and popular democracy illustrate clearly a basic agreement between the East and West regarding the acquisition of zones of influence.[118]

The Brotherhood also doubtless recognized the expediency of supporting the throne at this critical juncture.

Hussein issued an open letter to Prime Minister al-Nābulsī on February 2, 1957 warning about the threats of subversive elements and Communism and serving notice that "the honeymoon of the monarch and the nationalists" was over. The letter stated:

> Imperialism, which is about to die in the Arab East, will be replaced by a new kind of imperialism. If we are enslaved by this, we shall never be able to escape or overthrow it. We perceive the danger of Communist infiltration within our

---

114 See Chapter One for background. See Satloff, *From Abdullah to Hussein,* 152–154 for a detailed discussion of these elections.

115 Again, two of these were Yūsuf al-ᶜAẓm and ᶜAbd al-Raḥmān Khalīfah. For a breakdown of the election results see Aruri, 135.

116 See Chapter One for background. For a detailed account, see Aruri, *Jordan,* 134–146.

117 See Satloff, *From Abdullah to Hussein,* 161, where he points out, although Hussein was a committed anti-Communist, the primary issue here was domestic politics rather than Communism.

118 *Al-Kifāḥ al-Islāmī,* February 15, 1957.

Arab home as well as the danger of those who pretend to be Arab nationalists while they have nothing to do with Arabism.[119]

There is evidence that the king showed the letter to the Brotherhood before its publication to be sure of their support.[120] And a response from Khalīfah in *al-Kifāḥ al-Islāmī* praised the letter for its rejection of international Communism and "adherence to Islamic principles."[121]

During the political crises of April and May of 1957,[122] with the king's dismissal of the National Socialist government, the crushing of the alleged military coup by General Abū Nuwwār and the weeks of violent demonstrations against the regime and its alliance with the United States, the Brotherhood continued to stand by the king. It held a number of mass rallies in support of the monarch and praised his decisions on behalf of Islam, attacking the misguided policies of the National Socialist government.

The Brotherhood's strategy of supporting the palace had paid good dividends. With the imposition of martial law and the dissolution of parties in May of 1957, the Muslim Brotherhood was the only remaining legal political organization in the country. Supporting the monarchy had not only assured the Brotherhood's legal status but also had given it an edge over its secularist competition.

Al-Kifāḥ al-Islāmī

The Brotherhood engaged in little intellectual activity in the 1950s. This can be explained in part by the youthfulness of the movement and the limited intellectual legacy left to it by its merchant founders. It can be explained further by the priorities of the intellectuals and professionals who assumed the leadership of the Muslim Brotherhood in 1952. In deciding to transform the movement into (for all intents and purposes) a political party and to join parliamentary life, the leadership committed itself to action and strategy rather than theoretical work. At the same time, the limited education of the Brotherhood's target recruitment audience militated against sophisticated intellectual activity.

---

119 H.M. King Hussein of Jordan, *Uneasy Lies the Heady* (New York: Bernard Geis Associates, 1962), 133.

120 Aruri, *Jordan*, 139.

121 *Al-Kifāḥ al-Islāmī*, February 8, 1957.

122 See Chapter One, p. 31–32 for more information. See also Satloff, *From Abdullah to Hussein*, chapters nine and ten, for a detailed analysis of these events.

The movement's only significant publication in this period was the weekly *al-Kifāḥ al-Islāmī,* which appeared for a short time in 1954 and again in 1957. A brief review of this publication, the "official mouthpiece of the Muslim Brotherhood,"[123] reveals the Brotherhood's tendency to resort to bombastic rhetoric which contradicted its fundamentally moderate and reformist nature. The use of such rhetoric can be understood in the context of the politically volatile nature of the times. In the parliamentary context it can be seen as nothing more than inter-party "mud-slinging." In spite of this, the publication is also revealing in highlighting the issues which were of most importance to the Brotherhood at this time: the battle against nationalist and Communist forces in Jordan and the Middle East as a whole, and the need to tackle the corruptive influences of these on governmental, educational and social institutions. Although the paper was outspoken in criticizing government policy, it balked at directly assailing the king himself.

The first three numbers of *al-Kifāḥ al-Islāmī,* which appeared in 1954, were concerned with several major issues: British power in Jordan and especially the role of Glubb Pasha, the threat of American imperialism, and government corruption.[124] The first run of *al-Kifāḥ al-Islāmī* contained the kind of vitriolic attacks on the government of Abū al-Hudā which led to the paper's banning after the publication of only three issues. The paper's opposition to British influence made it popular all over Jordan, not only within the limited circles of the Brotherhood.[125] The headline on the first page of the first number blared: "The servants of Glubb Pasha are enemies of freedom." This issue featured a particularly unflattering photo of Glubb in profile next to an article condemning the corrupt influence of the British in the military. Glubb was referred to as "nothing but an enemy." A general warning was issued to the British on the same page: "Beware, shameless foreigner, beware, the people know your true nature

123 Ziyād Abū Ghanīmah, *Dirāsah Wathā'iqiyyah fī Ṣaḥīfat al-Kifāḥ al-Islāmī* (Amman: al-Maktab al-Islāmī, 1991), 1.

124 The interventionary role of the censor cannot be overlooked. The microfilm of the newspaper is in extremely poor condition and large sections are almost completely white. This is probably because of poor reproduction rather than the clumsy "white out" tactics of the censors which are still used today in Jordan. It is not uncommon to open the latest issue of the current Muslim Brotherhood publication, *al-Ribāṭ,* and find an article inelegantly "blanked out" by the Ministry of Information.

125 Ziyād Abū Ghanīmah, *Dirāsah Wathā'iqiyyah, 11.*

and have revealed your power."[126] In its second issue the newspaper continued its diatribe against the vileness and corruption of British rule with the headline "The English octopus throttles the Arab countries." On this page the British army was accused of conspiring with Israeli soldiers and recruits at the border.[127] The third and final issue, censored by the government, attacked Glubb under the headline "To those who are responsible," pouring scorn on "those who have welcomed him into our country " because he represents the vileness and "trickery of those distant lands of the world."[128]

Warnings about increasing American influence in Jordan are prominent in the first three issues. The Brotherhood focussed on the American Point Four development and aid program. The headline of the first issue reads "The American Point Four is for the benefit of the Israeli state," and the article goes on to accuse the Americans of using the Point Four as a cover for espionage activities with Israel.[129] Moreover, an article on Point Four in the second issue claimed that "the majority of those responsible for the organization of the Point Four in Jordan are Jews or their clients."[130]

The Palestinian issue was given little direct attention in this publication. However, it has already been noted that this issue was not given special attention in the Brotherhood's political statements at this time. Ziyād Abū Ghanīmah has defended this omission, arguing that there was no need to stress the Palestinian problem in particular as there was at that time general consensus on how to approach its resolution.

> Although the Muslim Brethren take the position that the Palestinian problem is an Islamic issue which concerns all Muslims . . . and the sole solution to it is through the path of jihād . . . the general atmosphere in that period of time did not necessitate concentration on the actual struggle because the general opinion of Jordanians, Palestinians and then Arabs was agreed on: the

---

[126] *Al-Kifāḥ al-Islāmī,* August 9, 1954.

[127] Ibid., August 19, 1954. This refers to border conflicts between the Israelis, the National Guard and the Arab Legion. The British controlled-Arab Legion was accused of providing insufficient defense of the border. See, for example, Satloff, *From Abdullah to Hussein,* 79.

[128] *Al-Kifāḥ al-Islāmī,* August 26, 1954.

[129] The article stated that these services "dispatch [ed] photographs, figures and data about the agencies and departments of the government and the people including detailed maps of areas subordinate to American imperialism," and "all this information goes first to Israel."

[130] *Al-Kifāḥ al-Islāmī,* August 19, 1954.

acceptance of war as the only means of liberating Palestine; no Arab was ready to accept the idea of urging any manner of reconciliation with the Jews.[131]

Because of this general atmosphere, the paper assumed that the Palestinian issue was generally incorporated into the whole anti-imperialist debate.

Government corruption was a third prominent theme. The first issue discussed the general "outbreak of bribery and corruption in government institutions" and accused many government officials of bribery and patronage.[132] The second number was critical of the "boldness of the government in censoring the publications of political parties,"[133] and the third issue took a direct swipe at Prime Minister Abū al-Hudā, declaring that his rule bore the stamp of greed and exploitation. Abū al-Hudā's government was accused of "choking the freedom of the press with the banning of party newspapers." The editors went on to say that they had anticipated the closure of *al-Kifāḥ al-Islāmī* because it had "exposed the vileness of this age in which the country is ruled with the iron hand of the English and the guns of the Americans," and in which the prime minister was a pawn in the hands of the West, supporting only publications which "give American and English perceptions of the news."[134]

The second run of *al-Kifāḥ al-Islāmī* (January 11-October 11, 1957) featured a variety of issues: the increased prominence of America on the Middle East political stage, continuing British and French interference in the regime, the evils of Nasserist, Baᶜthist, and Communist ideologies, Muslim peoples' resistance to imperialism, and some domestic social issues, especially education.

The first number of the second run attacked the American role in the region with a denunciation of the Eisenhower Doctrine "promulgated by the U.S. under the pretext of the great void in the Middle East after the

---

131 Ziyād Abū Ghanīmah, *Dirāsah Wathā'iqiyyah,* 13. This statement seems to be an over-generalization. There were clearly differences in the Jordanian-Palestinian community regarding the solution to the Palestinian problem, for example, whether the defeat of Israel necessitated the formation of a pan-Arab entity. However, Abū Ghanīmah's point here should be taken as a comparative one relating to the political climate in Jordan in the early 1990s. In the 1990s the Brotherhood has opposed the option of peace initiatives as a way of resolving the Palestinian-Israeli conflict. In the 1950s conflict was more widely accepted as a means of liberating Palestine from Israeli control.

132 *Al-Kifāḥ al-Islāmī,* August 9, 1954.

133 Ibid., August 19, 1954.

134 Ibid., August 26, 1954.

contraction of British influence." The same number warned of the replacement of the British and French by American imperialists who "shake hands with the Jews on one side and with Arabs on the other."[135] An editorial by Yūsuf al-ᶜAẓm on February 15 declared:

> America has finally removed the veil which covered its face and has proved to be an imperialist state. It is an invisible and slow type of imperialism disguised in economic projects, financial and technical assistance, to be followed by control, exploitation and human destruction.[136]

Al-ᶜAẓm also levelled an attack at the Soviet Union:

> Soviet attempts to extend their influence and establish control in the name of equality and popular democracy illustrate clearly a basic agreement between East and West regarding the acquisition of zones of influence.[137]

A later issue (June 22) renewed the assault on Point Four referring to "the fairytale of American aid and dollar backing" and "American efforts to infiltrate the area through financial aid."[138]

Meanwhile, the paper was still preoccupied with British influence in the region as demonstrated by headlines such as "British control great," and "British power invades the circle of government in Maan."[139] The sixth number exhorted the English to "get out of Mafraq and all our lands . . . get out!" referring to the "disgraceful agreement," the Anglo-Jordan Treaty of 1946.[140] The second run of *al-Kifāḥ al-Islāmī* gave more attention than the first to the Palestinian problem in the light of condemning Israeli activities in Gaza and the neglect of Palestinians by other Arab leaders. "Do not forget the enduring battle for Gaza!" exhorted one headline on January 11th.[141] A long article on the front page of the seventh number asked:

> What are they doing in Gaza and Rafah and Khan Yunis? What are the Jews doing there? . . . They have killed men and plundered property and insulted women and strangled infants and humiliated our sons and brothers.[142]

---

135 *Al-Kifāḥ al-Islāmī,* January 11, 1957.

136 Ibid., February 15, 1957.

137 Ibid.

138 Ibid., June 22, 1957.

139 Ibid., January 18, 1957.

140 This treaty granted Jordan independence but allowed the British to retain considerable financial and military control. See Chapter One for background.

141 *Al-Kifāḥ al-Islāmī,* January 11, 1957.

142 Ibid., February 1, 1957.

Nūrī al-Saʿid of Iraq,[143] a favourite target of the Brotherhood for his cooperation with the British, was referred to as the "despot" who had signed the pro-Western Baghdad Pact. Headlines encouraged the people of Iraq to prepare for a major revolution, as "the Euphrates and Tigris boil with hatred of the tyrant."[144] And the front page on June 8 pointed to evidence against Nūrī al-Saʿid, alleging that the "Iraqi Petroleum Company is cooperating with Israel." The same page included coverage of the Algerian revolutionary struggle, referring to the atrocities of the French against the freedom fighters of Algeria.[145]

On the domestic front, the paper concerned itself with a number of social issues including the status of women, economics, workers rights, and especially education. *al-Kifāḥ al-Islāmī* was concerned with pulling the rug out from under the feet of the Communist Party, which boasted a following in the labour movement.[146] A section of every issue entitled "With the Workers" was devoted to labour issues, especially from the viewpoint of workers' rights. A section on February 1, 1957 dealt sympathetically with a bakers' strike[147] and an article on February 15th told the story of a worker who died accidentally by colliding with a phosphate transporter, under the headline "Victim of Negligence in the Phosphate Company."[148] In line with its commitment to labour issues, *al-Kifāḥ al-Islāmī* also called for the opening of an employment office.[149]

Analyses of economic issues usually supported the "underdog" against corruption in and abuse by government. Authorities were accused of "corruption in the phosphate industry,"[150] and the economy minister was held responsible for deceiving the people regarding the failure of the economic plan in Jordan.[151]

---

143 Nūrī al-Saʿīd was the prime minister of Iraq until 1958.

144 *Al-Kifāḥ al-Islāmī,* January 11, 1957.

145 Ibid., June 8, 1957.

146 Ziyād Abū Ghanīmah, *Dirāsah Wathāʾiqiyya,* 72.

147 *Al-Kifāḥ al-Islāmī,* February 1, 1957.

148 Ibid., February 15, 1993.

149 Ibid., June 1, 1957.

150 Ibid., January 18, 1957.

151 Ibid., February 8, 1957.

Women's issues were only discussed to a very limited degree, reflecting the Brotherhood's generally male-dominated agenda.[152] But the Brotherhood did venture so far as to say that women should not be prevented from associating with men:[153]

> We do not want a return to the past, to an old era and lifestyle . . . and it is inevitable that women associate closely with men and become acquainted with men to the greatest possible degree. A man who prevents his wife from just associating with another man must fear that she will love another man.[154]

Education was at the forefront of the Brotherhood's agenda. The movement seemed concerned that education in Jordan was losing its Islamic content. *al-Kifāḥ al-Islāmī* proclaimed that a headmaster in Amman had ordered primary teachers to stop children from praying. One teacher was accused of deleting the word "Islam" from history books and another of making fun of the sayings of Muḥammad.[155] The newspaper also expressed concern about the activities of secular parties in the government schools. "Destructive Elements in the Midst of Education in the Name of Freedom and Socialism," read a headline of March 15. Interference of secularists was blamed for one teacher's leaking of final exam questions in Irbid, and for a case in Nablus where "a teacher illustrates to students a theory corroborating the non-existence of God."[156]

Al-Kifāḥ al-Islāmī provides an overview of the different political and social issues which preoccupied the Brotherhood in the late 1950s. In the broadest sense these issues were linked to one overriding theme: the wickedness of Western influence on the Islamic world at international, national, and local levels. But the paper offered no serious Islamic solutions to the problems created by Western influences in state and society. More than anything, it is a reflection of the Brotherhood's first "hands-on" experience of life amidst the tumult of day-to-day Jordanian politics in the 1950s. And yet parliamentary politics was not a major focus

---

152 This issue will be dealt with in the discussion of the movement's thinking in the 1980s and 1990s when the role of women has come to the forefront of political discourse.

153 An attitude which was more liberal than that professed by the Muslim Brotherhood in the 1990s.

154 *Al-Kifāḥ al-Islāmī,* February 8, 1957.

155 Ibid., March 1, 1957.

156 Ibid., March 15, 1957. The Brotherhood's approach to education and the ways in which it has influenced the education system in Jordan are discussed in detail in Chapter Three.

for the Brotherhood in the 1950s. During the period under discussion, the movement concentrated on education and the mobilization of grass-roots support. This it undoubtedly achieved, as attested to by its triumphant reemergence on the political scene in the 1980s. How the Brotherhood organized and recruited its support base is the subject of the next chapter.

Chapter Three
Building the Electoral Base

In the three decades between the dramatic events of 1957 and the parliamentary elections of 1989 the Muslim Brotherhood did not have a high profile on the political stage. But this period was critical in the expansion of the Brotherhood's grass-roots organization and in the creation of a broad support base. This chapter examines these developments in three sections.

First, it discusses the Brotherhood's organization with special emphasis on the period since the 1967 war. The Arab defeat caused widespread disillusionment with pan-Arab and socialist perspectives. This created an ideological climate favourable to the Brotherhood. The Brotherhood's position was further bolstered by the weakening of the PLO in the civil war of 1970–71, since the PLO was the Brotherhood's major competitor for Palestinian support. There followed the decade of stability and economic prosperity of 1973 to 1983 in which the Brotherhood kept a low profile and devoted itself to the development of its organization and grass-roots network.

Officially, the Jordanian movement was and remains administratively subordinate to the Egyptian Muslim Brotherhood. In fact, the movement has functioned autonomously. It has, however, maintained close organizational linkages with the Palestinian Brotherhood and this has assured that Palestinian issues have remained at the forefront of the Jordanians' agenda.

Second, this chapter reviews the recruitment strategies of the Brotherhood in public and (its own) private institutions. It is argued that these strategies were enhanced by the movement's legal status which gave it relative freedom in comparison with other Islamist movements in Jordan and elsewhere in the Arab world, and allowed the Brotherhood to build a mass support base by the elections of 1989.

The third section of this chapter analyzes the nature of the movement's support base and appeal. Growing sympathy for the Brotherhood was suggested by a general Islamic revival of the 1980s and activities on university campuses. Tangible evidence of the Brotherhood's popular appeal is to be found in the election results of 1984 and 1989. Analysis of the evidence shows that the Muslim Brotherhood's membership and leadership continue to be dominated by professionals and students and that the movement reflects the hopes of an emergent professional class for political power. It is also demonstrated here that the Brotherhood maintained a broad base of support that transcends class and regional divisions. Of particular significance in this regard is the vagueness of the Brotherhood's ideology, a feature it shares with other Islamist movements and one that allows it to appeal to the populace at a variety of levels. This chapter also argues that Palestinian support, in particular, was a key factor in the Brotherhood's popularity, as demonstrated in the electoral success in the 1980s.

Overall, this chapter addresses the evolution of the movement's relations with the state in these few decades. It concludes that these were characterized by peaceful coexistence up to 1984. But in the mid-1980s the Brotherhood became more forthright in its demands for democratization and Islamizing reforms. The Brotherhood's outspoken demands for reform soured relations with the regime after 1984. Although these relations were temporarily mended in time for the movement's participation in the elections of 1989, a subtle shift had occurred in the dynamics of the Brotherhood's relations with the monarchy. The movement, emboldened in 1989 by a strong show of public support, was less easily coopted by the regime.[1]

Organizational Structure: The Usrah Cell

The movement's basic organizational unit since the 1940s has been the *usrah* cell. These cells of five to ten individuals were introduced by the Egyptian Muslim Brotherhood in 1944 as a system of cooperative families (*niẓām al-usrah al-taᶜāwunī*). They are considered by Mitchell to be "the keystone of the organizational power of the Muslim Brotherhood" in Egypt.[2] Such family cells have been effectively deployed by all Muslim Brotherhood and many other Islamist organizations in the recruitment and education of membership and in developing and sustaining kinship bonds among members.[3]

---

[1] The relations between the Brotherhood and the regime after 1989 are discussed in Chapter Four.

[2] Mitchell, *The Society*, 32.

[3] Because of the secret conditions under which some branches of the Muslim Brotherhood have had to operate, detailed information on their grass-roots organization is scarce. The Egyptian structure has been duplicated by Muslim

The organization of the usrah cells, the basic unit of the Brotherhood's grass-roots structure, is simple. Members of the cells recruit individuals at a highly individualized and personalized level. The idea is to create a bond of friendship as a means of drawing an individual into the cell. Usrah members have sought out recruits mostly in mosques or educational institutions. They start by gradually developing acquaintances with potential recruits. One Brotherhood sympathizer described this manner of recruitment:

> I will find an individual, I will find that he might be suitable. . . . I will give him a book to read and discuss some of the issues with him. . . . Then, if I find him responsive, I will provide him with more books and invite him to my house for dinner. . . . If I find that he is ready I will raise the level of interaction with him and talk about the general issues of my country. . . , that we are Muslims and the system is not so good, that we should do something to improve it.[4]

At this point the potential recruit's opinion of the Muslim Brotherhood is sought and if s/he is still responsive, then s/he would be invited to a discussion circle at a "pre-usrah" level. Discussions are led by a "responsible individual" whose duty it is to assess the suitability of recruits and "to make sure they are good Muslims."[5] According to Muslim Brotherhood members, considerable time is spent in study groups in discussions led by the cell leader (*naqīb*). The naqīb is responsible for the spiritual and moral education of the cell members. Particular emphasis is placed on the member's personal and social behaviour and on the reconstruction of his/her "Islamic personality."[6] The members of a cell

---

Brotherhood organizations in Syria and Palestine. With regard to Syria, see Umar Abd Allah, *The Islamic Struggle in Syria,* (Berkeley: Mizan Press, 1983), 106. For Palestine, see Mohammed K. Shadid, "The Muslim Brotherhood Movement in the West Bank and Gaza," *Third World Quarterly,* 10 (April 1988): 664. This system of organization has also been replicated by other Islamist organizations, such as the Tunisian Mouvement de Tendance Islamiste, which organized students in *ḥalaq* (study circles), based on the same principle. See Marion Boulby, "The Islamic Challenge: Tunisia Since Independence," *Third World Quarterly* 10 (April 1988): 590–614.

[4] Malkāwī, interview.

[5] Ibid.

[6] ʿAzzīzī, Malkāwī, and Muslim Brotherhood member of parliament Ḥamzah Manṣūr, interview, tape recording, Amman, Jordan, 30 June, 1992. Similar methods have been employed in Egypt by the Islamic Liberation Organization, and the Muslim Group studied by Ibrahim. See Ibrahim, "Anatomy," 438, where he notes the recruitment mechanisms employed by cell members: "Typically, the older members observe young worshippers in the college or neighbourhood or mosque. If the persons appeared to be deeply religious (especially if they observed prayer) they would be

are encouraged to develop their kinship bonds within the usrah, to attend weekly branch meetings and to spend at least one whole night of the month reading and praying together. Usrah members are often grouped according to age and are sexually segregated.

It should be emphasized that the existence of usrah cells does not imply that the Brotherhood has been involved in revolutionary underground activity. The cell structure has been employed by anti-regime Muslim Brotherhood organizations such as in the cases of Syria, the West Bank and Gaza, and has been effective as a means of organization and indoctrination.[7] But the use of the cells in themselves does not suggest subversive, anti-regime activity. In the Egyptian case, the usrah cells were not designed to support clandestine political activity. The Egyptian movement's underground activities during the 1940s were associated with the formation of another, "secret apparatus" (*al-jihāz al-sirrī*). This secret organization was first formed after clashes between the Muslim Brotherhood and the regime in 1948 and there is little information about it except that "it was secondary to the tightly-knit, well-disciplined, and coordinated membership-at-large."[8] There is no indication that the Jordanian Muslim Brotherhood ever developed a secret apparatus. Nor did the movement have any reason to do so in light of its essentially cooperative relations with the regime.[9]

The cells are part of a complex hierarchical organization. Each group of four or five cells forms a division headed by a *raqīb* (supervisor). The raqib is then responsible to a regional branch executive. Branches existed in all the main urban centres of the East Bank by the end of the 1940s including Irbid, Salt, Karak, Madaba, Zarqa, and Amman. After 1948 they expanded into refugee camps on the East and West banks.[10] In the

---

approached to attend religious discussion after prayers. It was during these discussions that the potential member was considered already to be or capable of becoming politically conscious."

[7] See Shadid, "Muslim Brotherhood in the West Bank and Gaza," 664, regarding the usrah cells in the West Bank and Gaza, and Abd Allah, *The Islamic Struggle,* 106 where he discusses the creation of cells of followers.

[8] Mitchell, *The Society,* 200–205.

[9] The security services have always been aware of the cells and have for the most part left their members alone. Occasional persecution of the Brotherhood by the secret police (especially since the 1980s and on the university campuses) probably explains elements of secrecy in recruitment and membership activities.

[10] Refugee camp branches were established in the camps of Aqbat Jabr, Irbid, Arrub and Askar.

ensuing decades the movement has increased the number of branches in urban centres and developed branches in the University of Jordan, Yarmūk University, and other post-secondary institutions. Its branch network also extends further into rural areas of the South.

Branch executives, elected by all members in any region, are in charge of important administrative duties: the budget, collection of membership fees and financial donations, the coordination of activities, and supervision of the Muslim Brotherhood's extensive medical, educational and charitable institutions. During the 1989 and 1993 election campaigns, the regional executives were responsible for organizing and mobilizing support in their zones. This they did through various channels, working through institutional infrastructures of mosques, schools, university campuses and medical centres, as well as through the use of big assemblies, discussion meetings, and street banners.[11]

The regional committees have considerable administrative autonomy but they do not have political authority. They serve to execute the policy agenda of the executive. Regional executives do have an indirect say in policy, however, because they elect the members of the national *majlis al-shūrā* (parliament or consultative body of the Muslim Brotherhood).[12] The membership of the majlis al-shūrā reflects proportionately the size of each region and has approximately 30 members. Neither the identity nor number of majlis al-shūrā representatives is publicized. The meetings take place in different locations around the country. It is not clear how often the majlis al-shūrā meets.

The Brotherhood's political policy decisions are made, at least in theory, at the level of the majlis al-shūrā, and then implemented by the executive committee.[13] This executive committee is selected from the majlis al-shūrā by the chief executive, the general supervisor (*al-muraqīb al-ʿāmm*). The executive committee controls policy making. Today in Jordan the general supervisor, the aged Khalīfah, serves merely as a figurehead.[14]

---

11 ʿAbdallāh ʿUqaylah, Muslim Brotherhood MP, interview, tape recording, Amman, Jordan, 26 July 1992.

12 The exact number and identity of regional representatives was withheld by Brotherhood sources.

13 The policy decisions are only made public when deemed appropriate by the executive as, for example, where they pertain to issues under discussion in the Jordanian media or parliament.

14 See Cohen, *Political Parties*, 145, where he notes in this regard that from 1954 to the mid-1960s Khalīfah was the undisputed leader (general secretary) of the

The Muslim Brotherhood is an international organization which maintains strong linkages between its branches. Officially, Muslim Brotherhood organizations internationally have been subordinate to the Egyptian general director. But for the most part, although they tend to support each other when possible, as will be discussed below, the organizations have maintained independence in administration and policy.[15]

The relationship between Jordanian and Palestinian branches, on the other hand, is unique and their histories have overlapped significantly. They have been administratively united and have influenced each other's ideological development. As the Palestinian issue has been central to Jordan's state development, so too has it been a major preoccupation of the Jordanian Muslim Brotherhood.

The first Muslim Brotherhood branch on the West Bank was founded in Jerusalem on October 26, 1945 by Saᶜīd Ramaḍān. By 1947 there were 25 branches in Palestine.[16] In Gaza the Muslim Brotherhood evolved at the end of the 1948 war under the influence of Egyptian soldiers who were members of the Muslim Brotherhood.[17] Under Egyptian control until 1967, the Gazan organization had little political freedom and worked for the most part underground. It maintained closer contacts with the Egyptian than the Jordanian or West Bank Muslim Brotherhood.

After Jordan annexed the West Bank in 1950, the West Bank Muslim Brotherhood was absorbed under the control of the Amman offices. The West Bank movement had expanded in the post-war era, extending numerous branches through the Hebron area in Jenin, Qalqiliya, Anabta, Sura, Sur Bahir, Tubas, Kafr Burqa, and Jericho.[18] In Amman, Khalīfah

---

movement in Jordan. In mid-1963, however, the title was also applied to Yūsuf al-ᶜAẓm, a leading activist in the movement. It seems that by this time Khalīfah no longer played an active role in the movement's affairs and was regarded as a sort of "honorary leader." Cohen states, "But there was no doubt that Khalīfah was the Brotherhood's most important figure during its first fifteen years and left a strong personal mark on the movement. Branch leaders used to make what amounted to pilgrimages to Amman, simply to consult with him; and his presence at a branch meeting or party conference was always assiduously sought."

15 See Abd Allah, *The Islamic Struggle,* 91 and Abu Amr, *Islamic Fundamentalism,* 11, where they discuss the relative independence of Muslim Brotherhood organizations in Syria, West Bank and Gaza.

16 Abu Amr, *Islamic Fundamentalism,* 3.

17 Ibid., 7.

18 Ibid., 3.

maintained little administrative control over these West Bank branches who, for the most part, ran their own affairs.[19]

The Israeli occupation of the West Bank in 1967 disrupted the Muslim Brotherhood organization. Although the East and West Bank movements remained officially united, in reality Amman exerted even less control than before.[20] In the mid-1970s the Gaza branch of the Muslim Brotherhood was united organizationally with the East and West Bank movements. This change reflected the fact that, considering Gaza's new status under Israeli occupation, the Brotherhood there was no longer part of the Egyptian movement.[21] The Gaza Brotherhood now worked in closer coordination with the West Bank movement. Contacts were also developed with Brotherhood members inside Israel.[22] Again, the Palestinian Brotherhood continued to receive guidance from Amman but was allowed considerable autonomy.

The next significant development came with the founding of Hamās at the beginning of the Palestinian *intifāḍah* in 1987. Hamās was formed by members of the Muslim Brotherhood in Gaza. The idea behind the formation of Ḥamās was to create a special organization from the Muslim Brotherhood to take responsibility for participation in the intifāḍah. The intifāḍah marked a significant change in the Muslim Brotherhood's approach to the Palestinian question. For the first time the movement condoned and participated in armed struggle, abandoning the position that the time had not yet arrived for the jihād. A seemingly new organizational framework such as Ḥamās served the useful purpose of justifying this ideological shift. The Palestinian Muslim Brotherhood eventually became submerged within Ḥamās.[23] But the creation of Ḥamās

---

19 Cohen, *Political Parties*, 157.

20 Kamāl Rashīd, editor of *al-Ribāṭ*, interview, tape recording, April 14, 1992, Amman, Jordan. Rashīd is a Palestinian native of Jaffa who became a member of the Muslim Brotherhood as a student in Nablus in 1958. He was studying in Damascus when the war broke out in 1967 and was unable to return to the West Bank. He remembered 1967 as "a period of movement and division and troubles and problems" in the organization and said that the Brotherhood in Amman "left the situation to those brothers in the West Bank to arrange themselves. They left it to them, depending on their treatment. . . . The situation was different from one city to another city in the West Bank. There was a good organization. . . . When Amman could tell them what to do they did and otherwise they left them to their own devices."

21 Abu Amr, *Islamic Fundamentalism*, 10.

22 Ibid., 22.

23 Abu Amr, *Islamic Fundamentalism*, 63–67.

did not indicate a secession from the Muslim Brotherhood, and the Ḥamās movement still belongs to the Jordanian Muslim Brotherhood organizationally. The Muslim Brotherhood Parliamentary headquarters in Amman are also Ḥamās headquarters. Senior members of the Ḥamās Politburo are almost permanently in residence there. The relationship between the Jordanian Muslim Brotherhood and Ḥamās is a cooperative one. The Jordanians do not interfere with Ḥamās policy.[24]

Interlaced with the Muslim Brotherhood's organizational structure is a complex network of educational, religious and charitable institutions. These have played a key role in the mobilization of Brotherhood support amongst all social classes and are discussed next.

Recruitment Through Muslim Brotherhood Institutions

The Muslim Brotherhood was concerned from the time of its founding in Egypt with spreading its influence through educational, charitable and religious institutions. In the 1930s Ḥasan al-Bannā established a centre of activity in Ismailiyya which has provided a model to all other Brotherhood branches. The Ismailiyya headquarters raised money for a mosque to which were added boys' and girls' schools and a youth club. All new Egyptian branches were subsequently founded on the same pattern: the establishment of a headquarters followed by the creation of a project such as a school, club, medical clinic or social centre.[25]

In subsequent decades, Muslim Brotherhood organizations throughout the Arab world have established networks of socioeconomic institutions and services rendered under the catchword "Islamic" and providing an alternative to state institutions.[26]

The Jordanian Brotherhood established its first schools after the annexation of the West Bank. The unification of the two banks led to expansion and modernization of the education system with a drive to hire more teachers and build more schools. The 1952 UNESCO report on education in Jordan notes, "In view of the crying need for more schools, teachers and other persons interested in education have opened private schools, and these have proved very successful."[27]

---

24 Ibrāhīm Ghūshah, interview.

25 Mitchell, *The Society*, 9.

26 For further discussion of such institutions in Egypt, see Saad Eddin Ibrahim, "Egypt's Islamic activism in the 1980s," *Third World Quarterly* 10 (April, 1988) 632–657.

27 UNESCO, *International Yearbook of Education*, 1952 (Paris: UNESCO, 1952), 193.

Yūsuf al-ʿAẓm founded the Brotherhood's first elementary school in Amman in the early 1950s. Around the same time the Muslim Brotherhood founded a school in Karak.[28] Schools were also established in some refugee camps including Aqbat Jabr, where Khalīfah set up a school in 1955.[29] These schools were elementary rather than secondary institutions because of the generally low level of education in Jordan at this time and the high demand for entry-level schools in order to increase the literacy rate.

The number of Muslim Brotherhood schools did not significantly expand beyond this level until the 1970s, in the context of the Brotherhood's renewed emphasis on support base development.[30] But even then, the schools did not expand rapidly. By 1992 there were only 30 combined elementary and secondary schools run by the Brotherhood, out of approximately three thousand schools countrywide. There are two reasons for this. First, the Muslim Brotherhood focussed more of its attention on recruiting support through the public school system than in developing its own schools. Secondly, these schools did not seem to have extensive appeal for the Jordanian population. The alternative schools followed the same curriculum as the state institutions, except for providing additional religious instruction and an "Islamic orientation," and were not considered academically superior.[31] The state school curriculum itself offered a strong religious program by the late 1980s.[32] Besides, the state schools were free, while the Brotherhood-run schools charged fees.

---

[28] Peter Gubser, *Politics and Change in Al-Karak, Jordan* (London: Oxford University Press, 1973), 119.

[29] Plascov, *The Palestinian Refugees*, 136.

[30] Isḥāq Farḥān, Muslim Brotherhood member, leader of the Islamic Action Front, interview, tape recording, 15 February 1993, Amman, Jordan.

[31] Although these alternative schools came under the administration of the Islamic Charitable Center, they, like all schools in Jordan, fell under the jurisdiction of the Ministry of Education. As such, they were subject to fairly close regulation by the ministry which required them to follow the basic guidelines of the state curriculum and reviewed their teaching standards annually. Teachers in all the Brotherhood's schools were recruited and vetted by the Islamic Charitable Centre where they undertook special training courses.

[32] As a result of the influence of the Brotherhood in the Ministry of Education to be discussed below.

An example of Muslim Brotherhood schools are the five Dār al-Arqām schools in and around Amman. These schools supplement the ministry curriculum by teaching five rather than the specified three classes in religious instruction per week. The extra lessons in religious studies focus on Islamic ritual and practice rather than strict theological study. Children are instructed in practical matters such as how to pray and how to wash themselves before prayer. "We give three classes and add two to see reactively the children's absorption of the material. We try to activate them and teach them how to build ideas into action," explained the schools' director, Yūsuf al-Sakīd.[33]

Outside the religious studies classes, focus is geared to the inculcation of Islamic values and behaviour. Emphasis is placed on the behaviour of the individual in society. Students are taught to follow what al-Sakīd referred to as an "Islamic lifestyle." Male and female students are separated from the first grade.[34] In the girls' school all teachers and 90% of students, even in the earliest grades, wear some form of "Islamic head covering." During the month of Ramaḍān even the youngest children are encouraged to fast. Al-Sakīd emphasized the importance of "Islamic family values" and explained that female students at the secondary level take courses in housekeeping and cooking as part of their "concentration on Islamic heritage."[35]

The Brotherhood's youth clubs and organizations have played a more important role than their schools in recruiting support for the movement. The Brotherhood's boy scouts, *al-firaq al-kashfiyyah,* have been active since the 1940s. The Scouts are modelled on Ḥasan al-Bannā's Rovers organization (*al-jawwālah*). The principle behind the Rovers was "the inseparability of the healthy body from the healthy mind" and its main focus was on athletics.[36]

In the Jordanian case, activities at Scout meetings are also primarily athletic and social, with little emphasis on religious instruction. Scouts engage in outdoor activities such as hiking and camping, and indoor games such as ping pong and chess. The Scouts provide a conduit for

33 Yūsuf al-Sakīd, Director General of the Dār al-Arqām schools which are run by the Islamic Charitable Centre, interview, tape recording, Amman, 21 February, 1993.

34 Except in one of the schools where, due to space limitations, boys and girls are in the same classroom through to the third grade.

35 Al-Sakīd, interview.

36 Mitchell, 200.

attracting young students to the movement. Many of the men who became prominent in the Brotherhood in the 1950s and 1960s first became acquainted with the movement through this organization as well as through the schools.[37]

Recruitment Through Public Institutions

The Muslim Brotherhood's most effective method of spreading its influence has been through public institutions. The Brotherhood's success in garnering support through the state education system, in particular, can be attributed to the availability and accessibility of schools for recruitment purposes. Not only was there a proliferation of schools due to the country's efforts to expand education after World War II, but, as Waterbury points out, "The school, like the mosque, has the advantage of being an institution within which it is very difficult for authorities to control political activities among people who congregate in a perfectly legal manner."[38] Gubser has noted that in Karak during the 1950s the school provided an arena within which the central government and alternative political parties could vie for influence over a new generation:

> The central government has used the schools to create a sense of identity in the individual as a Jordanian and an Arab, as well as for social development and economic advancement. The various political parties have propagated their opinions and ideologies through the reaches among their members. It is the schools as much as any other force which have created the educated middle stratum, a group with significantly different social and political attitudes from the remainder of the population.[39]

From the 1950s onwards the Muslim Brotherhood was critical of the state education system, finding it to be poisoned by Western influences

---

[37] ʿAzzīzī, interview. He recalled the early days of the movement's organization, when he was a boy of 12 and was eager to join the Scouts: "My elder brother got involved with the movement and became a member of the Scouts. . . . Seeing my elder brother wearing this Scout dress I looked forward to doing the same thing." In 1949–50 he attended the Scouts' meetings along with about 60% of his classmates. The Scouts offered activities "which attract young people . . . a social club, a chess club, ping pong." ʿAzzīzī emphasized that there was "no religious instruction" at the social club meetings. Lectures on Islamic themes apparently took place in different venues such as public lecture halls or at weekly branch meetings. Yūsuf al-ʿAẓm, in a separate interview, recalled attending the meeting in the 1940s in Jebel Amman and the activities there included "sports, lectures on Islam, and how to revive the heritage."

[38] Waterbury, *A Political Economy,* 131.

[39] Gubser, *Politics and Change,* 119.

and insufficient in the area of religious instruction. The education program was Western-oriented and run with the collaboration of the United States Point Four Program and the British Council.[40] The Ministry of Education emphasized Western pedagogical techniques and an empirical approach to education. In 1962 the Ministry stated that it was "exerting great efforts to make teachers practice modern methods and to adopt the modern philosophy of education which considers the child as the centre of the educational process."[41] Indeed, the same year the Ministry changed its name by replacing *al-maʿrifah* (knowledge or science with clear religious overtones) with *al-tarbiyah wa al-taʿlim* (education and teaching in the purely technical sense). The Brothers saw this change as proof of the alienation of the kingdom's education system from religion.[42] Their position was that the teaching of science should be incorporated within an Islamic educational system which would bring up well-rounded human beings from a moral and spiritual as well as intellectual point of view. The casting aside of Islam in the education system threatened a whole generation. And this was of greatest concern to the Muslim Brotherhood because it was, after all, a priority of the movement to educate a generation which would work to Islamize society.[43]

Members of the Brotherhood were able to infiltrate the Ministry of Education during the 1960s. This gave them access to the development of curricula and the appointment of teachers.[44] As a result they were gradually able to implement a curriculum with a stronger religious component.[45] This took them several decades to achieve, but by 1987 the ministry's statement of principles and objectives had acquired strikingly more Islamic undertones:

---

40 And later by the USAID. Point Four was its precursor.

41 UNESCO, *International Yearbook on Education, 1962* (Paris: UNESCO, 1962): 206–208.

42 Cohen, *Political Parties,* 184

43 For a discussion of the Muslim Brotherhood's critique of Western education see Emmanual Sivan, *Radical Islam: Medieval Theory and Modern Politics* (New Haven: Yale University Press, 1985), 6–10.

44 For a description of the administrative structure of the Ministry of Education see UNESCO, *International Yearbook on Education,* 1983, 117.

45 See Day, *East Bank/West Bank,* 48, where he argues, "The Ministry of Education came under the control of Islamic enthusiasts in the early 1960s and a strong religious program in the schools has resulted."

> The philosophy of education is derived from the Jordanian constitution which states that: "Islam is the religion of the country, and Arabic is the official language." The main aspects of the educational philosophy are: Faith in God; inculcating the morals of the Arab nation; unity and freedom in the Arab nation; promotion of world cultural development; social justice; democracy; and individual respect and dignity.[46]

Teachers sympathetic to the Brotherhood played a significant role in mobilizing student support. As mentioned above, many members of the Muslim Brotherhood today were exposed to the movement at primary or secondary school in the 1940s or 1950s.[47] Teachers at elementary and secondary levels were able to attract support for the movement either by encouraging students to join social clubs such as the Scouts organization or through religious education classes. Their work did not necessarily bring new members to the movement. But at least it created a pool of potential recruits, individuals sympathetic to the Brotherhood's ideology.

The young and impressionable could be easily affected by their teachers and peers even in cases where their families were not particularly religious. A young woman member of the Islamic bloc[48] at the University of Jordan sharīʿah college described how she was affected by her religious studies teacher in elementary school:

> I grew up in an ordinary family. I first wore just a scarf and then my mother didn't even wear a scarf and my father didn't pray. My religion teacher at school my first day told us about paradise and hell and that good people go to paradise and the girls who didn't wear a scarf, they didn't go there. . . . She awakened

---

46 UNESCO, *International Yearbook on Education 1987–1990* (UNESCO: Paris, 1990), 39–42.

47 ʿAzzīzī, interview. He recalled the influence of teachers and other students as early as the late 1940s in encouraging them to join social clubs where they played ping pong and chess. Yūsuf al-ʿAẓm became involved with the Muslim Brotherhood while attending preparatory school in Maan, and at high school in Amman in 1945–46 he attended lectures given by the Brothers and joined a youth club. Muḥammad al-Bannā (interview) said that he was first acquainted with the Muslim Brethren through a lecture given by Egyptian missionaries which he attended as a secondary student in Irbid. Isḥāq Farḥān (interview) was recruited directly into a cell as a student in Salt. Ziyād Abū Ghanīmah (interview) became aware of the movement in elementary school when he was ten years old.

48 Islamic bloc (*kutlah Islāmiyyah*) is a general term used to describe supporters of the Muslim Brotherhood and other Islamist groups.

something inside and my parents agreed [that she could wear the *ḥijāb* or headcover]. . . ."[49]

Students themselves have played a major role in attracting each other to the Muslim Brotherhood. For example, a female student at the sharīʿah college described her experience in the following way:

> I grew up in Amman and my family was not very religious. . . . But when I met some friends they affected me somehow . . . friends at elementary school when I was six years old . . . my teachers and my friends. My friends were from Syria. When they are little they are very religious. When I was 11 or 12 I wore the ḥijāb. My family refused at first; they said I am too young but I insisted on wearing it. . . . I insisted and after that I convinced them at home. My big sister wore ḥijāb after me when she was at university and I have a little sister and when she was 11 I convinced my mother to let her wear ḥijāb. . . . After I was religious I affected my family.

This student said she was pleased when she arrived at the university to find a community of what she described as "religious" women at the University of Jordan.[50]

The university campuses have been always among the most significant centres for Muslim Brotherhood recruitment. They have attracted students through a variety of activities. Some, such as bus trips or picnics, are strictly social. But the majority focus on education and cultural development and include book fairs, art exhibits, and discussion groups on Islamist themes.

Beyond the scope of general social or educational activities, the Muslim Brotherhood organizes direct recruitment into usrah cells on the university campuses. The University of Jordan functions as its own region within the national administrative organization.[51] Students and faculty

---

49 Anonymous student Islamic Bloc member #1, interview, tape recording, Amman, Jordan, 3 August 1992.

50 Anonymous student member of the Islamic bloc, #2, interview, tape recording, Amman, Jordan, 3 August 1992. Identification with a community plays an important part in the attraction of the Muslim Brotherhood on university campuses. Although women have played an insignificant role politically in the Muslim Brotherhood organization, they are becoming increasingly prominent in its campus organizations. The movement's female support base is analyzed below.

51 The region seems to be administered by some senior faculty whose identities are kept secret. Faculty involvement in general is kept quite secret and the researcher was not able to acquire information about this. Presumably, secrecy is explained by fear of reprisal by the security services. ʿAbdallāh ʿUqaylah (interview) stated that in the late 1980s many members of the movement lost their jobs. He said that after serving in the government from 1984 to 1988 he was not permitted to return to his position in the

belong to a network of usrah cells on the campus. The activities of these cells are concerned with the affairs of the Muslim Brotherhood at the university, their political agenda, distribution of pamphlets, organization of demonstrations, recruitment of new members. University of Jordan members all belong simultaneously to another usrah which deals with issues in their home branch. The university branches of the Muslim Brotherhood were politically significant in the period before democratization because they were the only forum in which the organization could speak openly.[52]

As in the national organization, women and men on university campuses work within separate usrah cells.[53] To some extent the men and women coordinate usrah activities on the campus, although they mostly manage to do this without actually being in the same room. Men have traditionally dominated the leadership of the student organization but women are now gaining some ground. In the newly elected students' union there are 14 women from the Islamic bloc.

Muslim Brotherhood activities on the campuses have gradually led to the movement's prominence in professional associations filled with university graduates. Today the Islamists hold a majority in nearly all these old "leftist castles"[54] except for the legal and medical associations which remain the most stalwart holdouts of the centrist professional elite. In June 1991 the Islamists won control of the executive board of the Pharmacists Association with seven out of nine seats on the executive committee.[55] In March of 1993, the Jordanian Bar Association barely held out against an onslaught by Islamists who managed to secure four out of ten seats. This was the first time in 30 years the Islamists won seats on the prestigious board.

Faculty of Education at the University of Jordan: "I was delivered from that by the mukhābarāt (security services)."

52 Anonymous students, #4 and #5, interviews.

53 The history of women in the national organization is discussed below.

54 Phrase used by Layth Shubaylāt (interview, tape recording, Amman, 29 April 1992) who said "Islamists are powerful in the professional organizations, to say that they dominate is an exaggeration, but the tide is coming and these are the old leftist castles." By "leftists" he is referring to a few Marxists and many nationalists who dominated the professional syndicates up to the 1980s.

55 Beverley Milton Edwards, "A Temporary Alliance with the Crown: the Islamic Response in Jordan," *Islamic Fundamentalisms and the Gulf Crisis,* James Piscatori, ed. (Chicago: American Academy of Arts), 106.

The Brotherhood's success on the campuses is attested to by the political supremacy today of the Islamic bloc in Jordanian universities. The Muslim Brotherhood was active in the student and faculty populations from the time of the founding of the country's first university, the University of Jordan in 1962.[56] But it did not gain major influence until the mid-to-late 1970s, when it started to make significant gains at the expense of the leftists in student council elections.

The Muslim Brotherhood is politically dominant today on all Jordanian university campuses. For example, at the nation's largest university, the University of Jordan, the Islamic bloc gained dominance in the faculties of sharīʿah and science in the mid-1970s.[57] By the late 1980s, the Muslim Brotherhood-dominated Islamic bloc held a majority in elected student associations of nearly all faculties of the University. In 1993 the sharīʿah faculty was still more heavily dominated by the Islamic bloc than any other. Interestingly, the sharīʿah faculty today has the highest proportion of women Islamists.

By the late 1980s the Islamic bloc controlled student associations in all faculties with two exceptions—the faculty of law and the faculty of physical education. The law faculty has been traditionally the domain of the Westernized upper classes. The faculty of physical education has no enrollment of female Islamists (presumably due in part to considerations of modesty). Female Islamists are regarded as a key factor in the bloc's support base, as will be discussed below.

Recruitment Through Mosques

Mosques provide important centres for Brotherhood recruitment, although the Jordanian ʿulamāʾ have not played a significant role in the movement's leadership as they have, for example, in the Syrian case where they were the earliest founders of the Brotherhood.[58] The Jordanian ʿulamāʾ have been relatively unpoliticized. A factor in this is that their institutions have not been attacked by the state as they have, for example,

---

[56] Fuʾād Tārūrī, student at the University of Jordan, interview, tape recording, student at the University of Jordan and Islamic bloc member, Amman, Jordan, 15 April 1992.

[57] Ibid.

[58] Batatu, "Syria's Muslim Brethren," 117. Batatu links the ʿulamāʾ with the economic interests of Sunnī Arab small traders who have played a dominant role in the Syrian Muslim Brotherhood.

in Tunisia.[59] But the ʿulamāʾ have been used by the Jordanian Muslim Brotherhood to mobilize support, especially through Friday sermons. The mosques have been important centres for developing grass-roots constituencies (as focal gathering points) for communities and centres for charity work and education. Mosques have also been useful for educating and mobilizing support in rural areas where other institutions were not available.

Mosques have been used by the Brotherhood since its founding. As early as 1955, security services monitored both the content of Friday sermons and activities of preachers.[60] After the 1967 war, the Brotherhood focussed on mosques as centres for education in the context of a major political awareness drive.[61] The Brotherhood increased its influence in the mosques in the 1980s. There were two main reasons for this: first, a proliferation of mosques and an increase in mosque attendance in the context of a wave of general Islamization,[62] and secondly, the infiltration of the Ministry of Religious Affairs by the Muslim Brotherhood.[63] As the Jordanian ministry exerts considerable control over mosques, this infiltration considerably enhanced the Brotherhood's influence. By law, the ministry is empowered to appoint mosque preachers, orators and teachers.[64] The ministry gives preachers orientation sessions and organizes periodic meetings with workers in mosques, often under the patronage of the minister himself.

Circumscribing Brotherhood influence within the mosques was an issue in the legalization of political parties. Article six of the 1992 draft law

---

[59] In Tunisia, the ʿulamāʾ have played a significant role in Islamist movements after they suffered the abolition of their sharīʿah courts in 1956 and the loss of all independence. In Egypt, as in Jordan, the ʿulamāʾ have not come under direct attack by the state and have not been politically active in Islamist organizations. As Emmanual Sivan has commented, "[t]he Muslim Brotherhood has always disdained the ʿulamāʾ as a class for having failed to accomplish its historical duty as a guardian of the conscience of the faith, whether out of pusillanimity or opportunism." See Boulby, "The Islamic Challenge," 591–596, and Sivan, *Radical Islam*, 52.

[60] Cohen, *Political Parties*, 150.

[61] Rashīd and ʿUqaylah, interviews.

[62] These factors will be discussed in more detail below.

[63] Day, *East Bank/West Bank*, 48, where he notes, "The membership of the Brotherhood numbers in the many thousands. It enjoys a strong influence over the mosques and in the Ministry of Islamic Affairs and Holy Places and the Ministry of Education."

[64] Antoine Messara, "La régulation étatique de la religion dans le monde arabe: le cas de la Jordanie," *Social Compass*, 40 (April 1993): 581–588.

which defines political parties prohibits them from undertaking political activity in schools and religious institutions.[65] This law was clearly directed against the Brotherhood. Isḥāq Farḥān, leader of the Front, stated that the party would not use mosques and would abide by the law, in spite of the good deal of support attracted by the mosques historically.[66] Yet, in spite of government interference, the Brotherhood still retains a country-wide network of mosques.

Mobilization of Support: The Appeal of the Muslim Brotherhood

In the 1980s the Muslim Brotherhood became a significant player on the Jordanian political stage, rallying its social base for an impressive showing in the elections of 1989. The movement was able to mobilize electoral support in the context of three major factors. First, the economic downturn of the early 1980s fuelled political and economic discontent on which the Brotherhood was able to capitalize. As discussed in Chapter One, rapid socioeconomic changes in the 1970s had produced a more educated, urbanized, and politicized Jordanian population, frustrated by economic recession and autocratic rule. The Brotherhood, as an increasingly outspoken advocate of democracy, captured some of their support.

The students of the Islamic bloc were particularly forceful in their demands for democratization of university politics and the establishment of a national students' union. These demands brought them into conflict with the regime which feared the prospect of Islamist domination of a national students' body.[67] In 1990 University of Jordan students voted in a committee charged with the task of working to establish a union. The Islamists won 96% of the vote with the remainder going to monarchists and nationalists. Similar elections took place at all other Jordanian universities with the Islamists achieving large majorities. At this point the government forbade any further move to establish a national union.

In a more successful attempt, students at the University of Jordan held elections in May of 1992, returning a student council in which the Islamists won 64 out of 80 seats. This student council, in coordination with other university student councils, undertook the task of organizing a

[65] *The Jordan Times*, June 30, 1992.

[66] Farḥān, interview.

[67] Layth Shubaylāt, interview. Anonymous student members of Islamic bloc, #3, #4, interview, tape recording, Amman, Jordan, 26 July 1992.

national students' union. Once again, the government tried to discourage student unionization and the king even visited the University of Jordan to try to persuade the administration that elections were not needed. But the elections were permitted to proceed in the wake of student demonstrations and the loudly-voiced criticism of the popular Islamist member of parliament Layth Shubaylāt who accused the king of "interfering" with the affairs of the universities. In 1993 students at the University of Jordan elected a Muslim Brotherhood student council. Of those who voted, 88% supported Islamists.[68]

The regime's concern with the implications of Islamist political activism in universities has been indicated by secret police surveillance and harassment of students. Although the majority of the students associated with the Islamic bloc are in fact Muslim Brotherhood supporters, these students choose not to admit their affiliation publicly, fearing reprisal from the security services.[69] One student told this researcher:

> No one at the University of Jordan will agree to meet you under the headline of Muslim Brotherhood. Here in Jordan we have democracy but . . . the students don't like to have the name Muslim Brotherhood. . . . In their activities they may work with them but they will say not. . . . They are afraid to say they are Muslim Brotherhood although they are.[70]

---

68 Anonymous students #3 and #4 and Layth Shubaylāt, interviews.

69 Estimates by students suggest that support for the Muslim Brotherhood lies somewhere between 70% and 90% with only about 1% support for the Liberation Party. The rest are referred to loosely as "independents," presumably those who are not politically committed or affiliated to a national organization. There is, unfortunately, no exact data on student membership of the Islamic bloc. But the majority of students interviewed at the University of Jordan indicated that they saw little difference in political or social goals between the Muslim Brotherhood and the Islamic bloc. The issue was primarily one of making the commitment to political affiliation and the security risks entailed.

70 Many other students at the University of Jordan also admitted that although their sympathies lay with the Muslim Brotherhood they were afraid to affiliate openly. "I agree with [the Muslim Brotherhood] but really I have some special circumstances . . . some security reasons with the government . . . it is a very weak democracy," said one. (Anonymous student member of the Islamic bloc #5, interview, tape recording, Amman, Jordan, 3 August, 1992.) "Students who state openly that they belong to the Muslim Brotherhood have problems with the government. . . . The security services watch the university everywhere," said another. (Anonymous student member of the Islamic bloc member #6, interview, tape recording, Amman, Jordan, 3 August, 1992.)Prominent student activists at the forefront of the union movement have been harassed, detained and threatened by the security services. Threats have generally

The development of the Muslim Brotherhood's support base is therefore directly linked to the rapid expansion of education in Jordan since World War II, as discussed in Chapter One. In Jordan, as in other Middle Eastern states, the education system has contributed in the past two to three decades to the rapid growth of white-collar civil servants and professionals.[71] Since the early 1980s Jordan has faced an increasingly acute problem with unemployment, as it has been unable to absorb the growing ranks of would-be professionals and civil servants. The economic frustration of this younger generation of secondary and university students has made them particularly amenable to recruitment by the Muslim Brotherhood throughout the last decade.[72]

A second factor in the building of the Brotherhood's support base was the decline in popularity of the Pan-Arabists and then the PLO. The post-war era produced widespread disillusionment in the region with pan-Arabist and socialist perspectives. For the Muslim Brotherhood, the setback of 1967 was regarded as a clear defeat for secular, nationalist, and socialist trends. In Egypt, the movement condemned the defeat of 1967 as "divine revenge" against the regime for its incarceration and torture of

---

taken the form of warnings that if the student does not withdraw from the brotherhood, s/he may have difficulties with the government bureaucracy in the future obtaining visas or employment. Female members of the Islamist bloc are not usually harassed by the secret police, perhaps because so far they are not taken seriously. This is likely to change, however, with the increased prominence of female student supporters of the movement. One prominent student member of the Islamic bloc was arrested in his house and questioned for two days by the security forces. He told the writer:

> They came to my house and said I had to come. They said that if I didn't give up this thing (work with the Islamic bloc for the establishment of a union) . . . this will have a future dimension, that it would be difficult for me to get a job. I was asked many questions about the Islamic movement and my relationship to it.

On another occasion he was arrested with other students staging a peaceful demonstration in support of a students union in front of the parliament building. "They just asked a lot of questions for that day. Democracy is limited," he said. (Anonymous student member of the Islamic bloc #7, interview, tape recording, Amman, Jordan, 26 July, 1992.)

[71] Waterbury, *A Political Economy*, 100.

[72] The attraction of students to Islamist movements has been widely noted. Nikki Keddie has pointed to the presence of a "large, alienated, educated class" as a major factor in encouraging the development of Islamist movements in general. This occurs especially, she argues, in cases where the existence of such a class coincides with "a significant break with traditional culture" as in Jordan which undertook a Western-inspired development plan. See Nikki Keddie, "Ideology, Society and the State in Post-Colonial Muslim Societies," Halliday and Ahlavi, *State and Society*, 16–17.

Muslim Brotherhood members.[73] In this atmosphere the Jordanian Brotherhood was encouraged to expand its activities. It founded the Islamic Charity Association, which supervised a growing network of educational and social institutions.

It was also active, as it had been in 1948, amongst the Palestinian refugees.[74] Although it was appreciated for its charitable work, the Brotherhood did not attract much Palestinian political support at this time.[75] The post-war years in Jordan saw the increasing prominence and radicalization of the PLO.[76] Its specifically Palestinian nationalism was favoured by many disillusioned with proposed solutions to the Palestinian problem under an Arab banner.

The Muslim Brotherhood, both in Jordan and the Occupied Territories, was ideologically opposed to the PLO on more than one ground. Tensions between the PLO and the Muslim Brotherhood had their roots in the 1950s when the Brotherhood supported King Hussein against the challenge of National Socialists.[77] The Brotherhood, critical of nationalist and socialist ideologies, was hostile to leftist elements such as the Popular Front for the Liberation of Palestine (PFLP) and the Democratic Front for the Liberation of Palestine (DFLP) within the PLO. The Brotherhood was closer ideologically to Fatah but became increasingly alarmed by what it perceived as Fatah's gradual abandonment of its Islamic leanings.[78] The Brotherhood believed that the salvation of Palestine could not come about without the revival of the Islamic faith. Its

---

73 Ibid., 11.

74 Kamāl Rashīd, editor of *al-Ribāṭ*, interview, Amman, April 14,1992. He mentioned that after 1967 the Brotherhood's "first work was to offer charity to the Palestinians here and those abroad to whom we could send money."

75 Most of the Jordanian Brotherhood's work with the Palestinians was charitable. However, there are some indications that the Brotherhood was involved after 1967 with military training and guerilla operations. Fatḥī Malkāwī was certain about this in an interview: "Of course, the most important item on the agenda of the group at this time was the Palestinian problem and directly after the war they started doing some military training and established some groups as *fedayīn* and so I think that after the 1967 war the main issue was how to attack the Jews and the Jewish state." It was not possible to corroborate this information with other sources. The Muslim Brotherhood deny involvement in any military activity since the 1948 war, stressing their gradualist, non-violent methods.

76 See Chapter One, 38, for a summary of events leading up to the 1970–71 civil war in Jordan.

77 As discussed in Chapter Two.

78 Abu Amr, *Islamic Fundamentalism*, 28.

program for the liberation of Palestine required the education of a new generation capable of waging jihād against the enemy.[79] The Brotherhood used this explanation to justify its rejection of armed struggle as a solution to the Palestinian problem. This position also reflected the Brotherhood's non-confrontational posture on both sides of the Jordan River. On the West Bank, the Muslim Brotherhood argued that if it became involved in armed struggle then this would only give the Israelis a pretext for striking at them. In Jordan, the Muslim Brotherhood doubtless wished to avoid overt confrontation with the regime.

During the civil war of 1970–71 the Muslim Brotherhood did not join with the PLO in openly challenging the Jordanian regime, although some members participated in the resistance before 1970 under the cover of the Fatah umbrella.[80] They have provided various explanations for why they did not publicly support the PLO, including the refusal of the PLO to allow them to do so, the lack of support for their ideological position, and their criticism of the PLO's provocative actions which caused King Hussein to strike at them.[81]

In any case, the civil war weakened the PLO, severing its ties with the Occupied Territories. This served in the long run to bolster the Muslim Brotherhood's ideological position. The 1973 war was also a factor in heightening Islamist consciousness in Jordan and throughout the Arab world. The war was fought during the month of Ramaḍān under the code-named "Badr" (the name of a battle in which the Prophet Muḥammad was victorious over idolaters in 623), and the limited victories of the Egyptian troops were attributed by Islamists in general to their lack of religious faith.[82] The war also strengthened the Muslim Brotherhood's position regarding the PLO. The PLO at this time opened the door for diplomatic solutions and began to consider the establishment of a national authority on any piece of land freed from Israeli occupation, rather than demanding sovereignty over all of traditional Palestine. This so-called "two-state solution" was harshly criticized by the Muslim Brotherhood. As the PLO's status declined in the context of continued failures and allegations of corruption, the Brotherhood's standing among Palestinians rose.

---

[79] Ibid., 37.

[80] Ibid., 41.

[81] Ibid.

[82] Abu Amr, *Islamic Fundamentalism,* 11.

Thus, the Brotherhood had, for the first time, the potential of harnessing extensive Palestinian political support.

The 1980s saw the rise of Palestinian discontent in Jordan specifically. Tensions between Palestinians and Transjordanians which had been submerged during the decade of prosperity now resurfaced. The 1980s were also characterized by increased disillusionment with the PLO, in the wake of its 1982 ouster from Lebanon. Many Palestinians living in Jordan, especially those in the refugee camps, felt that the Arabs were ineffective in the face of Israeli intransigence. The outbreak of the intifāḍah in 1987 reinvigorated Palestinian nationalism which the Brotherhood was for the first time able to channel into political support.

A third major factor in the increased appeal of the Brotherhood was the success of the Iranian revolution, which had contributed to a heightened consciousness of Islam and a more generalized Islamic revival throughout the Middle East in the late 1970s and early 1980s. Signs of an Islamic revival in Jordan have been evident from the early 1980s on.[83] This "new Islamic manifestation,"[84] described as "the appearance of an amorphous but very real movement back to Islam by many people from all levels of society,"[85] was evidenced in increased wearing of Islamic dress, an upsurge in mosque attendance, and a proliferation of mosques.

The upsurge in mosque attendance coincided with a mosque building boom in Amman.[86] This boom far exceeded population requirements since, according to Rogan, parity was achieved by 1979 between urban expansion and mosque construction.[87] The popular movement was

---

[83] There may be considerable argument over the meaning of "Islamic revivalism." Here the concept of Islamic revival is understood, as John L. Esposito has described it, in its broadest sense: "Islamic revivalism in its broadest sense refers to a renewal of Islam in Muslim personal and public life. Its manifestations include an increase in religious observances (mosque attendance, Ramadān fast, wearing traditional Islamic dress); a revitalization of religious publications and media programming; calls for the implementation of Islamic law; creation of Islamic banks; and the growth of Islamic organizations and activist movements." See John L. Esposito, "Islamic Revivalism," Occasional Paper No.3 in *The Muslim World Today*, American Institute for International Affairs (Washington: 1993).

[84] Day, *East Bank/West Bank*, 48.

[85] Ibid., 48

[86] This phenomenon is analyzed by Eugene Rogan, "Physical Islamization of Amman," *Muslim World* 76 (January 1986): 24–41. He discusses two parallel trends: the symbolic effort on the part of the Jordanian government to devise a standard of Islamic architecture for Amman and a popular expansion in mosque building.

[87] Ibid., 36.

parallelled by a government initiative to define, develop and apply an Islamic architectural formula to the city of Amman. A law of 1981 established a committee charged with the preservation of architectural and environmental heritage and with providing guidance for modern buildings to follow Arab and Islamic architectural lines.[88] Nevertheless, mosque building, Rogan argues, was "an overwhelmingly popular movement with only a minimum of government participation."[89]

Those individuals who participated in or were conscious of an Islamic revival were not necessarily predisposed to vote for the Muslim Brotherhood. Jordan's Islamic revival, like most Islamic revivals, was an amorphous phenomenon, influenced by a variety of social, economic, political and cultural factors. The motivations of individuals or groups choosing to attend the mosque or wear the veil cannot be generalized and should not be correlated with conscious political or social dissatisfaction or a predisposition to join an Islamist movement. Such individuals can only be regarded as providing a potential support base for the movement. This viewpoint is echoed by Waltz in her analysis of Islamist appeal in Tunisia. In surveying the Islamic revival in Tunisia and its relationship with the Islamist Tendency Movement, she commented:

---

88 By identifying itself with Islamic tradition, the monarchy sought to capture the Islamic revival so that it would not be channelled into political opposition. As John Voll wrote of the monarchy's relations with revivalist Islam at this time, "The key to survival appears to be a careful reaffirmation of the Islamic tradition along with a renewed emphasis on nationalist causes." [See John Obert Voll, *Islam, Continuity and Change in the Modern World* (Boulder, Colorado: Westview Press, 1982), 292.] In 1980, King Hussein stated regarding the government's concern with the preservation of Islamic heritage:

> We live in the historic centre of the Muslim world, and are keenly aware of the need to associate our sense of identity with the best that Islamic history and tradition have to offer. The plans for the present are to seek innovation in a world beset by an expedient tendency to imitate blindly. . . . We are conscious of our aesthetic heritage and of the need for its practical manifestation. ["The Aga Khan Award for Architecture, "Places of Public Gathering in Islam," *Proceedings of Seminar Five* in the series Architectural Transformations in the Islamic World. Held in Amman, Jordan, May 4–7, 1980 (Cambridge: Aga Khan Awards, 1980), 15.]

Hussein had always emphasized the Islamic legitimacy of Hashemite rule, had been adept at accommodating religious forces in Jordanian society and hoped to coopt the revival. [Rogan, "Physical Islamization," 31.]

89 Ibid., 36. According to Rogan, the Ministry of Religious Affairs' role in mosque construction was limited to approving the site and plans and providing tax exemptions on cement and steel.

> Because it is difficult to know where personal piety ends and support for the Islamists' social goals begins, one must be cautious in interpreting such developments as signs of increased Islamist influence. Nevertheless, there is within this sensitized population a new predisposition to read Islamic tracts and to hear out those who have committed themselves politically. While this population cannot be identified as members or even supporters of such groups as the MTI, they nonetheless form a latent base of support which could someday be of political importance.[90]

Likewise, the observer must be cautious in over-determining the political or religious significance of the wearing of the veil. As Dr. Samīrah Fayyāḍ, a prominent Jordanian female Islamist and ex-member of the Muslim Brotherhood commented to the researcher:

> You see more Islam amongst the young university women than there really is. Many girls wear Islamic dress but it doesn't mean a real commitment to Islam. It's becoming more of a national costume than a commitment. . . . Some women wear it and they don't even pray. We had a national costume which was embroidered and complicated. Islamic dress is cheaper and more available and it serves the purpose of covering the body of the woman. That's why many fathers insist on their daughter wearing this and they don't believe much in the religion; it is just a conservative tradition.[91]

Nevertheless, the increased wearing of the veil is a clear reminder of the increased popularity of "the Islamic alternative."

---

[90] Susan Waltz, "Islamist Appeal in Tunisia," *Middle East Journal* 40 (Autumn 1986): 657.

[91] Dr. Samīrah Fayyāḍ, interview, tape recording, Amman, Jordan, 28 March, 1992. Likewise, Souhayr Belhassen, "Femmes tunisiennes islamistes," *Annuaire de l'Afrique du Nord*, 1979 (Paris: CNRS, 1981): 138–143, found that the choice of wearing the ḥijāb was not necessarily correlated with piety or political ideology. Belhassen interviewed a street sample of twenty women wearing the ḥijāb and encountered several women who indicated they had learned nothing of Islam from their homes and came to wear the ḥijāb only after having been influenced by friends or after having read an Islamist pamphlet. Nevertheless, since the late 1980s it has become increasingly possible to differentiate those women who are members of the Islamic bloc by the particular style of Islamic clothing that they wear. The "sisters" tend to dress in a "uniform" including a coat, gloves and a veil which covers all of the head and in many cases all of the face except for the eyes, while other young women may wear only a headscarf, or a coat with no gloves or some other variation on the theme. For the author, a telltale visual sign of the popularity of the Islamic bloc at the University of Jordan was the sight of two thousand identically uniformed women attending an Islamist lecture in April 1992.

The 1984 By-Elections

The first real indication that the Muslim Brotherhood had acquired a popular base came with the parliamentary by-elections of March 1984. As discussed in Chapter One, three main factors precipitated the calling of the elections: demands for democratization; Hussein's manoeuvring to challenge the PLO's exclusive position and to press the organization to join with Jordan in diplomacy towards a peace settlement with Israel; and the practical consideration that since the last elections, held in 1967, eight candidates had died.

Hussein recalled parliament on 5 January 1984. The first act of the newly-called parliament was to pass a constitutional amendment allowing elections to take place on the East Bank but not, because of Israeli occupation, on the West Bank. The eight members of parliament who had died would be replaced by direct election. Of the eight seats to be filled in the East Bank, two were reserved for Christians, leaving six open for contest by Muslims. The government permitted free elections in order to gauge public opinion.[92] However, mass meetings, public rallies, loud-speakers and posters in the streets were prohibited.[93]

These elections were meaningful in gauging public opinion, not only because they were free, but also because of significant changes in the electorate. This was the first opportunity for women to vote.[94] (They were enfranchised in 1974.) It was also the first chance for Jordanians in the 20–37 age group to vote.[95] One-hundred two candidates ran in total. They, including Muslim Brotherhood members, ran independently, since political parties remained illegal.

For the Brotherhood, the decision to participate in the 1984 elections was a logical continuation of its long-term pragmatic strategy. It looked benignly upon parliamentary representation as a means of increasing its influence in Jordanian society, although it did not necessarily view parliamentary democracy as a satisfactory end in itself.[96] The dominant issues in the campaign were the liberation of the Occupied Territories, increased democratization, and the development of national industries

---

92 Robins, "Politics and the 1986 Electoral Law," 192.

93 Day, *East Bank/West Bank*, 52.

94 Women were not allowed to run as candidates, however.

95 Layne, "Elections," 118.

96 The political goals of the Muslim Brotherhood are discussed in detail in Chapter Four.

and agriculture to revitalize the economy.[97] Muslim Brotherhood and independent Islamist contenders focussed on the Palestinian issue, taking the stalwart position that "no one has the right to negotiate away an inch of Palestine,"[98] and rejecting compromise diplomatic solutions with Israel with slogans such as "No to Camp David and no to Reagan," and "No solution to the Palestinian question except through Islam."[99]

There was considerable shock amongst the political establishment when the elections resulted in three Islamist members of parliament. Two of these, Dr. Aḥmad al-Kufāḥī and Dr. ʿAbdallāh ʿUqaylah, were members of the Muslim Brotherhood. Dr. al-Kufāḥī, a professor at Yarmūk University, received over 30% of the vote in Irbid in a field of nineteen candidates. He won a majority of 10,687 votes over a candidate from the nationalist left.[100] Irbid had been identified with growing Islamist popularity and a group of Islamist candidates had been elected to the municipal council the previous December. ʿUqaylah, a lecturer at the University of Jordan, won against two other candidates in the southern district of Tafileh. The most outstanding victory was gained by Islamist independent Layth Shubaylāt, the former president of the Jordanian Engineers Association, who triumphed over thirty-five rivals in the upper class Third Circle constituency of Amman.[101]

These results were the first indication of increased Islamist political popularity amongst varied sectors of the population, including professionals and the business elite of Amman's elegant Third Circle constituency and a relatively uneducated and rural population in Tafileh. The Irbid constituency contains a more varied distribution of the population along class lines. Without a breakdown of the vote it is impossible to state definitively where the Islamists' support was based. However, Irbid is the home of Yarmūk University which has been a centre of the intellectual Islamist movement in Jordan. The constituency also includes a large Palestinian refugee camp. Although the turn-out for the 1984 by-election was not great in the camps, the Islamists were popular for their strong stand on the Palestine issue. *Al-Ra'y* newspaper noted that the refugees tended to choose ideological candidates rather than those

---

97 Layne, "Elections," 118.

98 Shadid, "Muslim Brotherhood in the West Bank and Gaza," 668.

99 Day, *East Bank/West Bank*, 50.

100 Robins, "Politics and the 1986 Electoral Law," 191.

101 Shubaylāt, interview.

relying primarily on kinship, and commented that in these elections, "[P]art of the refugees voted in support for [sic] leftist candidates, and others supported candidates with strong religious orientation."[102] It is likely, given the low ebb in the popularity of the PLO at this time, that the Islamists' agenda on Palestine played an important role in their electoral appeal in 1984. It also seems that although the Palestinian issue was of supreme importance to the Muslim Brothers anyway, they made a conscious effort to highlight it in the campaign so as to garner the maximum electoral support.

Both the government and unseated traditional candidates reacted with alarm to the election results. The previous incumbent of Shubaylāt's Amman constituency had been Anwar al-Ḥadīd, from the Ḥadīd section of the Balqāʾ tribes. The Ḥadīds, with their considerable influence based on land owned in and around Amman, had viewed the seat as a family right.[103] The unseating of al-Ḥadīd reflected the gradual process of tribal fragmentation, a process that helped to widen the Brotherhood's support base. As the range of tribal authority shrank, tribespeople tended to vote more and more as individuals and on an ideological rather than tribal basis.[104]

The presence of Islamists in the parliament made life uncomfortable for the government.[105] Emboldened by their new role in parliament, the three Islamists joined with three or four other deputies to form a bloc in the lower house. They attacked the government on human rights issues, the activities of the security services, public sector corruption, and the continuance of martial law. ʿUqaylah and Shubaylāt concentrated their attacks on the security services, hoping to cause maximum embarrassment to Prime Minister Aḥmad ʿUbāydī, who was a former interior minister and head of the security services. "The Prime Minister was only able to stem the tide by specifically outlining the security threats the kingdom was suffering. Thus he had been forced to reveal the instability and strain to which the country was prone."[106]

---

102 *al-Raʾy*, 25 July 1984.

103 The Ḥadīd section have been close to the Hashemite family since 1923 when they supported ʿAbdallāh against a rebellion of most of the Balqāʾ tribes. See above, Chapter One.

104 See Layne, "Elections," 128.

105 Day, *East Bank/West Bank*, 49.

106 Robins, "Politics and the 1986 Electoral Law," 193.

The government did not ignore these direct attacks. The king, in the wake of the elections, may have realized for the first time the possible threat of the Brotherhood to the regime's stability. Accordingly he took steps to try to limit the Brotherhood's influence in the period up to the 1989 elections.

In 1980 the king had used the Muslim Brotherhood as a pawn in foreign policy. In an ongoing dispute with President Ḥāfiẓ al-Asad of Syria, he had allowed the Jordanian Brotherhood to establish paramilitary bases near the Syrian border which were used to facilitate training of Syrian Brothers.[107] The king, in the context of improved relations with al-Asad, then took the unprecedented step of directly attacking the Muslim Brotherhood on these grounds in a speech of 1985. He stated:

> The truth was revealed to me. . . . Some of those who had something to do with what had taken place in Syria in terms of bloody acts were among us and had sought shelter in the houses of a minority which had deviated from the truth {and} dressed up our religion.

He went on to deliver a thinly-veiled warning to the Brotherhood:

> I should warn this misguided handful of people, which abused our confidence, that there is no place among us for the treacherous, the wicked, the conspirator, of those who receive orders from enemies and coveters, or for the corrupt who try to harm our commitments and pledges to those near or far.[108]

After this speech members of the Brotherhood were subject to harassment by the security forces. Many senior members of the Brotherhood lost their jobs, and some had their passports taken away. ʿUqaylah was forced to resign his post as parliamentary deputy in 1988 after criticizing the intelligence department's campaign against the Brotherhood. He was prevented from returning to his teaching post in the faculty of education at the University of Jordan.[109]

But the period of hostility reached an end in the spring of 1989 when the king made it clear that he wished to resume cooperative relations with the Brotherhood. The king realized, no doubt, the necessity of continuing

---

107 This was denied by members of the Muslim Brotherhood in interviews with the author. This denial can perhaps be attributed to the Brotherhood's sensitivity to the regime's (and Western) perceptions of them and hence their desire to dissociate themselves as much as possible from military operations.

108 "King Hussein's letter to Prime Minister on Anti-Syrian Group" (Excerpts from 10 November letter, read on Jordanian television) in *BBC, Summary of World Broadcasts* ME/8106/A2 (November 12, 1985).

109 ʿUqaylah, interview.

to coopt the Brotherhood in the context of intensifying political and economic tensions in his country. The king faced mounting criticism for not implementing democracy. Economic hardship and anger at political corruption in the government sparked serious riots and disturbances in the south of Jordan. These prompted the government to initiate a program of political liberalization, leading to the elections of November 8, 1989.[110]

The 1989 Elections

The election campaign was a lively affair characterized by a proliferation of pamphlets and banners and boisterous rallies. This was the freest campaign in Jordan's history. The only (and significant) restraint placed on the candidates was that political parties remained illegal. This meant that the majority of the 652 candidates ran as independents. The large number of candidates (over eight candidates per seat) could be attributed to several factors: the absence of political parties, the breakdown of tribal cohesion without the substitution of alternative groups, the fact that these were the first elections in almost thirty years.[111] In the absence of legal political parties, groups of candidates attempted to form lists. Only the Brotherhood was able to form a nationwide list, while leftists and Arab nationalists failed to unite.[112] The Brotherhood also had the advantage of being able to campaign publicly as a legal organization.

The Brotherhood greeted the 1989 campaign with enthusiasm, seeing the participation in elections as an opportunity to expand its influence. The campaign gave it the opportunity to mobilize the extensive grass-roots constituency it had built up over the decades, with branches and regional committees coordinating meetings and rallies at local levels.[113]

Again, the dominant issues on the agenda of all campaigners were the deepening economic crisis, the need for political liberalization and the abolition of martial law, and support for the intifāḍah. The Brotherhood incorporated all of these elements in its campaign, although placing greater emphasis on the Palestinian problem and solidarity with the intifāḍah. Key to the movement's strategy was the adoption of the slogan

---

110 For an account of the factors favouring political liberalization and events preceding the elections, see Chapter One.

111 Abu Jaber, "1989 Parliamentary Elections," 74.

112 Ibid., 75.

113 ʿUqaylah, interview.

"Islam is the solution," which vaguely described Islam as a solution to all of Jordanian and Palestinian political, economic, and social woes. The slogan was popular and accessible to many Jordanians. As ʿUqaylah pointed out, "Adoption of the slogan was a major factor in our campaign . . . after all 97% of Jordanians are Muslim."[114] Some of the Brotherhood's campaign rallies attracted thousands, with Islamic slogans ringing in the air, especially after Friday prayers in front of the mosques. "Scarved women, children wearing green headbands and bearded men of all ages distributed leaflets, and its rallies, under the slogan 'Islam is the solution' were packed."[115] "No to the West, no to the East, Islam is my path" was the popular chant of supporters.[116]

Even taking into account the Brotherhood's good organization and grass-roots base, its success in the 1989 election defied all predictions. It returned twenty out of twenty-six candidates and together with fourteen Islamist independents made up an Islamic bloc of thirty-four out of eighty parliamentary seats.[117]

Muslim Brotherhood deputies reflected the social profile of the movement's leadership since the 1950s. The majority were well educated professionals and academics, many possessing post-graduate degrees from Western universities. Regarding their ethnicity, two thirds of the Brotherhood candidates were of East Bank origin. Seven were of Palestinian ethnicity. This number may not seem significant until it is compared with the total number of representatives of Palestinian origin, only twelve out of an eighty-seat parliament.[118] The Brotherhood's candidates were selected by the majlis shūrā with particular attention paid to the suitability of candidates according to ethnicity or clan affiliation.[119] Thus the majority of Muslim Brotherhood candidates of Palestinian

---

114 Ibid. This figure is inaccurate. The 1996 *World Almanac and Book of Facts* estimates a Sunni Muslim population of 92%.

115 Lamis Andoni, "King Hussein Leads Jordan into a New Era," *Middle East International* 363 (17 November 1989): 3–4.

116 Ibid.

117 Ibid. Thirteen seats went to leftists, pan-Arab nationalists, reformers and liberals, and the remaining 31 seats were held by traditionalists, rural community leaders, former officials and Bedouin candidates. Nationalists and leftists formed a Democratic Bloc shortly after the convening of the house in an attempt at counterbalancing the Islamists.

118 See Abu Jaber, "1989 Parliamentary Elections," 91 for a table defining deputies by district, ethnic/religious origin, political classification and winning intensity.

119 Abū Ghanīmah, interview.

ethnicity were elected in Amman and Zarqa, areas with a high concentration of Palestinians.

Before turning to analysis of the Muslim Brotherhood's support base, it is worth highlighting several factors which favoured the movement's success in these particular elections. The Brotherhood clearly derived an advantage from its legal status. It was able to campaign publicly as, to all intents and purposes, a political party. While there were indications that the leftists had considerable popular support, the fact that they were prevented from running on party platforms severely limited their campaigning potential. The Brotherhood also benefitted from tribal fragmentation as a result of the expansion of the state and urbanization. Although tribalism remained a significant feature of Jordanian society, tribesmembers were more and more attracted to ideological candidates. Often candidates armed with different ideologies competed within the same tribe.[120]

Furthermore, the Brotherhood's Palestinian support was boosted by the failure of the PLO to participate in the elections. In the wake of Jordan's disengagement from the West Bank, Palestinian political activists debated whether or not they should establish political parties in Jordan. The concern, echoed by the PLO, was that the Jordanian regime might try to find a way to use these parties to weaken the PLO.[121] The Jordanian regime, in the meantime, emphasized that it was the PLO and not the parliament that should represent the Palestinians, and discouraged them from running as candidates. Prior to the elections the PLO issued an official statement, asking candidates to refrain from exploiting its name in the campaign. The official absence of the PLO from the elections helped the Brotherhood to rally the support of Palestinian activists, especially in light of increased radicalism with the outbreak of the intifāḍah.[122] The Brotherhood's mobilization of support surprised the regime, which had underestimated the extent to which "fundamentalism and Palestinian activism would merge and reinforce each other's strength to such an unprecedented degree."[123]

It can be concluded that in the 1989 elections the Brotherhood derived considerable benefit from the fragmentation and multiplicity of other

---

120 Abu Jaber, "1989 Parliamentary Elections," 78.

121 Garfinkle, "Nine Lives," 96.

122 Abu Amr, *Islamic Fundamentalism*, 68.

123 Garfinkle, "Nine Lives," 97.

candidates as well as its grass-roots organization. However, the fact remains that the Brotherhood was not only successful by default; it had its own tremendous popular appeal which must be analyzed.

Appeal and Social Base

The election results provide some useful, if limited, data on the support base of the Muslim Brotherhood. The results do not include information on gender breakdown or occupation. They also gauge only the political decisions of the less than 40% of the population that voted.[124]

The results are most revealing in indicating that the Brotherhood mobilized regionally broad-based and inter-class support. Admittedly, the Muslim Brotherhood's parliamentary seats were concentrated in the major urban centres of Amman, Irbid, and Zarqa.[125] Nonetheless, the movement also won representation from the more rural constituencies of Tafileh, Balqa and Karak.[126] Analysis of this regional breakdown of the Brotherhood's vote highlights its ability to appeal to all social classes and both Palestinians and Transjordanians. The Brotherhood was elected in the urban centres of Amman and Irbid which have the kingdom's highest concentration of Palestinians, ranging from the wealthiest to destitute camp-dwellers. The movement also won seats in the richest constituencies of Amman, home of the East Bank and Palestinian business elite.[127] The Brotherhood was also elected in the central and southern, Transjordanian-dominated towns of Tafileh, Karak, and Maan where tribal ties and allegiance to the crown had historically been the strongest.

---

124 Abu Jaber, "1989 Parliamentary Elections," 84.

125 The Brotherhood won 10 of its seats in Amman, 3 seats in Irbid and 2 seats in Zarqa. For detailed statistics see Abu Jaber, "1989 Parliamentary Elections," 81–82.

126 The Brotherhood won 2 seats in Tafileh, 1 seat in Karak and 2 seats in Balqa' Governorate.

127 The Muslim Brotherhood did not win a seat in Amman's Third Circle, the "Champs Elysees" of Amman where Islamist independent Layth Shubaylāt triumphed in 1984 by-elections and 1989 elections. In this riding, Shubāylat, an outspoken critic of the absolutism of the regime and the lack of democratization in Jordan, won the support of upper class leftists and other secularists, as well as that of Christian men and women. This support was in some ways personal more than ideological in its basis. Shubaylāt is a highly charismatic individual and well respected in professional circles as an engineer. Nonetheless, the fact that he was able to win twice as many votes as the democratic leftist in second place points to the increased legitimacy of Islamist political discourse amongst professional classes.

The existence of the Muslim Brotherhood's wide support base clearly defies any single universal economic or political explanation of the movement's appeal. Such explanations can be found more easily in the cases of Islamist movements which not only represent but are dominantly supported by the interests of one social class or group. For example, in the Syrian case, Hanna Batatu has tied the Muslim Brotherhood with the interests of urban Sunnī trading and manufacturing middle and lower middle classes.[128] But purely economic or political explanations of Islamist appeal have their limitations. As noted, Islamism is a complex phenomenon with a multiplicity of explanations. Particularly problematic are analyses of Islamist appeal which rest on presumptions of unbelief and regard Islamist ideologies as only secondary phenomena involving material gain or class interest.[129] Such analyses tend to discount the sincerity of belief and its importance in shaping the social, cultural and political realities in which people live.[130]

---

128 Batatu, "Syria's Muslim Brethren," 115.

129 As Eric Davis has noted, to insinuate that Islamism is merely the "opiate of the masses" does an injustice to the sociopolitical realities of countries in which Islam is a major force and also to the sophistication of much Marxian analysis. Davis states that "while the concept of Islamic society is unacceptable in its reified form, so too is the reduction of Islam to social class or false consciousness and hence its treatment as epiphenomenon." Eric Davis, "The Concept of Revival and the Study of Islam and Politics" in Barbara Stowasser, ed., *The Islamic Impulse* (London: Croom Helm, 1987): 37–57.

130 Martin E. Marty and P. Scott Appleby, eds., *Fundamentalisms Observed,* (Chicago: University of Chicago, 1991), 624. Craig Calhoun has also pointed out that the presumption of unbelief has been widespread in the social science community. He says, "Few eras have been shaped more profoundly by religious activism than the last fifteen years. But the presumption of unbelief is so basic to much of modern academe that it is hard for scholars to take religion altogether seriously—especially in the study of advanced industrial societies. That an understanding of economic action is essential for sociologists and political scientists is all but unquestioned; that religion should be accorded similar centrality is all but unconsidered." Craig Calhoun, ed. *Comparative Social Research: A Research Annual.* Religious Institutions (London: JAI Press, 1991), x. As Martin and Appleby have pointed out:

> Analysts commit a serious error, however, if they assume that fundamentalism is, as one former State Department official put it during a public conference, "essentially a sociopolitical protest movement sugarcoated with religious pieties". Standing behind some of the most spectacular blunders of the foreign policy establishment have been a number of errors in judgement, including the smug assumption that secular rationality is the system underlying all forms of discourse; the tendency to underestimate the capacity of well-educated people for religious sensibilities, and the unwillingness or failure to appreciate the genuine alterity of the religious consciousness.

For Jordanians, the vast majority of whom are Muslims, the Muslim Brotherhood held wide appeal through the religious and cultural authenticity of its Islamist discourse.[131] As has been discussed, the movement's latent support base was fuelled by a general climate of Islamic revival starting in the late 1970s and early 1980s. In the election campaign of 1989, the Brotherhood capitalized on this climate with the vague but reassuring slogan "Islam is the solution." Thus, people were able to associate a vote for the Brotherhood with a vote for "Islam," whatever meaning Islam had for them. Or they were able to vote for the Muslim Brotherhood as a vote for democracy first and Islam second.[132]

The Brotherhood shied away from references to an Islamic state and indeed focussed on the general compatibility of Islam and democracy. Thus, it risked less chance of alienating those who might fear an Islamic revolution. It was able to draw into its net Palestinian and Transjordanian supporters (including members of the Transjordanian elite) whose primary concern was democratization rather than Islamization. In a similar way, as has already been noted, the Brotherhood was able to attract the following of Palestinians whose concern may well have been with the liberation of the Occupied Territories first and Islamic solutions second. Likewise, the Muslim Brotherhood drew support from the poor of the Palestinian refugee camps and the East Bank rioters of Maan whose votes could be interpreted as demands for improvement of their economic status.

Thus, it is clear that the Brotherhood was able to cast its net widely to win broad-based electoral support in 1989. The question remains, however, regarding the appeal of the movement to two groups: professionals who dominate the leadership, and students, or would-be professionals, who comprise its most prominent membership.[133] The

---

131 Michael Gilsenan, "Popular Islam and the State in Contemporary Egypt," Halliday and Alavi, *State and Society*, 175. Gilsenan notes the widespread appeal of Islamist ideology in his analysis of popular Islam and the contemporary state in Egypt where he states: "For many occupying quite different class and status positions, only one total conception of social order, one language, retained its pristine and unqualified authenticity: Islam."

132 The Muslim Brotherhood's parliamentary platform and ideology in the 1990s are analyzed in Chapter Four.

133 A general profile of the Muslim Brotherhood's leadership was obtained from a list of the membership of the preparatory committee of the Islamic Action Front in 1992. This list included twenty names, stating their ages and occupations. The average age of the members was fifty, suggesting that most of them were not active in the

predominance of professionals and students (especially of those with science education) in Islamist movements has been widely noted by scholars.[134] The appeal of Islamist ideologies to professionals may be attributed in part to the nature of their training, which stresses logic and inductive reasoning. Islamist discourse may be particularly attractive to them not only due to issues of cultural authenticity, but also because it claims to be based on universal truths. It stresses the importance of logic and careful thought rather than personal observation or authority. As Gilsenan has described their point of view:

> Technocratic, seeing themselves as without ideology, trained in the concept of the neutral quality of scientific knowledge, there are problems to be solved and solutions available. Yet, in their own eyes they are constantly hedged around with a society of a singularly unscientific and irrational dimension that resists their world view. It lacks control. They have risen through a university career themselves. Knowledge for them has been the key to advancement. What now prevents the realization of what they know should be done for society is the irrational nature of that society itself. It is religious law which can rationalize and order Egypt![135]

It is interesting to note in this context Layth Shubaylāt's description of coming to terms with Islamist thinking in the late 1960s:

> I was working as an engineer in Rome, I did not have any Islamists around me, can you imagine, but I had this subject in my brain because my thinking accepted the logic of religion. It was my lust and outgoingness that did not accept it. To achieve serenity I should respect my brain. I took that decision slowly and my friends deserted me and I started a new life.[136]

A similar argument can be used to explain the particular attraction of students in science faculties to the Jordanian Muslim Brotherhood and to Islamist organizations throughout the world. But the appeal of the Muslim Brotherhood to students has extended far beyond the science faculties, for a number of reasons. Students are the most highly politicized group in society. As has already been noted, they have been strong in their

---

movement until the 1950s or 1960s. The breakdown of occupations was as follows: four university professors, one teacher, one engineer, two lawyers, two doctors, five members of parliament (three of whom were educated to the Ph.D. level). For a table of this information see Markaz al-Urdunn al-Jadīd, *Dalīl al-Ḥayāt al-Ḥizbiyyah fī al-Urdunn: Jabha al-ʿAmal al-Islāmī* (Amman, Jordan, 1993), 73.

134 See Gilsenan, "Popular Islam," 183; Ibrahim, "Egypt's Islamic Activism," 436; Waltz, "Islamist Appeal," 667; and Abu Amr, *Islamic Fundamentalism*, 16–17.

135 Gilsenan, "Popular Islam," 183.

136 Shubaylāt, interview.

demands for liberalization and are amenable to the Muslim Brotherhood's political platform. They are economically frustrated as many, after years of education, now face the grim prospect of unemployment or underemployment. As the would-be generation of future professionals, they identify with the Muslim Brotherhood's leadership and especially with its demands for a larger stake in the future of the state. These frustrations and demands could also be channelled by leftist or nationalist movements, but, as noted, these movements have not attracted significant numbers of students in recent decades, due to the discrediting of Western-inspired socialist and nationalist ideologies in the Arab world since 1967. The economic setback experienced by Jordan in the 1980s further fuelled criticism of the Western model of development pursued by the regime.

In this regard, a psycho-social explanation of the Brotherhood's appeal to students is most convincing. Alexander Zghal was one of the earliest proponents of psycho-social explanations of Islamist appeal amongst Tunisian youth. He saw that young Tunisians were in the market for an ideology that could reaffirm their economic and cultural self-worth. Students were alienated not only by economic problems but also by Western cultural models. They were, in a sense, on a quest for positive identity.[137] Youth is the time when individuals sort out their identity and university students, often alone and away from home for the first time, are particularly in need of a sense of community.[138]

Thus the Muslim Brotherhood offered a channel for the expression of economic and political discontent, a critique of Western-inspired ideologies, and a solution to the quest for identity or cultural authenticity. The usrah cells offered a sense of community and solidarity which could bond students to the movement at a social as well as ideological or spiritual level. As one female Islamic bloc student noted, "One of the best

---

[137] Alexander Zghal, "Le retour du sacré et la nouvelle demande idéologique des jeunes scolarisés," *Annuaire de l'Afrique du Nord,* 1979 (Paris: CNRS, 1981), 201–221.

[138] Students interviewed made frequent reference to the quest for identity. Anonymous student member of the Islamic bloc #3 argued that the problem was not to escape the influence of Western culture but rather to define an authentic Muslim identity. "The problem," he said, "is how we can understand a system, how we can live with a system. The problem here is how we live, the problem isn't Western culture. . . . We want Islam, OK, but what does Islam mean? . . . Now we want to have our entity, our culture. . . . I want to discover my cultural identity."

things about joining this movement was the community I found when I reached the university."[139]

Women have comprised at least 50% of the Islamic bloc's student membership since the late 1980s. Jordanian women generally were regarded as a significant source of electoral support to the Brotherhood in 1989, both according to the movement and to observers. Estimates of the proportion of female voters supporting the movement in the 1989 elections have run as high as 80% but are, of course, difficult to verify. Electoral support came from women of all levels of society, barring the female population which is educated to the post-graduate and/or professional levels. These women may fall into two categories: secularist and Westernized; or possessing an Islamist agenda but rejecting male political dominance of the Brotherhood and what they see as a male authoritarian agenda.[140]

Women did not become actively involved with the Brotherhood until the 1980s, and from that time have functioned as an entirely separate subsection.[141] Those women involved in organizing usrah cells or study groups have been mostly relatives of male members. These women have had little say in running their own affairs at a grass-roots level. At the national or regional institutional levels, women have had no representation. However, it is important to take into account in this regard that women across the board have played an insignificant role in Jordanian political life. They were not granted the right to vote until 1974 and voted for the first time in the elections of 1984. In the elections of 1989, women candidates ran for the first time. Out of the registered 652 candidates there were only twelve females, none of whom was elected.[142] The first woman was elected to Jordan's parliament in 1993.

Thus, the Muslim Brotherhood has not been unique in Jordanian society in discouraging an active organizational role for women. The Islamic Action Front claims to encourage female participation.[143] In fact,

---

139 Anonymous Islamic bloc student #1, interview.

140 As Fayyāḍ stated, "I don't know how many women there are with more than a BA. . . . Some of them are educated but most of the prominent women in society are not of their movement." She said that the upper class women in Jordanian society are in general too Westernized to support this movement and those feminists with an Islamist agenda will not be committed to a male-dominated movement.

141 Ibid.

142 Abu Jaber, "1989 Parliamentary Elections," 80.

143 Farḥān, interview.

women played no prominent role in the party up to 1993. And Dr. Samīrah Fayyāḍ, who left the movement because of the extent of male domination within it, commented:

> [The Brothers] always say that Islam [is] fair to women, giving them the right for employment. . . . In reality you can see that they are over-protective. I mean they don't want to give women all that Islam gave them. They are so protective of women that they deprive them of having an active role in the society, you see, because they don't want them to be exposed to anti-Islamic effects or influences.[144]

But, attitudes of professional and highly educated women towards the Muslim Brotherhood may be gradually changing, if the movement's growing popularity amongst female students on university campuses is any indication. As mentioned above, although the campus organization remains male dominated, women are gradually gaining ground politically.

The issue of the appeal of Islamist movements to women has been a contentious one, especially as many women have seen the adoption of an Islamist ideology as a step backwards in social and economic terms. The Muslim Brotherhood supports the education of women and their right to employment. However, the movement puts particular emphasis on the responsibility of the woman as a wife and mother. These responsibilities are regarded as taking priority over other employment. As noted in the earlier discussion of Muslim Brotherhood schools, female secondary students take courses in housekeeping and cooking as part of "their Islamic heritage." At the University of Jordan, women's book exhibits and discussions focus on issues of women and the family in Islam. A course is offered in the sharīʿah faculty on the practical application of Muslim family law.

The subordination of women's careers to their role in the family has caused some analysts to reject the admissibility of an economic explanation for the appeal of Islamist movements to females.[145] But it is again important to consider the limited economic opportunities for women in Jordanian society as a whole. As Abu Jaber commented in his analysis on the failure of women candidates to win even one seat in the 1989 elections:

> Remarkable, though not necessarily surprising, is the fact that none of the women succeeded to secure a seat in the Parliament. Again, there are many

---

144 Ibid.

145 Waltz, "Islamist Appeal," 664.

> reasons, some rooted in the traditional, conservative society that Jordan remains to be despite obvious advances. Many Jordanians appear to continue to believe that while women have the right to study and to work, the most suitable occupation remains to be the one of mother and wife. Ironically, it seems that many women voters also held on to that belief and voted along their husbands', fathers' or brothers' suggestions.[146]

Thus, women who chose to affiliate themselves with the Islamic bloc should not be viewed as necessarily taking a step backwards in economic terms.

It can be argued that joining the movement provides young women with considerably more freedom and independence in Jordanian society. They do not have to experience the harassment often endured by young Jordanian women who choose to wear Western-styled clothing. In this context, their decision to wear the ḥijāb may persuade their parents to allow them more freedom in the public arena.[147]

The Islamist sisters at the University of Jordan follow a lifestyle which prescribes conservative dress and segregation from male students in almost all activities. A strict segregation policy is enforced in the classrooms of both the sharīᶜah and science faculties, with male students occupying the front rows. Informal segregation of the sexes occurs in other classrooms on campus or in lecture halls where women supporters of the Islamic bloc are present. Male and female members of the Islamist bloc organize separate social activities.

Some young women take the segregation policy to such an extreme that they will not even converse with male students. "There is not any reason to be together," a female Islamic bloc student at the faculty explained. "We think that if you mix boys with girls this will lead to temptation, we'll be thinking about boys."[148]

---

146 Abu Jaber, "1989 Parliamentary Elections," 80.

147 Fayyāḍ, interview.

148 Anonymous Islamic bloc student member #2. This attitude was officially dismissed by Isḥāq Farḥān. Farḥān referred to this sort of segregation as a misunderstanding of Islam "by some Muslims who say that a woman doesn't talk to a man or vice versa. . . . This is not Islamic. . . . They can attend classes and gatherings with men and it still can be called Islamic behaviour. But the non-Islamic behaviour is for a man and a woman to be alone together one on one." Regardless of Farḥān's official statement to this researcher, the Brotherhood has consistently petitioned through the Ministry of Education for the segregation of male and female students at all educational levels. And in the households of Muslim Brotherhood members visited by the researcher, women usually remained out of sight.

Psycho-social alienation is a particularly compelling explanation for the appeal of the Islamic bloc to female students. For these women students as much as the men, the usrah cells provide a sense of community and identity. Female students interviewed by the researcher exhibited close bonds with one another and emphasized the significance of friendship as a central aspect of belonging to the movement.

For young women in Jordanian society today, the quest for authentic identity is even more complex than for men. They have been confronted with the image of Western women and with a previous generation which shunned the ḥijāb.[149] This may explain why, in seeking to define their own identity, they are particularly preoccupied with the alleged moral superiority of Muslim women and the depravity of their Western counterparts.[150]

In concluding, analysis of the Brotherhood's mobilization and recruitment strategies demonstrates how this movement has worked to garner support through private and public educational, social and religious institutions. In a reflection of the primary concerns of the Brotherhood's professional leadership, it has focussed more of its recruitment activities on education than in any other area.

The Brotherhood's mobilization tactics have been similar to those employed by other Islamist organizations. However, the movement benefitted greatly from its legal status in expanding its influence in public and

---

149 See Waltz, "Islamist Appeal," 699, where she refers in the Tunisian context to women's experience of social dislocations created by the meeting of Western and conventional values: "No one feels these contradictions more than do young women raised with the notion that their bodies are the symbol of their families' honour. In a world full of sexual temptations (for which women in Tunisian society bear full responsibility), where within the sanctioned value system even platonic relationships between unmarried men and women are admitted with reluctance, the retreat to the ḥijāb or "Islamic dress" is perhaps the only course of guaranteed safety. . . . The ḥijāb and the face unadorned with makeup send a clear message that the woman inside is observing conventional norms, not the new."

150 One of the first topics raised by Muslim sisters at the sharīʿah college in discussion with the researcher was the incidence of abortion in Israel and the United States. Anonymous student #1 stated: "Last night I read a book and I wrote some notes on how women are treated in other civilizations. . . . I read about the Jews. They said that the woman was only responsible for getting Adam from Eden. Also I have exact numbers of how many children are aborted in America. . . ." An art exhibit organized by the Muslim sisters and attended by the researcher was designed to depict non-Muslim, especially Jewish, women in a negative light. One drawing showed a woman with fangs and the face of the devil. Written across her face were the words "*al-marʾah al-yahūdiyyah*" ("the Jewish woman").

private institutions, giving it a relative advantage over other Islamist movements which have been forced to function underground.

Analysis of the movement's social base reveals that the movement captured the electoral support of a wide spectrum of Jordanian society. In this light, it is argued that explanations of the Brotherhood's appeal which rest on any single economic or political factor must be rejected.

This analysis concludes that the Brotherhood's appeal may be attributed to a wide variety of economic, political, and psycho-social frustrations along with the role of Islam as a component of authentically Jordanian discourse.

It is maintained, however, that there are two groups which are of particular significance to the Brotherhood's social base. First, there is a new generation of educated and politicized Transjordanians, disillusioned by grim economic prospects in the 1980s, lack of political liberalization, and Jordan's Western-oriented state development. Second, there is a generation of Palestinians disillusioned with the performance of the PLO and its perceived continuing failures.

Finally, this analysis has noted a souring of relations between the Muslim Brotherhood and the Jordanian regime in the 1980s. This occurred in the context of the movement's electoral success and its outspoken demands for democratizing and liberalizing reforms. The further deterioration of these relations in light of the regime's increasing recourse to strategies of containment rather than cooptation are explored in the next chapter.

CHAPTER FOUR
THE MUSLIM BROTHERHOOD IN THE JORDANIAN PARLIAMENT, 1989–1993

This chapter examines the experience of the Jordanian Muslim Brotherhood in the parliament of 1989–1993. First, an overview of the Brotherhood's ideological perspective in this period demonstrates that it had undergone little intellectual development since the 1950s. The Brotherhood remained committed to action rather than theory, boasting no significant thinkers and only one publication, the weekly newspaper *al-Ribāṭ* ("The Bond"). The most salient feature of the Brotherhood's ideology remained its ambiguity, a feature shared with other Arab Islamist movements. The Brotherhood offered Islam as a general solution to Jordan's socioeconomic problems but offered few concrete suggestions for reform beyond the demand that the state, and the Islamic people as a whole free themselves from Western domination. In this latter context the Brotherhood was clear on the issue that Jordan should break economic ties with the West and refuse to participate in Arab-Israeli peace negotiations. Israel continued to be viewed as an outpost of Western imperialism in the Middle East. For the Brotherhood no compromise with Israel was possible and the only solution to the Palestinian problem was the liberation of all territory west of the Jordan River from Israeli control.

The Brotherhood's specifically political agenda also remained ill-defined. The movement provided no clear blueprint of a future Islamic order, referring only, in the tradition of the Egyptian Brotherhood, to the implementation of sharīᶜah through the process of shūrā (consultation). The ill-defined nature of the Brotherhood's ideology reflected, as it had in the 1950s, the movement's desire to avoid alienating the regime by the adoption of goals counter to its political interests. The movement publicly stressed its acceptance of the monarchy and sought to justify this acceptance in Islamic terms. It espoused the implementation of sharīᶜah through gradual reform and rejected violence as a means to this end. As it had done in 1954, the Brotherhood chose to work within parliament for pragmatic reasons, i.e., in order to increase its political influence. But in the context of Jordanian demands for democratization and the political liberalization of the state in the 1980s, the Brotherhood, in contrast with the 1950s, now made much of the compatibility of its political goals with liberal democracy. In this context it stressed the central role of the Islamic principle of shūrā as being similar to the notion of parliamentary representation.

The second section of this chapter analyzes the practical experience of the Brotherhood in the parliament of 1989 to 1993, and the movement's relations with the regime in this period. In these years the Jordanian regime moved increasingly away from a policy of coopting the Brotherhood to one of containment. The regime adopted this policy in the context of its pursuit of limited, state-directed liberalization intended to coopt oppositional forces. The Muslim Brotherhood became a specific target of the regime for several reasons: its wide social base and large representation in parliament, its efforts to implement an Islamizing agenda which ran counter to the regime's pro-Western domestic and foreign policies, and its advocacy of increased pluralism, public liberties and governmental accountability. While the attainment of liberal democracy was not the Brotherhood's ultimate goal, the movement nonetheless served as a liberalizing force in Jordanian politics.

An analysis of events in the 1989 to 1993 period demonstrates the ways in which the regime effectively contained the Muslim Brotherhood in the parliamentary process. They included denying it representation on cabinet, resorting to constitutional provisions allowing for executive veto of lower house legislation, introducing a National Charter limiting the activities of political parties, suspending parliament, and lastly, in the months before the election of 1993, imposing an election law designed to limit the electability of Islamists and favor rural/tribal interests loyal to the regime.

There was only one brief period during these four years in which the Brotherhood was allowed to maximize its potential in parliament. During the Gulf crisis (1990–1991) the regime forged a brief alliance with the Brotherhood in recognition of its ability to mobilize Jordanian popular opinion in support of Saddam Hussein. The Brotherhood was given seats on cabinet and through these it was able to maximize both its political influence in parliament and its ability to mobilize popular support through grass roots networks. The Brotherhood ministers also moved to implement Islamizing reforms such as the gender segregation of public employees. But the Brotherhood's influence was short-lived. In June 1991, in the wake of the Gulf crisis, King Hussein moved at once to contain the Brotherhood, firing the cabinet. The king had two major motives in this regard. First, he was eager to repair relations with the United States and to involve Jordan in a Western-sponsored Middle East peace process, both of which the Brotherhood publicly opposed. Second, his regime was anxious to curtail the Brotherhood's moves to implement sharīʿah in Jordan.

A review of the Brotherhood's record in parliament shows that its achievements in the area of Islamizing reform were limited due to the short duration of this period in cabinet and the king's use of executive veto to block legislation. The Brotherhood came under criticism by those supporting its agenda for its failure to introduce Islamizing reforms. It also came under attack by supporters and opponents alike for its failure to find concrete solutions for socioeconomic problems. Such criticisms are justified, but it is important to emphasize the severe limitations placed on the Brotherhood by the regime. And it is also significant to note that in the 1989 to 1993 period, the Brotherhood did effectively demonstrate (as it has argued in its own defense) its willingness and ability to work within the parliamentary system and its adherence to reformist methods. In 1992 the movement formed the Islamic Action Front party, not only to conform to the regulations imposed by the National Charter but also with an eye to improving its performance in parliament.

Pragmatic as always, the Brotherhood continued to avoid confrontation with the regime throughout this four-year period. This chapter concludes with the observation, however, that the Brotherhood's pursuit of reform through parliamentary means did not serve it well in the 1989 to 1993 period. Following the elections of 1993 its representation was substantially reduced in the legislature, although it still retained considerable popular support from Transjordanian and Palestinian constituencies opposing the regime. And although the Jordanian monarchy had been effective in containing the Muslim Brotherhood for the time being, a significant question remains as to how long the regime will be able to maintain a stranglehold on the liberalization process and repress the constituencies represented by the movement. Furthermore, although it seems unlikely that the Jordanian Muslim Brotherhood will move in the near future towards a more radical agenda, the Jordanian regime's curtailment of the movement may fuel the growth of more radical Islamism in Jordan.

Ideology

The Muslim Brotherhood's ideological perspective in the early 1990s, changed little since the 1950s, reflects a lack of significant intellectual development in these four decades. The Brotherhood's only significant publication was the newspaper *al-Ribāṭ,* which is mostly devoted to political issues in the Arab/Islamic world and deals in particular with two issues: its strong support for other Islamist movements in Algeria, Sudan, and Tunisia, and its opposition to the Arab-Israeli peace process. For example, in an interview with *al-Ribāṭ* entitled "What happened in Sudan is similar to what happened in Algeria" Ḥasan al-Turābī explained how in both regimes attempts were made at opposing free expression of Islam. In both cases "Islam was adopted by the majority" and "minority forces" tried to reject the "Islamic project." Yet, in Sudan the military acted "in favor of the spread of Islam" by defending the government while in Algeria the military forces acted against Islam.[1] In a later edition Ḥasan al-Turābī is praised by *al-Ribāṭ* as "the great Muslim Arab thinker" leading "a revolution not only for Sudan but for the whole Islamic nation."[2] In other examples on February 4, 1992 Muslim Brotherhood member Ḥamzah Manṣūr wrote an editorial in support of the Algerian Islamic Front's "peaceful" means against a government insistent on shedding blood.[3] The banned issue of February 17, 1992 contained an article criticizing Tunisia's repression of the Islamist group *Al-Nahḍah.*[4] *Al-Ribāṭ* was licensed in 1991 with Greek registration, enabling the Jordanian authorities to treat it as a foreign publication. As a result the newspaper has been subject to harsh censorship by the regime.[5] In 1992 four numbers of the newspaper were confiscated by the government. According to the publishers of *al-Ribāṭ,* the government has routinely censored articles critical of the Arab-Israeli peace process or of Arab leaders' repression of Islamists.[6] In discussing these issue, *al-Ribāṭ* has been critical of the government indirectly. However, the paper does not openly challenge the Jordanian regime on domestic policy, due to both censorship and its desire to avoid confrontation with the government. "We don't criticize Jordan except within the context of the peace talks," commented *al-Ribāṭ* editor Kamāl Rashīd.[7]

---

1 *Al-Ribāṭ,* March 18, 1992.

2 *Al-Ribāṭ,* June 9, 1992.

3 *Al-Ribāṭ,* February 4, 1992.

4 *Al-Ribāṭ,* February 17, 1992.

5 Kamāl Rashīd, interview.

6 *Jordan Times,* February 17, 1992.

7 *Jordan Times,* February 20, 1992.

The newspaper rejects the Arab-Israeli peace process and other conciliatory means for ending the Palestinian problem. "Ḥamās will lead the people in an Islamic revolution!" declared *al-Ribāṭ*. "Successful action is taking place with the mobilization of the jihād in the streets of Palestine."[8] It considers the peace initiative to be an extension of Western imperialist ambitions following the Gulf War and called for "no submission to the American conditions which minister the current peace process."[9] A Brotherhood/Ḥamās pamphlet outlining the movement's position on Palestine declared:

> However, our enemies have not been content with the gains they achieved [in the Gulf War]. They are endeavouring, with all the powers they possess, to make more gains through forcing the Arab and Muslim people to recognize the Zionist enemy and give Palestine away to the Zionist enemies of the Muslims. In exchange for such a recognition and such a concession the enemies are offering us nothing but useless crumbs and morsels.[10]

This pamphlet spells out the position of the Brotherhood and Ḥamās quite clearly. They refuse to bargain over the land of Palestine because it is the holy land of Muslims. They view the relinquishment of Palestine as an act of treason and betrayal of the trust of God who says in the Qur'ān: "O ye that believe! Betray not the trust of Allah and the Apostle, nor misappropriate knowingly things entrusted to you." Palestine does not belong to Palestinians alone but to all Muslims and cannot be conceded by Palestinians or any Muslim government. "Those who want to sign a peace accord with the enemy delude themselves if they believe that such an accord will put an end to the conflict," as it will only enable the Jews "to pounce upon the Muslim people, destroy them and accomplish their dream of establishing their greater state from the Euphrates to the Nile." The Muslim people must unite and reassert itself in jihād against the Zionist enemy and support Ḥamās in its battle against "the Jewish war machine."[11]

---

8 *Al-Ribāṭ*, December 29, 1992. The Muslim Brotherhood's changing ideological perspective towards armed struggle in Palestine was noted in Chapter Three, in the context of the organizational links between Hamās and the Jordanian movement.

9 *Al-Ribāṭ*, March 18, 1992.

10 Ḥamās, *Mawqifunā min al-taswiyah: bayyān al-Murshid al-ʿĀmm li-al-Ikhwān al-Muslimīn ḥawla uṭrūḥat al-taswiyah li-al-qaḍiyyah al-filasṭīniyyah* (al-Maktab al-ʿĀmm: Amman, 1991), 23.

11 Ibid., 23–36

Beyond the Arab/Islamic worlds, *al-Ribāṭ* is mainly concerned with a critique of the United States and other Western influences. These are presented in fiery and vitriolic language reminiscent of *al-Kifāḥ al-Islāmī* (see Chapter One). For example, a July 1992 article entitled "Islamists Reject US Pressures" raged:

> The United States—the leader of the new world order that was devised to suppress nations, plunder their wealth, and break their will—is still persisting in bolstering its hegemony over our Arab and Islamic nation and dealing with its countries one at a time. . . . That this plotting targets the rising Islamic awakening is no secret to anyone, since this awakening represents an impregnable bulwark in the face of plans that aim at humiliating the nation, fragmenting its ranks, controlling its wealth, and creating infighting and sedition among its sons.[12]

Another article accused the United States of repressing Islamists:

> You [Islamists] are in for an unprecedented witch-hunt and campaigns of repression. Nixon explicitly stated that US interests in the region reside in oil and the Zionist entity. This means that you pose a threat to both, and so the repression will be all the more ferocious. . . . The regime has, since the end of the Gulf crisis, played the role of the cat's paw to coerce Arab parties further into the American camp. Moreover, that regime has been waging a pitiless, all-out war against Islamists wherever they are.[13]

The paper also objected to the participation of the American ambassador in the official opening of a school funded by USAID (although it is interesting to note that the Muslim Brotherhood did not object to the USAID funding itself):

> While we know that the school is part of a project that has been established with the assistance of USAID, we believe that the US ambassador's participation, particularly at this time, is a serious precedent that we reject and condemn and we warn against the negative impact it may have. . . . It is no secret . . . that this visitor is the representative of the United States, which the Jordanian people and their deputies unanimously agree was the leader of the aggression against our Arab nation. . . .[14]

The newspaper *al-Ribāṭ* is similar to the *al-Kifāḥ al-Islāmī* of the 1950s in that it provides only superficial highlights of the Brotherhood's opinions. *Al-Ribāṭ* gives us little information regarding the Brotherhood's conception of Islamic themes relevant to state and society. One of the few

---

12 *Al-Ribāṭ*, July 7, 1992.

13 *Al-Ribāṭ*, February 4, 1992.

14 *Al-Ribāṭ*, June 9, 1992.

areas in which the Brotherhood's ideology has remained crystal clear has been in its critique of the negative influence of the West on Islamic mores and social institutions. Its attitude in this regard is at once assertive and defensive, attacking the West for trying to impose itself on the Islamic world and articulating the right of Muslims to live according to their own traditions and norms. As Brotherhood spokesman Ziyād Abū Ghanīmah stated:

> All we want as Muslims is to live as we want to live. Your problem in the Western world is that you want us to live as you want—you are trying to force us to live as you want to live.[15]

The Muslim Brotherhood in the 1989–1993 period criticized many aspects of Jordanian foreign policy for being in collusion with the imperialist West. The movement's goal was to undercut Western supremacy, prevent further Western colonization and introduce a new international Islamic world order to replace the imperialist world system.[16] The movement focussed on two major issues, Jordanian economic reliance on the International Monetary Fund, and Jordanian participation in the Madrid Peace Process. With regard to the former, the Brotherhood, regarding the West as filled with "capitalist greed and colonial hatred,"[17] proposed that Jordan and other Arab states break free from the international capitalist system, improve inter-Arab trade, and work towards the establishment of an Arab/Islamic common market.[18] Muslim Brotherhood members of parliament have also called for an international Islamic economic system. They say that such a system, based on Islamic principles of wealth distribution and the prohibition of usury, would include an Islamic stock market and pan-Islamic currency.[19] It should be noted that the Jordanian Muslim Brotherhood has not provided a clear blueprint or design of this system.

The Brotherhood's program for Jordan's internal transformation is somewhat ambiguous. In 1989 the movement declared its goal of implementing sharīᶜah:

---

15 Abū Ghanīmah, interview.

16 Markaz al-Urdunn al-Jadīd, *Dalīl al-Ḥayāt,* 107.

17 *Jordan Times,* January 5, 1993. Political statement issued by the Muslim Brotherhood.

18 Markaz al-Urdunn al-Jadīd, *Dalīl al-Ḥayāt,* 106.

19 Dr. Aḥmad al-Kufāḥī, statement in parliament as reported by the *Jordan Times,* January 4, 1993.

> Our domestic policy is based on God's sharīʿah and on carrying out God's rules. . . . We are confident that all the masses of our people would like to see Article Two of the Jordanian Constitution, which stipulates that Islam is the religion of the state, applied fully in all aspects of their political, economic, military, financial, and educational life.[20]

The specifics of the implementation of sharīʿah in society were detailed only in cases of family and personal conduct. Thus it was prescribed that a woman

> has the right to own property, work and participate in developing the society within the limits set by Islam, on condition that this does not overwhelm the duty of the woman towards her home, husband and children.[21]

The Brotherhood also hinted that it supported the forced veiling of women, as implied in this excerpt from an interview of ʿAbd al-Munʿīm Abū Zant (Muslim Brotherhood deputy for Amman's second constituency) by journalist Suʿād al-Silāwī in November 1989:

> (Al-Silāwī) Are you going to seek the passing of a law banning women from leaving their homes with their heads uncovered?
>
> (Abū-Zant) The issue of women's playing up their charm is a flagrant encroachment on public rights. Misbehaviour will occur whenever women display their charm or disgracefully mix with men.[22]

The Brotherhood has declared a "war on corruption," calling on society to combat "the means for moral deviation and punish the committers of sin." It called for a ban on alcohol consumption, "resisting moral degeneration represented by bawdiness and use of makeup," closing down dance halls and clubs, banning the publication of pornographic materials, and "cleansing the radio and television of perverse items" and of any programs "contrary to Islam." The movement also demanded the revision of the school and university curricula and textbooks "by removing all that is contrary to Islamic tenets and focusing on the noble Islamic values." The Brotherhood believes in segregating the sexes and "resisting coeducation at universities and community colleges,

---

20 *al-Raʾy*, October 25, 1989.

21 Ibid.

22 *Ṣawt al-Shaʿb*, November 14, 1989.

explaining its harmful effects and dangerous role in perverting the youths within the educational institutions."[23]

Otherwise, the Brotherhood spelled out few tangible prescriptions for socioeconomic reform. The movement focussed on describing problems, rather than advocating solutions.[24] For example, the Brothers made much of the "great disparity in the income of individuals" and the serious problem of unemployment, but offered only the prescription that:

> One of the first duties of the representatives is to study this dangerous situation and work with the executive authority to find solutions to this problem. This requires delving into the heart of the matter and removing all the barriers that might stand in the way of a solution, because the results of unemployment are disastrous.[25]

The movement also emphasized the principle of economic justice and called vaguely for "a return to the Islamic method" in order to achieve this. This method included a review of the tax system to "achieve equality between the wealthy and the poor."[26]

The Brotherhood, as in the 1950s, continued to emphasize that change would come through gradual means and the education of a new, Islamically-oriented generation. The leadership has stated that its "main target is to achieve Islamic rule in Jordan. Government by sharīʿah. We proceed step by step, not by using force."[27] The movement remained emphatic about pursuing a strategy of non-violence. In the words of Khalīfah:

---

[23] Ibid. In parliament, the Brotherhood tried but was unsuccessful at implementing laws requiring segregation of the sexes in government buildings, universities and schools.

[24] The Jordanian Muslim Brotherhood is not unique in this regard. See Asʿad Abu Khalil, "The Incoherence of Islamic Fundamentalism: Arab Islamic Thought at the End of the Twentieth Century," *Middle East Journal*, vol. 48 (Autumn 1994), 677–94: 691 where he observes "It is fair to say that Islamic fundamentalist programs—if one can call them that—suffer from ambiguity. The leaders of Islamic fundamentalist groups insist that the Qurʾan has all the answers." (691) He noted that these movements tend to be specific only in areas of worship. An examination of the program of the Islamic Salvation Front (FIS) shows that they talk about considering issues but rarely address them outright. Likewise, Shaykh Muḥammad Faḍlallāh of Lebanon's Ḥizballāh parliamentary bloc responded to a question about agricultural programs in South Lebanon, with "We do not need a program; the Qurʾān is the program."

[25] *Al-Raʾy*, October 27, 1995.

[26] *Al-Raʾy*, October 25, 1989.

[27] Abū Ghanīmah, interview.

> We as a group are opposed to violence as a way to resolve political differences. We condemn such reckless acts, which can do no good, but rather harm the pillars of security, economy, virtue and humanity.[28]

As in the Brotherhood's early days, the right of the king to rule is never publicly questioned: "The king is the king of all Jordanians, we respect the rule of the king," is the Brotherhood's official line.[29] The king's rule is respected by virtue of its foundations in the Arab world and in Islamic history (a reference to the Hashemites' Sharifian descent). But the monarch, although near to the Muslim Brotherhood in "Islamic beliefs and values," is viewed as requiring guidance to set him on the track of reforming society in accordance with sharīᶜah. "We try to advise and bring forward advice and reform," explained Khalīfah. "Any situation will not be as bad if the government listens to us . . . the king is a Muslim and Islam preserves all governments."[30]

The Brotherhood's public acceptance of the monarchy reflects its pragmatic nature. The movement is anxious not to be perceived as a threat to the regime at home or abroad and is eager to maintain its legal status. "There is fear on the part of the West of the brothers because they don't understand sharīᶜah . . . and that we are working step by step," observed Brotherhood member of parliament Ḥamzah Manṣūr.[31] In a similar vein, after the elections of 1989, member of parliament and senior Brotherhood member Dr. ᶜAlī al-Ḥawāmdah made the statement:

> The Islamic trend and Muslim Brotherhood deputies who now occupy seats in the Jordanian parliament do not seek to change the regime but to help it rectify educational, moral, and economic matters in the country through dialogue and persuasion.[32]

Another Brotherhood member of parliament, Dr. Yūsuf Ḥassūnah, commented:

> I think that a lot of people have been threatened by this movement . . . but the people who have seen us involved in the political life in this country have

---

28 *Ākhir Khabar*, December 1993, 5.

29 Ibid.

30 Khalīfah, interview.

31 Dr. Ḥamzah Manṣūr, interview, tape recording, Amman, Jordan, June 30, 1992.

32 FBIS, Paris Radio Monte Carlo, 1200 GMT, 12 November 1989.

> changed their minds. . . . We are not fanatics, we are moderate and we are very useful to them and this country.[33]

The movement's conception of an Islamic polity has likewise remained ill-defined. The vagueness of the blueprint for a future Islamic state is partly due, as indicated above, to the movement's desire not to alienate the regime by proposing any specific model of government. In this regard, senior members of the Brotherhood have gone so far as to question even the desirability of transforming Jordan into an Islamic state. They have argued that Jordan is not suitable for Islamic statehood while it is on the front line in the confrontation with Israel. The Israelis would not tolerate the transformation of Jordan into an Islamic state. The argument is also advanced that Jordan should not become an Islamic state because it would thereby risk losing American economic support.[34] The Brotherhood's adoption of a public position so far from its critique of Western capitalism indicates how far the movement is willing to go at times in order to placate the regime. As one Brotherhood sympathizer commented:

> My understanding is that they are trying hard to convince the government that it is not the goal of the Brotherhood to change the political system in this country and I think they are serious about that because they do not consider Jordan a good place for an Islamic government. Jordan is small . . . so to establish an Islamic state will be very dangerous even if Islamicization exists. They want gradual change—their main political goal is to convince the government that they are not a political threat.[35]

In a second sense, the Brotherhood's vagueness about a future Islamic political order served to broaden the movement's electoral base, as noted in Chapter Three. The Brotherhood's slogan served it well in the 1989 election, offering Islam as a comprehensive solution to society's woes:

> Islam is the solution to all the nation's political, social, economic and moral problems. Its course is: Reforming the Muslim, then the Muslim family, then the Muslim people, then the Muslim government will apply God's sharīʿah,

---

33 Yūsuf Ḥassūnah, Muslim Brotherhood MP, interview, tape recording, 23 August 1992, Amman, Jordan.

34 As Abū Ghanīmah stated, "We think that Jordan in the current conditions is not a suitable place to be an Islamic state. Because, first of all the Jews will interfere in the first moment, and second, because financially we cannot find money to cover the needs of the country because now all the budget for Jordan is from the US and the Saudis and they will never fund us."

35 Malkāwī, interview.

> demand what is right and forbid what is wrong. Thus, it will meet the condition of righteousness. . . .[36]

Such generic use of the term sharīʿah by Islamist movements in general is unique in the contemporary era, as was recently elucidated by Ann Elizabeth Mayer:

> Rather than treat the sharīʿah as a body of specific and highly technical rules, contemporary Muslim fundamentalists tend to transform it into an ideology, thereby treating it as a scheme for reorganizing society that, because of its divine origins, can serve as a panacea for political, economic and social ills. In its conversion for use as a political ideology, the sharīʿah has inevitably become simplified and politicized; its elaborate jurisprudence and the complex and extensive rules worked out by the premodern jurists have been slighted in its fundamentalist formulations.[37]

This, of course, avoids the possibility of alienating those whose notions of Islamic society may differ from those of the Brotherhood.

Given the vagueness of the Brotherhood's public statements, it is difficult to envision the type of government they hope to implement. The writings of their Egyptian mentors shed some light. A theoretician having considerable influence on the Brotherhood was Rashīd Riḍā (d. 1938). A major preoccupation of Riḍā was how to construct a model of Islamic rule which would meet the challenges of twentieth century life. His terms *dawlah* (state) or *al-ḥukūmah al-Islāmiyyah* (Islamic government) made new additions to Islamist discourse.[38] The main tenets of Riḍā's theory were that the political, social and economic affairs of state could be regulated by a constitution which is inspired in its general principles by the Qurʾān, sunnah and historical experience of the first four caliphs. The head of state (caliph/imām) is a *mujtahid* (interpreter) aided in his judicial capacity by the *ahl al-shūrā* ("the people who loose and bind"). The ahl al-shūrā is a body of highly trained jurisconsults who elect the caliph. They represent the community and are guardian of the state's Islamic character, ensuring that the decisions of the ruler are in accordance with sharīʿah. For Riḍā, the sharīʿah was adaptable to every time and place, maintaining overriding authority in society. But he also allowed for a realm of civic law (*qānūn*), subordinate to the sharīʿah which may evolve

---

36 *Al-Raʾy*, October 25, 1989.

37 Ann Elizabeth Mayer, "The Fundamentalist Impact on Law, Politics and Constitutions in Iran, Pakistan and Sudan," Marty and Appleby, eds., *Fundamentalisms and the State* (Chicago: University of Chicago Press, 1993), 10.

38 Enayat, *Modern Islamic*, 69.

through human reason in cases where there is no clear provision in the Qur'ān or the Sunna.[39]

Riḍā's vision of the Islamic state was adopted by the Egyptian Muslim Brotherhood with some modifications. Muḥammad al-Ghazzālī's concept of an Islamic state differed from that of Riḍā in denying the necessity or permissibility of human legislation. Divine sovereignty must be enforced if the state is to be more than nominally Islamic. Ghazzālī insisted on the all-pervasiveness of sharīʿah in social, economic and political life.[40] The political structure of the Islamic state was to be bound by three principles: the Qur'ān is the constitution, government rests on the principle of consultation (shūrā), and the ruler is bound by sharīʿah and the will of the people.[41] Al-Bannā was very clear on this relationship between the ruler and the people, describing it as a "social contract" (*ʿaqd ijtimāʿī*) in which the ruler is defined as a "trustee" (*ʿamīl*) and "agent" (*ajīr*).[42]

This conception of a "social contract" raised the issue of the nature of the ruler in an Islamic state. Monarchical or dictatorial government seemed out of the question on the principle that the ruled could eliminate the ruler if s/he broke her/his contract with the people. Likewise, the notion of theocratic rule is eliminated because the authority of the ruler to rule comes from people, not from God. In fact, the Egyptian Muslim Brotherhood has been unclear about who should be granted the rulership. The movement has tended to put emphasis on the nature of the governance rather than the person who governs; its major criterion of rulership is the ability to govern in accordance with Islamic principles.

The general principles outlined by Ghazzālī leave considerable ambiguity regarding exactly what sort of political system an Islamic state would comprise. Overall, the Egyptian Muslim Brotherhood tended to emphasize Islamic principles of government rather than the actual system to be established. A parliamentary system was viewed by al-Bannā and al-Hudaybī as just one type conforming with the principles of consultation and social contract.

We find strong influences of the ideas of Riḍā, al-Bannā and Ghazzālī on the Jordanian Muslim Brotherhood's perception of Islamic rule

---

39 Hourani, *Arabic Thought,* 233.

40 Enayat, *Modern Islamic,* 89.

41 Mitchell, *The Society,* 246.

42 Ibid., 247.

(although these are rarely acknowledged by the Jordanian movement). Like the Egyptians, the Jordanian Muslim Brotherhood has since the 1950s advocated the ultimate establishment of a pan-Islamic entity and today the movement continues to emphasize the universality of Islam and its concern with the fate of all humanity, referring often to the "Muslim nation." As Kamāl Rashīd, editor of the Muslim Brotherhood newspaper *al-Ribāṭ* expressed it:

> It is a kind of circle to deal with Palestinian affairs, Arab affairs, Muslim affairs. For us it is the same kinds of circles inside each other. We must deal with all of these circles and later on we are asked to deal with the problems of human beings wherever they are all over the world. . . . In our Qurʾān and in our Islam we must be with a human being whether he is Muslim or not.[43]

But the Jordanians, again like the Egyptians, while transcending nationalist boundaries in theory and making reference to a global Muslim community, accept state boundaries in fact. This is an approach shared by most contemporary Islamist movements, as Sami Zubaida noted:

> [Even when Islamist movements] explicitly reject all modern political methods as alien imports from a hostile West, their various political ideas, organization and aspirations are implicitly premised upon the models and assumptions of modern nation state politics.[44]

Like Ghazzālī, the Jordanian Brothers conceive of three principles underlying Islamic rule: the Qurʾān, sharīʿah, and shūrā. The movement's aim in establishing Islamic rule is, as simply stated by Ḥamzah Manṣūr, that "all Muslims must be ruled through the Qurʾān and God."[45] The implementation of legislation which is in compliance with sharīʿah is thus the central feature of the reform program of the Muslim Brotherhood.[46] The movement calls for the "control of society's public domain by the Muslim majority through the implementation of sharīʿah."[47] Muslim Brotherhood members of the Jordanian parliament have declared that Jordan is well on the way to becoming an Islamic society in the sense of conforming with some aspects of sharīʿah (as in the area of family law). But further Islamizing reforms are required for Jordanian society to run in

---

[43] Rashīd, interview.

[44] Sami Zubaida, *Islam and the State*, 69.

[45] Manṣūr, interview.

[46] Markaz al-Urdunn al-Jadīd, *Dalīl al-Ḥayāt*, 105.

[47] Manṣūr, interview.

accordance with sharīʿah in such areas as banning of coeducation and alcohol consumption and illegal banking (usury).[48]

The Brotherhood's notion of the majority rule of sharīʿah is tied closely with the concept of shūrā (consultation) as a mainstay of Islamic government. As noted, the Jordanian Brothers conform to the idea that the ahl al-shūrā should act to ensure that the ruler follows the sharīʿah and as such reflects the will of the people. As discussed earlier, they have used this line of reasoning to underscore their role as legitimate advisors to King Hussein since the 1950s. More recently, in the 1980s and 1990s the Brotherhood has sought parallels between the principle of shūrā and parliamentary democracy, an approach also shared with the Egyptian Muslim Brotherhood and other contemporary Islamist movements.

The Muslim Brotherhood's Ultimate Goals

In the democratic spirit, the Islamic Action Front, the Brotherhood's political party, in its founding charter called for a model of democracy that could be initiated throughout the Arab world.[49] But while much has been made by Islamists of the correspondence of shūrā with parliamentary rule, in fact, the traditional shūrā council is endowed only with the right to judge right and wrong on the grounds of Islamic validity and on the basis of common good.[50] This ideal, as Gudrun Kramer has pointed out, "amounts to an expertocracy" and "not a political assembly representing conflicting opinion and interest."[51]

In this context, Muslim Brotherhood deputy Shāykh Muḥammad al-ʿAlawīnah implied in an interview with the newspaper *Ṣawt al-Shaʿb* that a multiparty system might only be a stage on the way to the establishment of Islamic rule:

> If freedom and multi-parties are meant to reveal the truth, then they are not objectionable and an urgent need. However, if they are meant to be, as in most countries of the world, "parties just for the sake of having parties" and for highlighting a certain character, then I think this is selfishness conflicting with

---

48 Hassūnah, interview.

49 Markaz al-Urdunn al-Jadīd, *Dalīl al-Ḥayāt,* 106.

50 For a discussion of the role of consultation consensus in the Islamic concept of the state see Abu-l-Ala Mawdudi, "Political Theory of Islam," 252–260 and Fazlur Rahman, "The Islamic Concept of the State," 261–271 in John Donahue and John Esposito. eds. *Islam in Transition* (New York: Oxford University Press, 1982).

51 Gudrun Kramer, "Islamist Notions of Democracy," *Middle East Report* (July-August 1993), 2–8.

> the teachings of Islam. I have no doubt it will be a harmful experience but we are trying through it to reach a better state of affairs.[52]

The "state of affairs," although undefined, seemed to be something other than pluralist democracy. Ziyād Abū Ghanīmah seemed to confirm this when he stated in an interview with the author: "We agree to pluralism and democracy although we believe that shūrā is better."[53]

Like the Egyptian Brotherhood, members of the Jordanian Muslim Brotherhood have implied that parliamentary democracy is just one of any number of (undefined) systems which could correspond with shūrā and sharīᶜah. Following on the theory of Riḍā that the sharīᶜah is applicable in every time and every place, the Jordanian Brothers maintain that almost any kind of political system could be acceptable "as long as it does not contradict the main lines of Islam—equality, justice, respect for God, power and worship."[54] As Islamic Action Front leader Isḥāq Farḥān explained:

> We are not after a ready-made model of thought to apply just abruptly and suddenly; we are after applying and implementing beliefs and knowledge of Islamic sharīᶜah as applied to the situation in time and place . . . taking time and place factors into consideration. . . . So sometimes we don't know how the state will evolve . . . but, for example, we believe in shūrā, in consultation and we think people should participate in taking decisions for the country. So the parliamentary process can be Islamic. But we are not after a certain model. . . . If the means are efficient in satisfying our goals we can say they are Islamic. If they do not then we just reject them and try other sets of procedures. In this way and in this part of our work we are pragmatic . . . and this, if I may say so, is not what we call compromise but the real adaptation of the foundations of our ideology to the requirements of modern times—the bridging of values and ideas with the practical requirements of modern times.[55]

From the statements above we can infer that parliamentary democracy is not the Muslim Brotherhood's final goal, although it is viewed as a political system within which transition to Islamic rule may take place. As far as can be gathered from the Brotherhood's limited pronouncements on the topic, the movement seems inclined towards the eventual establishment of a governmental system similar to a parliamentary democracy, incorporating a legislative assembly but fundamentally different in

---

52 *Ṣawt al-Shaᶜb*, November 21, 1989.

53 Ziyād Abū Ghanīmah, interview.

54 Rashīd, interview.

55 Farḥān, interview.

the sense that sharīᶜah, being all-pervasive, would limit the scope for pluralism and popular sovereignty.

On the issue of pluralism, Brotherhood members tend to strike a defensive position. For example, Muslim Brotherhood member al-ᶜAlawīnah stated in an interview:

> Regardless of religious differences, our task in the House of Representatives is to deal with new developments, and all deputies are entitled to participate in discussing all the proposed issues or finding a suitable solution to them. Accusing us that we will forget about those who are non-Muslims in dealing with any topic is unjust and unfounded.[56]

Ziyād Abū Ghanīmah also maintained that Islamic rule would ensure the rights of the Christian minority in the private domain, respecting their role in society as the *ahl al-kitāb* (People of the Book):

> Islam is very clear on the relations between Muslims and non-Muslims. We believe in Jesus Christ and Moses. We believe that Christians and Jews are the people of the book and we are ordered by God to behave with them very kindly. . . .[57]

However, the Brotherhood's tolerance of the rights of Christians may not be as great as its members like to make out to the Western researcher.[58] The Brotherhood's calls for Jordanian national unity are framed within an Islamic perspective and the main focus of Muslim-Christian cooperation relates to "exposing Zionist ambitions and supporting the Christian Arabs in exposing Zionist endeavours at influencing Christians in the West. . . ."[59] Yet while the majority rule of sharīᶜah might guarantee some religious rights to Jordan's extremely small Christian minority, it would clearly limit the freedom of Muslim Jordanians choosing a different lifestyle from that prescribed by the Brotherhood. The Brotherhood makes much of the issue of personal freedom and declares that "securing public liberties is the duty of the

---

56 *Ṣawt al-Shaᶜb*, November 21, 1989.

57 Ziyād Abū Ghanīmah, interview.

58 As noted by Amnon Cohen, *Political Parties*, 129, the Brotherhood on the West Bank was officially more tolerant than in reality and "the Brothers displayed much of the traditional Islamic contempt in their dealings with the local Christian Arabs. In 1962, for example, the Christian director of the General Security Services in Jordan was dismissed from his post. The move was welcomed by the Brothers, who noted that in a state with an Islamic constitution it was unthinkable that the director of the security services should be anything but a Muslim."

59 Markaz al-Urdunn al-Jadīd, *Dalīl al-Ḥayāt*, 106.

state." The state should "guarantee the freedom of worship for every citizen, and also political and scientific freedoms, the freedom of expression, press, movement, and travel, and man's [sic] freedom to work, security, and protection from arbitrary detention."[60] But as already discussed, such freedoms would be constrained by the abolition of press and media considered to be in violation of "the Islamic law's spirit." Furthermore, the Brotherhood's declaration in support of "public liberties" is accompanied by the message, "We believe it is the right of every Muslim citizen, and in fact his duty to advocate Islam throughout the country."[61]

In the final analysis, it seems that the freedom of those choosing not to live in accordance with the Muslim Brotherhood's conception of sharīʿah would be curtailed in an Islamic polity. As Isḥāq Farḥān emphasized in response to the author's question about the tolerance of elements in society not conforming to sharīʿah:

> But, there again, your freedom ends where the freedom of others begins. So we will not permit the influence [of these deeds] on Muslim youngsters in public places.[62]

Popular sovereignty, a fundamental principle of liberal democracy, is likewise brought into question by Islamists who reject the logic of juridical positivism, maintaining that only God is sovereign.[63] Indeed, some Islamists have completely rejected the compatibility of liberal democratic and Islamic institutions because of the conflict between the principles of popular and divine sovereignty. Sayyid Quṭb maintained that Muslim

---

60 *Al-Raʾy*, October 27, 1989.

61 Ibid.

62 Farḥān, interview.

63 See the discussion of this in Addi Lahouari, "Islamicist Utopia and Democracy," ANNALS, *American Association of Political and Social Scientists (AAPPS)* 524 (November 1992): 120–132. It is important to emphasize that the notion of divine sovereignty does not imply that the state itself is theocratic in the sense that it wields divinely-sanctioned authority. The argument that the ruler derives his/her power from God and is therefore not accountable to the people has been advanced by Bernard Lewis and offered as a basis for challenging the compatibility of Islamic and liberal democratic ideals. (See Bernard Lewis, "Islam and Liberal Democracy," *The Atlantic Monthly*, (February 1993):89–98. In fact, Islamic rulers after Prophet Muḥammad have not held divine authority. Legitimacy of state acts was determined only by the sharīʿah, historically manipulated by the ʿulamāʾ. We must note here in this specific regard the emphasis placed by the Muslim Brotherhood on the idea of a social contract and the accountability of the ruler.

societies should not accept any political system imposed by the West. He regarded any notion of popular sovereignty as a usurpation of divine society, maintaining that Muslim society's only salvation was to restore divine rule:

> To declare God's sovereignty means: the comprehensive revolution against human governance in all its perceptions, forms, systems, and conditions and the total defiance against every condition on earth in which humans are sovereign . . . , in which the source of power is human.[64]

Starting from the same premise, Mawlānā Mawdūdī, founder of the *Jamā^cat-i Islāmī* in Pakistan, and a contemporary of Sayyid Quṭb, argued that Islam as based on divine sovereignty is the "very antithesis of secular Western democracy." But, he went on to argue that if democracy is conceived of in a more limited way with popular sovereignty circumscribed within the bounds of divine law, there is no incompatibility. In this case there is "theo-democracy":

> The executive under this system of government is constituted by the general will of the Muslims who have also the right to depose it. All administrative matters and all questions about which no explicit injunction is to be found in the sharīʿah are settled by the consensus of opinion among the Muslims. Every Muslim who is capable and qualified to give a sound opinion on matters of Islamic law is entitled to interpret the law of God when such interpretation is necessary. In this sense the Islamic polity is democracy.[65]

Significant among contemporary advocates of Islamic government is Ḥasan al-Turābī, leading ideologist of the Islamic National Front in the Sudan. Al-Turābī has long held that Islamic regimes can best come to power through democratic means.[66] Al-Turābī propounds a conception of democracy through which construction and interpretation of sharīʿah take place by political shūrā. His conception of shūrā denotes public participation in political affairs. The ruler's power is counterbalanced by the will of the people represented in the assembly. But the representation

---

[64] Yvonne Y. Haddad, citing Sayyid Quṭb, *Fī Zilāl al-Qurʾān* (In the Shade of the Quran) in "Sayyid Qutb: Ideologue of Islamic Revival," John Esposito, ed., *Voices of Resurgent Islam* (New York: Oxford University Press, 1983), 85.

[65] Mawdūdī, "Political Theory of Islam," in John Donohue and John Esposito, eds. *Islam in Transition* (New York: Oxford University Press, 1982), 253–4.

[66] Although he has not been averse to the use of violence to achieve power. The history of the movement in the Sudan is discussed below.

of the people is again limited by the prescriptions of sharīʿah.[67] There is no room within the consultative process for a dissenter who would question the legitimacy of sharīʿah. Al-Turābī essentially envisages a one-party system, arguing that political parties can lead to factionalism which oppresses individual freedom and divides the community.[68]

In contrast, the Tunisian leaders of al-Nahḍah (the Renaissance Party), Rashīd al-Ghannūshī and ʿAbd al-Fattāḥ Mūrū have espoused a conception of government which claims to allow further scope for popular sovereignty than that of Mawdūdī, seeing the state "as something not from God but from the people," with laws emanating from God for sovereignty resting in the hands of the people. They view multiparty elections and constitutional law as part of a "new Islamic thinking based on a fresh interpretation of Islamic sources."[69] Like the Muslim Brotherhood, the movement has emphasized non-violence:

> Ennahdha [sic] is a school of Islamic thought that aims to play a political role and has rejected and still rejects violence both physical and verbal and this has been its methodology. . . . We believe in giving everyone the chance to run for the government and we believe in giving the people the right to choose through voting in an environment of democracy and human rights.[70]

The position of the Jordanian Muslim Brotherhood seems close to those advocated by al-Turābī and al-Nahḍah. Although the movement does not publicly acknowledge its similarity to either of these, it has already been noted that *al-Ribāṭ* contains laudatory references to both. Therefore, in spite of its public protestations, it seems clear that the Jordanian Muslim Brotherhood does not ultimately seek a pluralist parliamentary system based on popular sovereignty. In the words of Fuʾād Khalīfah, Islamist Independent MP (and former Brotherhood member): "The syllabus they have is fixed . . . when they talk about democracy they are talking about theo-democracy. We have to be ruled by the teachings of God in every area."[71] Religious freedom in the private sphere will not be denied, and the citizenry will have an advisory role of some sort in the

---

67 Ahamad Moussali, "Hasan al-Turabi's Islamist Discourse on Democracy and Shūrā," *Middle Eastern Studies* 30 (January 1994): 57–61.

68 Martin Kramer, "Islam vs. Democracy," *Commentary*, 95/1 (January 1993): 35–42. As noted in Chapter One, Ḥasan al-Bannā also originally advocated the position that political parties were divisive.

69 Interviews with Mūrū and al-Ghannūshī cited by Esposito and Piscatori, 437–438.

70 Rashīd al-Ghannūshī, *Ḥarakat al-Ittijāh al-Islāmī* (Kuwait: Dār al-Qalām, 1987).

71 Fuʾād Khalīfah, interview, tape recording, Amman, Jordan, August 27, 1992.

government, but ultimate authority will rest with essentially unquestionable Islamic legal codes.

Some scholars have been very suspicious of the ultimate goals of Islamists. For example, as Nikki Keddie noted in a cynical assessment of the real intentions of the Tunisian Islamist movement:

> [T]he vagueness of the leader's discourse when he describes the second, Islamic, phase that follows the democratic phase, the militancy of the student followers of MTI who won control of the University of Tunis student union, and a secret document that has been published outlining their clandestine goals and tactics, indicate that democracy is just a way-station for the MTI.[72]

Similarly, William Zartman cited the agenda of the Algerian Islamic Salvation Front (FIS):

> Islamic parties and regimes are usually rather straightforward about their intentions, although not always to the Western press. Although the leaders of the Islamic Salvation Front (FIS) profess their devotion to democracy before Western journalists, they also tell local audiences that "democracy is heresy" and "all parties who subscribe to the Way can compete freely," clear statements of incompatibility with democracy. It should be remembered that the position of democracy and that of political Islam on the matter of open debate are similar but different in an important way. Both maintain that truth will prevail in open debate, but democrats are proponents of the debate whereas Islamicists are proponents of the Truth.[73]

The true motivations of Ḥasan al-Turābī have also come into question in the light of his recent record in Sudanese politics.[74] As Shukri A. Abed commented in a recent article:

> Many point out, naturally enough, that al-Turābī's declarations in support of democracy and protection of individual rights cannot be reconciled with the actions of the present Sudanese government, and they accordingly raise questions about the sincerity of his pronouncements.[75]

---

[72] Nikki R. Keddie, "Ideology, Society and the State in Post-Colonial Muslim Societies," Halliday and Alavi, *State and Society*, 19.

[73] William Zartman, "Democracy and Islam: The Cultural Dialectic," ANNALS, *American Association of Political and Social Scientists (AAPPS)* (November 1992):231–268.

[74] In June of 1989 Brigadier General ʿUmar al-Bashīr, supported hy the Islamic National Front led by none other than Hasan al-Turābī, forced the elected government of Ṣādiq al-Mahdī from power. Since then, the country has been under military rule, and the military government and its supporters have not hesitated to use violent means to suppress their opponents.

[75] Shukri A. Abed, "Islam and Democracy;" for an analysis of the policies of Numeiri in the Sudan, see John O. Voll, "Political Crisis in the Sudan" *Current History*, 89 (April

Other scholars are convinced that virtually all Islamists are anti-democratic, and conclude that the movements' real goals are to "highjack" democracy and impose authoritarian rule. For example, Martin Kramer wrote recently:

> Of the vast complex of democratic values and institutions offered by the West, the fundamentalists have thus seized upon only one, the free plebiscite, and even that is to be discarded after successful one-time use.[76]

Bernard Lewis ignores even the democratic rhetoric of Islamists, stating:

> For Islamic fundamentalists, democracy is obviously an irrelevance, and unlike the communist totalitarians, they rarely use or even misuse the word. They are, however, willing to demand and exploit the opportunities that a self-proclaimed democratic system by its own logic is bound to offer them. At the same time, they make no secret of their contempt for democratic political procedures and their intention to govern by Islamic rules if they gain power. Their attitude toward democratic elections has been summed up as "one man, one vote, once."[77]

Such extreme assessments about the intentions of Islamist movements in parliament are not well-grounded. They discount, for example, past participation in parliament by the Jordanian and the Syrian Brotherhoods. The concern about the gradual imposition of authoritarian rule may be taken more seriously if we look, for example, to the situation in the Sudan. But it is worth noting that although there are many examples of authoritarian rule legitimized by Islam, these have been and are typified by Arab dictators and monarchs currently in power in the Arab world rather than by elected Islamists.[78] Furthermore these negative

---

1990): 546 and John O. Voll, *Sudan, State and Society in Crisis* (Bloomington: Indiana University Press, 1993).

[76] Kramer, "Islam vs. Democracy," 38.

[77] Bernard Lewis, "Islam and Liberal Democracy," 91.

[78] For a discussion of how Morocco's King Hassan has used Islam to justify his authoritarian rule, see Henry Munson, *Religion and Power in Morocco* (New Haven: Yale, 1993) and M. E. Combs-Schilling, *Sacred Performances: Islam, Sexuality and Sacrifice* (New York: Columbia University Press, 1989). For an analysis of the role of Islam in the maintenance of the Saudi regime see, for example, James Piscatori, "Ideological Politics in Saudi Arabia," James Piscatori, ed., *Islam in the Political Process* (Cambridge: Cambridge University Press, 1983). For discussions of the use of Islamist ideologies by military regimes see, in the case of Pakistan, David Taylor, "The Politics of Islam and the Islamization of Pakistan," James Piscatori, ed., *Islam in the Political Process*, and Hamza Alavi, "Pakistan and Islam: Ethnicity and Ideology," Halliday and Alavi, *State*

characterizations of Islamists' objectives are often themselves used to justify the decisions of authoritarian elites to cancel elections and limit political liberalization. As John Esposito notes:

> After a decade of charging that Islamic movements did not enjoy significant support and would be turned away in elections (a prediction that none, however, had been willing to put to the test), governments in the Muslim world and the West alike were quick to voice a common concern that Islamic movements threatened to highjack the system.[79]

In Syria, for example, the Muslim Brotherhood in the 1940s and 1950s pursued a reformist policy and participated in elections. The movement became more radicalized in the early 1970s when it was denied parliamentary participation.

In Tunisia the al-Nahḍah party has pressured the regime since the 1980s for representative elections and a multi-party system. In 1989 the movement won a majority in parliamentary elections but results were gerrymandered so as to ensure the majority of the ruling al-Dustūr party. The movement has since been denied formal party status by the regime, (in spite of its widespread popularity), and for this reason boycotted the elections of 1990. The leader of the movement, Rashīd al-Ghannūshī, has remained in exile where his pro-democratic position has inspired many Islamists. In neighbouring Algeria, FIS victories in municipal and then national parliamentary elections raised the "spectre of an Islamist movement actually coming to power through the ballot box" leading to the intervention of the military in 1991 to close down the democratic process.[80]

The Muslim Brotherhood in Parliament, 1989–1993

This last point is of great relevance to the case of the Jordanian Muslim Brotherhood. The following analysis argues that the Brotherhood, although accorded legal status and permitted to play a role in parliament, was increasingly contained by the Jordanian regime in the 1989–1993 period. The regime's coercive policies towards the Brotherhood were manifested in the more general context of its limited, top-down

---

and Society. For an analysis of the Iranian regime see Said Arjomand, *The Turban for the Crown: The Islamic Revolution in Iran* (New York: Oxford University Press, 1987).

[79] Esposito in Bulliet ed., *Islam and Democracy*, 138

[80] For a discussion of Islam and democracy in Algeria, see Hugh Roberts, "The Algerian State and the Challenge of Democracy," *Government and Opposition* 27 (Autumn 1991): 575–93.

implementation of pluralism in these years. The Brotherhood became a specific target of containment by the regime for several reasons. First, the movement emerged as a threat to the dominance of the throne when it demonstrated its popularity in the elections of 1989. It led the largest and most powerful bloc in parliament. Second, the Brotherhood proved its ability to mobilize Jordanian public opinion during the Gulf War period to the extent that the regime was forced to accept the movement into the government. Third, the Brotherhood in parliament tried to implement an Islamizing agenda which was counter to the pro-Western inclinations of the Jordanian regime in its domestic and foreign policy. The Brotherhood opposed the efforts of the Jordanian regime at seeking an Israeli-Arab peace accord, again jeopardizing the government's relations with the West. Last, and by no means least, the Brotherhood was a forceful advocate of increased pluralism and governmental accountability.

The elections of 1989 were heralded optimistically by some as bringing considerable liberalization to Jordan, with the reinstatement of a role for the legislature and greater freedoms for the press and political organizations.[81] These elections marked the start of a formal process of democratic reforms and were followed by government measures allowing for the free functioning of political parties for the first time since 1956, the repeal of anti-communist legislation, and the loosening of restrictions placed on political opponents of the regime under martial law (such as confiscation of passports).

The second significant step in democratizing reform was taken by the regime in 1991 with the promulgation of the National Charter (*al-mīthāq al-waṭanī*). This charter committed Jordan to the development of a multi-party system, enhanced freedom of the press, and introduced greater civil liberties. The charter can be viewed as a contract between the regime and the people, guaranteeing a pluralistic system in return for the allegiance of all political parties to the monarchy. It establishes general guidelines for the exercise of pluralism and carefully lays out what political parties can and cannot do. In this sense the charter serves well to reflect the relationship between Jordanian state and society in which the government controls limited democratization from above. According to the charter, Jordanians have the right to establish political parties, "provided that their methods are peaceful" and that they have no financial or structural

[81] See for example, Michael C. Hudson, "After the Gulf War: Prospects for Democratization in the Arab world," *Middle East Journal* 45 (Summer 1991): 407–421.

affiliation with any non-Jordanian political party.[82] The charter was referred to by King Hussein as a sort of "social contract" which spelled out "the foundations on which the state was created."[83] Implicit in the "social contract" is the loyalty of political parties to a Jordanian national identity described as a parliamentary hereditary monarchy.[84] In this light, the National Charter was viewed legitimately by some analysts as creating "a ceiling for political ideology in the country."[85]

Such analyses reinforce the view that in the 1989 to 1993 period, liberalization remained a "guided process at best."[86] The king remained at the centre of the political system, holding the reigns of legal and executive power. The constitution empowered him to select the cabinet regardless of the composition of the parliament, and made the cabinet responsible to him rather than to the legislature.[87] The constitution also specified that all legislation be approved by the upper house and at the final stage could be accepted or vetoed by the king. Members of the upper house or senate were appointed by the king. On more than one occasion in the 1989 to 1993 period, the king showed total disregard for the parliamentary process. In June of 1991 and again in August 1993 Hussein arbitrarily dissolved parliament amid protests from the entire spectrum of political parties. Having dissolved the parliament in 1993 the king then moved to impose a new electoral law by royal decree, again incurring widespread objections from political parties.[88]

In spite of the measures taken to recognize political parties and repeal martial law, public freedoms were still considerably constrained in the 1989–1993 period. The principles of the National Charter endorsing pluralism and civil liberties seemed more relevant at the level of theory than practice. For example, only a month after the promulgation of the

---

82 Draft law on political parties, printed in *Ṣawt al-Shaᶜb*, Amman, Jordan, July 6, 1991.

83 *Jordan Times*, June 11, 1991.

84 Ibid.

85 Ibid.

86 See Abla Amawi, "Democracy Dilemmas in Jordan," *MERIP* 174 (Jan-Feb 1992): 26–29.

87 Many of the provisions limiting the power of parliament were inherited from the constitution of 1928, although some reforms were introduced in this regard in 1952. The constitution was designed by the British to produce a powerless legislature. See Chapter One.

88 The circumstances surrounding these decisions and their connection to the Muslim Brotherhood are discussed below.

charter, the regime arrested six activists of the Jordanian Communist Party Revolutionary Path on charges of slandering Prime Minister Muḍar Badrān.[89] The press, largely owned by the government, was subject to unofficial censorship, avoiding overt criticism of the regime. A case in point was the failure of all newspapers save the Muslim Brotherhood's *al-Ribāṭ* to publish a report by the Public Liberties Committee of the Chamber of Deputies, dated August 26, 1991. This report contained reports of torture of political detainees by the General Intelligence Department (mukhābarāt).[90] The daily newspapers printed only the denial of the committee's charges by the interior minister.[91]

The experience of the Muslim Brotherhood in the parliament of 1989 to 1993 and its relationship with the regime must be assessed here in this context of limited, elite directed liberalization. As discussed in Chapter One, Hussein's strategy in holding the 1989 elections was to coopt discontent from both Palestinian and Transjordanian sources. He envisaged a parliament with little autonomy, whose primary function would be to relieve political and economic pressures on his regime.

Hussein's strategy of holding the parliamentary elections proved a miscalculation in two regards. First, it underestimated the popularity of the Muslim Brotherhood and its ability to mobilize both Palestinian and Transjordanian support. Second, and relatedly, it failed to anticipate the extent to which a parliament dominated by the Muslim Brotherhood would take on an active and aggressive role in Jordanian political life.

Islamist domination of the lower house raised serious concerns for King Hussein. The non-Islamist members of the house, although forming an absolute majority, were too divided to act as a counterweight to the 34-member bloc of Islamists.[92] The Islamist bloc (including the Muslim Brotherhood and Islamist independents) was for the most part united on

---

[89] Amawi, "Democracy Dilemmas in Jordan," 27.

[90] *Al-Ribāṭ*, September 10, 1991.

[91] The relationship between *al-Ribaṭ* and the regime is discussed below. Muslim Brotherhood members were prominent in the Public Liberties Committee, as also referred to later in this chapter.

[92] On the left of the political spectrum, 13 deputies were elected, including nationalists and leftists, who joined to form a loose Democratic bloc, united in their opposition to Islamists. On the right were 22 traditionalists, with the remaining 11 deputies acting as independents. For a table classifying deputies elected see Abu Jaber, "1989 Parliamentary Elections," 81–82, where he notes the except for the Islamic bloc, most other classifications were fluid and only meant as a yardstick in the absence of political parties.

policies which ran counter to the Jordanian regime's agenda. In the Brotherhood's first statement to the Arab press following the elections, it summed up its two major goals as the total liberation of Palestine (including, of course, the state of Israel) and the implementation of sharīʿah. The Brotherhood said it would work "to unite the two banks of Jordan" and that "the decisive battle with the Jews will be launched from the East of Jordan." The movement also announced that it would work through parliament, using gradual and non-violent means "to amend the Jordanian laws that are not in harmony with Islam, and that they will not hesitate to seek the issuance of legislative laws banning alcohol and night clubs."[93] The Brotherhood spoke also of its commitment to the enactment of the Constitution and respect for public liberties:

> Our first demand will be on activating the Constitution articles, returning real power to the people, allowing them to participate in the running of the country, regaining the prestige of this power within the Constitution, restoring daily popular participation through the release of general liberties, and then discussing the economic crisis.[94]

Enactment of the Constitution also implied for the Brotherhood that Article 2, which stipulates that Islam is the state religion of Jordan, be "applied fully in all aspects of political, economic, military, financial and educational life."[95]

The king publicly praised the elections as signalling the beginning of Jordan's march of democracy. In doing so, he emphasized the ideological diversity of parliament, rather than the large representation of Islamists. He said in an interview with *al-Ḥayāt* in London:

> Elections were the first step in the political, democratic march in Jordan. I think the elections were free and fair, open to all sections of the community and they crossed the political and ideological spectrum. The elections marked the first step toward the realization of our aspirations.[96]

Hussein then made a goodwill gesture to the Muslim Brotherhood by appointing Muḍar Badrān, known for his conciliatory attitude towards the Brotherhood, as prime minister. At the same time, however, the king took steps to limit the Muslim Brotherhood's influence in parliament. He

---

93 FBIS, November 27, 1989.

94 Interview with Islamist bloc deputy Yaʿqūb Qarrūsh, *Ṣawt al-Shaʿb*, November 22, 1989.

95 *Al-Raʾy*, 27 October, 1989.

96 *Al-Ḥayāt*, November 17, 1989.

appointed a senate containing mostly members of the traditional East Bank elite in an effort to counterbalance Islamist and other oppositional elements.[97] This was a significant step in barring Islamizing reform initiatives because, as noted above, all legislation constitutionally required upper house and executive approval.

In another move, the king discouraged the Muslim Brotherhood from joining the cabinet. The Brotherhood demanded six portfolios in the new cabinet, including those of education, information, and religious affairs.[98] The Brotherhood was interested in these particular portfolios not only because of its major concern with such issues as religious affairs and education, but because they would allow its deputies greater access to mobilizing its grass-roots networks. On the instructions of the king, Prime Minister Badrān refused to give the Brotherhood the education portfolio, instead offering it the Ministry of Higher Education (which had the disadvantage for the Muslim Brotherhood that it did not supervise curricula). The Brotherhood refused to participate in the cabinet without the education portfolio, a tactic regarded with some criticism by observers.

Overall, the Jordanian regime's strategy in 1989 was to coopt the Muslim Brotherhood by allowing it a role on the parliamentary scene, at the same time containing its activities so that it would not be able to implement its Islamizing agenda. But the regime had not reckoned with the determination of the Muslim Brotherhood and the vitality of parliament. By the spring of 1990 parliament had taken on a life of its own as deputies, spearheaded by the Islamic bloc (and in particular the charismatic and outspoken independent Islamist Layth Shubaylāt) investigated allegations of corruption in the government and denial of civil liberties.[99] The Public Liberties Committee of the Chamber of Deputies was formed, dominated by members of the Islamist bloc. Questions were raised openly in parliament as to whether the real motive underlying the introduction of a National Charter was to control, rather than encourage the development of democracy. On the foreign policy front, again under the influence of the Islamists, parliament called for a new "eastern front" against Israel.

For the first time King Hussein's regime faced significant opposition from an East Bank constituency pressing for both greater democratization

---

97 Abu Jaber, "1989 Parliamentary Elections," 84.

98 Paris Radio Monte Carlo, December 5, 1989.

99 Hudson, "After the Gulf War," 419.

and Islamizing reform. And, for the first time since the civil war of 1970–71, the regime was also challenged by a radicalized Palestinian opposition under an Islamist banner. Hussein ultimately realized he could not intervene to try to control parliamentary opposition without risking a serious loss to his regime's credibility at home and abroad. He could not overlook the extent to which the attitude of the parliament was reflected in the Jordanian "street," emboldened by an atmosphere of political debate.

The Gulf War and its Aftermath

In this context, the outbreak of the Gulf crisis in the summer of 1990 played a definitive role in the recent history of Jordan, bringing the Muslim Brotherhood unprecedented political influence. In the early days of the crisis, the Brotherhood was critical of Iraq's invasion of Kuwait. This policy was in line with its historic antipathy towards the Baᶜth and affinity for the more conservative Saudi Arabia. The movement changed its views, however, with the stationing of Western forces in Saudi Arabia.[100]

By January 1991 the Brotherhood mobilized popular sentiment in support of Iraq through the use of its own grass-roots organizational base. The Brotherhood called on the king to support Iraq and began organizing anti-American rallies and demonstrations from mosques after Friday prayers. The groundswell of Jordanian public opinion in support of Saddam Hussein was enormous.

In parliament, the Brotherhood was able to solidify its position in alliance with a National Unity Front of democrats and nationalists and in the absence of dissenting opinion. In October, the parliament, led by Layth Shubaylāt, called for the regime to arm the people.[101] The popularity of the Islamists' position in parliament was further indicated by the election of a Muslim Brotherhood member, ᶜAbd al-Laṭīf ᶜArabiyyāt, as speaker of the house in November.

The rhetoric of the Muslim Brotherhood on the Gulf War was emotional and evocative, invoking the sayings of the Prophet Muḥammad

---

[100] Milton-Edwards, "A Temporary Alliance," 94.

[101] The regime did not want to do this and settled on a compromise by which Palestinians were given People's Army uniforms and trained by the regular army in secure training area. See Lamis Andoni, "Jordanians Clamor for Giving Weapons to People," *Christian Science Monitor,* October 18, 1990.

and portraying the battle as one between the Western and Islamic worlds. In its own statement the Brotherhood declared:

> The war did not start on 2 August. It began years ago when America decided to establish the new world order to prevent the establishment of the world Islamic order. The invasion decision is an old one. However, it was waiting for an appropriate pretext. Prophet Muḥammad, may God's peace and blessings be upon him, said the truth in his saying: You will be invaded by the yellow race under 80 banners, under which there will be 12,000 soldiers, as narrated by al-Bukhārī [one of the narrators of the Prophet's sayings]. There are approximately 700,000 soldiers in the Arabian peninsula now under the banner of Bush, who wants to increase this figure to 960,000 soldiers from the remainder of his reservists. . . .

In a dramatic warning to Western leaders, the Brotherhood went on to declare:

> O Bush, Baker and Major, the day of judgement has come, and God has sent you a nation that is experienced in war and fighting. A day in which God gave pride to Islam and raised the banner of monotheism, embroidered with Allāhu Akbar [God is Great].[102]

The king, in recognition of the powerful popular appeal and mobilizing force of the Brotherhood, as well as the need to react to intense public pressure, chose to placate the movement at this juncture by giving it a place in the cabinet. The Brotherhood was awarded five cabinet appointments, including the coveted education portfolio, religious affairs, health, social development and justice.[103]

On the international front, Muslim Brotherhood House Speaker ʿAbd al-Laṭīf ʿArabiyyāt was active in lobbying support for the Iraqi cause. He sent a cable of protest to the French government regarding its participation in the Western alliance.[104] He also sent messages to the Pakistani National Assembly, the Egyptian parliament, and the Turkish national assembly denouncing their support of the Western cause.[105] The Brotherhood's influence on the cabinet was also demonstrated by the Ministry of Trade's revival of trade with Iran. The minister affirmed in this

---

102 *Al Raʾy*, January 21, 1991.

103 *Jordan Times*, December 31, 1990.

104 *BBC SWB/ME/0982/7/8/* January 29, 1991.

105 *FBIS*, Amman Domestic Service in Arabic, January 19, 1991.

context Jordan's interest in the concept of an Islamic Common Market, a long time goal of Islamists.[106]

The Brotherhood's period of influence was short lived, however, lasting only six months. Having survived the Gulf War crisis, the regime turned in June of 1991 to reconsolidate its position at the expense of the Islamists. In general, the Jordanian regime found itself in a stronger situation after the war than in the previous year. The economy was showing signs of improvement. Foreign workers were being repatriated, creating work for returnees to Jordan. King Hussein's profile with the Palestinian population had improved considerably due to his strong stance against U.S. intervention. This allowed him to openly become involved in the Arab-Israeli peace process. In March 1991 the American congress had voted to cut Jordan's $55 million aid package due to his stance, although this decision was reversed by President Bush. In the ensuing months Hussein made it clear to the United States that he was eager to improve diplomatic and financial relations and it became clear that Jordan would play a major role in the peace process.

The king's decision to be involved in the peace process was a significant factor in his desire to limit the political influence of the Brotherhood who were, of course, strongly opposed to negotiations with Israel. The king took two important steps in June 1991 to circumscribe the Brotherhood's power. First, on June 17 he dismissed the cabinet of Prime Minister Badrān. He asked Foreign Minister Ṭāhir al-Maṣrī, a Palestinian supportive of a negotiated settlement with Israel, to form a new administration. Hussein then discouraged the Brotherhood from joining the government. The Brotherhood, as anticipated, refused to serve in a government which supported negotiations with Israel. In retaliation the Brotherhood tried, but failed, to lead a no-confidence vote in the parliament to defeat the government's accession.

The second important step taken by the king to delimit the Brotherhood's influence was the approval on June 9, 1991 of the National Charter. Limitations placed by the charter on external funding of Jordanian political parties were aimed in particular at the Muslim Brotherhood. The king acknowledged this in thinly-veiled references to Brotherhood, asserting that "the two contributors to the unsettling history of political pluralism in the Kingdom were outside control or financing and 'the conviction of each party at that time that it alone represented the

---

106 *FBIS*, February 25, 1991.

truth.'[107] He also commented, "Pluralism is the only guarantee against all forms of dictatorship and despotism, particularly despotism by one party. There is not a single party that can claim to possess the truth."[108] By opening up the political system to the organization of new parties the king signalled to the Brotherhood that the Islamic bloc would now face competition and that he would not allow the movement's influence to expand further.

The measures taken by the king in June of 1991 made it clear to the Muslim Brotherhood that its period of glory was over. In reviewing the movement's record in the January to June 1991 period it is clear that one of its most significant achievements was demonstrating its ability to mobilize popular support. The control of cabinet portfolios much enhanced the Brotherhood's mobilizational skills. During this six-month period the Brotherhood also proved its intention of carrying out Islamizing reforms, although its initiatives were limited. There are two major reasons for the limited nature of these reform initiatives. First, the Brotherhood ministers were preoccupied with the events of the Gulf War during this period. Second, the constraints placed on the Lower House by executive and senate veto ensured in the Spring of 1991 and afterwards that the Brotherhood's influence in parliament would be contained even in cases where the parliament approved draft laws endorsing Islamic reforms.

It did achieve control of investments of the Civil Defense Martyrs' Fund assets, and forced the national airline to stop serving alcohol on flights to other Muslim countries.[109] It obtained a government amendment banning the licensing of recreational centres, sports clubs and swimming pools that do not segregate men and women. But the Brotherhood was prevented from passing legislation prohibiting the production and distribution of alcohol. It was also unsuccessful in passing an amendment to the education law, banning co-education in Jordanian government and private schools. Likewise, the Brotherhood's advocacy of Islamic economic reforms fell on deaf ears.

Overall, the Muslim Brotherhood was most effective in working with other groups in parliament, for example, introducing legislation aimed at

---

107 *Jordan Times,* June 8, 1991.

108 "On the Record," *Middle East International* 402 (14 June, 1991): 14.

109 Mariam Shahin, "Ban on Coeducation Thwarted," *Middle East International* 446 (19 March 1993): 12.

government corruption and ministerial accountability.[110] The movement was prominent on the Committee for Public Liberties and its support was also instrumental in legislation including the Law of the Supreme Court which provided for any citizen to petition the court with a complaint about the government, and the Economic Crime Law which called for ministerial financial accountability.[111]

Tensions Below the Surface

After June 1991 the Brotherhood did not publicly challenge the measures taken against it by the regime. With a pragmatic eye to its self-preservation, the movement emphasized its policy of peaceful coexistence with the government. The Brotherhood made an effort to appease the regime, declaring itself ready for the time being to postpone Islamizing reforms and "to tune in with the society at large and avoid confrontation over issues which touch on the personal freedom of the more liberal Jordanians."[112] The Brotherhood expressed its concern that its policies in the cabinet of Prime Minister Muḍar Badrān may have caused Jordanians to fear its strength and emphasized that it would now adopt a more cautious attitude.[113] This approach of appeasement extended to parliament, where, for example, in January 1993 the majority of Muslim Brotherhood members voted in support of the government's International Monetary Fund draft budget despite their criticisms that it did not take into account what "God sanctioned and prohibited, adopting usury as one of it pillars."[114]

But in spite of the official state of coexistence between the Brotherhood and the regime, tensions simmered below the surface. The regime continued to monitor the movement closely through the intelligence services. The Brotherhood endured extensive censorship of

---

[110] Ḥassūnah, interview. When asked about the Brotherhood's achievements in parliament he said, "There is the legislation introduced to correct corruption. We have created laws such as the law which asks the administrator about his wealth." Likewise, Manṣūr pointed to the Brotherhood's contribution in enacting "general democratic laws" to ensure "the continuity of the democratic run [sic]."

[111] The Brotherhood's assessment and those of its critics regarding its implementation of Islamizing reforms is discussed below.

[112] Nermeen Murad, "Brotherhood Matures, Assumes New Positions in New Era," *Jordan Times*, December 30, 1991.

[113] Ibid.

[114] *Jordan Times*, January 5, 1993.

its weekly newspaper *al-Ribāṭ*. On February 17, 1992 the paper was banned. According to Jordanian authorities, they banned the issue because it "slandered some Arab leaders" (this issue included critical articles on Yāsir ʿArafāt and the Saudi regime).[115] A statement released by the editor of the newspaper Kamāl Rashīd claimed the issue was banned "because the paper talked about some Arab countries that practice repression and terrorism against the Islamic movements there, and because of the subjects dealing with (the Brotherhood's) rejection of the peace negotiations."[116] The newspaper was again banned on November 21, 1992. On this occasion the publishers of *al-Ribāṭ* claimed that the paper was banned because it contained an article about repression and torture conducted by the Tunisian authorities against the Islamists.[117]

In November of 1992 *al-Ribāṭ* published an editorial entitled "We and the Publications Department" (referring to the Ministry of Information). In this statement the newspaper's editors complained that they were continuing to suffer harassment by the Publications Department and asked the regime to tolerate dissenting views:

> What is strange and dumbfounding is that they ban us and grant permission to appear depending on their own criteria and without due consideration to dissenting views, as if *al-Ribāṭ* were expected to seek inspiration in its articles from their sensitivities, minds and desires. It seems that the paper is not expected to publish articles that fall in line with its policy which must reflect the fact that it is the mouthpiece of the Islamic Movement, the largest and most organized opposition group. . . . O publications and media officials, we have a pledge to make. We will neither slander, level charges, engage in character assassination, nor seek sedition and sensationalism. . . . In return for this, we want you to be democratic, and consequently to respect our ideas, and allow us to communicate them as we see fit, even if this were to run counter to your own views.[118]

Until the 1993 elections, tensions between the Muslim Brotherhood and regime were vented in the public forum mostly over seemingly insignificant matters. For example in June 1991 the minister of the interior decided to ban prayers in open fields. The reasons for this were not clear. The Brotherhood protested this development, describing it as "a dark cloud marring the democratic process in Jordan." After this event

---

115 *Jordan Times*, February 17, 1992.

116 Ibid.

117 *Jordan Times*, November 21, 1992.

118 *Al-Ribāṭ*, December 2, 1991.

the Brotherhood tried unsuccessfully to set in motion impeachment proceedings against the minister of interior.[119] In a similar case, the Muslim Brotherhood protested the decision of the Ministry of Interior to ban a festival of Islamic poetry planned by the movement.[120] But such protests over apparently minor issues belied the potential seriousness of tensions between the Brotherhood and the regime.

The Brotherhood's formation in December of 1992 of a political party, the Islamic Action Front (*al-jabha al-ᶜamal al-islāmī*) under the leadership of Dr. Isḥāq Farḥān, confirmed the movement's determination to keep on contesting elections and working through parliament. The formation of the Islamic Action Front (IAF) was necessitated by the provisions of the National Charter which legalized political parties but prohibited those with linkages outside Jordan. As the Muslim Brotherhood is an international organization it was incumbent upon the movement to create a new separate political entity. According to the Brotherhood the formation of the IAF was also necessitated by the fact that the movement was a group that concerned itself with "all aspects of life and thus cannot call itself a political party."[121] In accordance with the government's regulations the party would survive financially through donations and membership fees and would not accept external funding.[122]

The party's announced goals were, not surprisingly, identical to those of the Brotherhood. The party's founders were mostly Brotherhood members, although independent Islamists also joined. Party membership was open to Muslim and Christian males and females over the age of twenty-five. Indeed, the Brotherhood made a special claim to support the rights of women. The party by-laws stated that the IAF

> respects the female entity [sic] and will protect her legitimate rights . . . within the framework of an Islamic system and will allow her to participate in public

---

[119] *Jordan Times*, 18–19 June 1992.

[120] In an article in *al-Ribāṭ* Ḥamzah Manṣūr noted that the government had allowed many festivals and activities to be held by other organizations and asked the ministry of interior to "apologise for its irrational refusal" to allow the festival to take place. *al-Ribāṭ*, March 3, 1992.

[121] Statement by Ziyād Abū Ghanīmah reported in *The Jordan Times*, September 29, 1992.

[122] The government was concerned about the Brotherhood receiving funding from external sources, especially Saudi Arabia which had been rumoured to be supporting the movement for decades. The researcher has not been able to corroborate these rumours.

life in order to pave the way for the emergence of women's leadership in the political field.[123]

Nevertheless there were no women in the party's administration.[124]

The relationship between the Brotherhood and the Islamic Action Front was closer than the movement chose to admit. Although Farḥān maintained that the party had "no official coordination with the Brotherhood," it was clear that the party was dominated by the Brotherhood.[125] The structure of the party also mimicked almost exactly the organization of the Brotherhood. Isḥāq Farḥān, as general secretary, presided over an executive committee of seventeen elected by a parliament of 120 members, representing all the electoral districts of Jordan. Administrative branches of the party operated in each district often side by side with a Brotherhood branch.

The Brotherhood hoped that the formation of the IAF would help to improve its performance in parliament, but so far it has been unable to do so.

Assessment of the Muslim Brotherhood's Record

By the early months of 1993 the Brotherhood's political fortunes seemed to be in decline. The Brotherhood came under heavy criticism from all sides for its failure to deliver Islamic solutions to Jordan's economic and social woes. Some of the criticisms came from critics such as economist Dr. Fahd al-Fanik who was cynical about the Islamist platform from the beginning, finding in it no concrete solutions to political or economic problems. "Candidates of the Islamic solution are

---

123 IAF statement cited in the *Jordan Times*, December 9, 1992. In an interview with the author, Farḥān expressed his concern about the limited role of women, stating simply, "In principle we think we have done injustice to women but we are open to women. But because they are a minority in the sample of our founders they did not have a chance to be represented in the shūrā council or in the leadership. . . . This is a pity. I will do many things about it." Farḥān suggested the possibility of establishing a similar and parallel party organization for women having some links with the men's organization.

124 Farḥān told the researcher in April 1993 that there had been 12 or 13 female co-founders of the party. Efforts to contact these women or to establish their identities proved fruitless.

125 Shortly after its founding, the party experienced internal tensions between Islamist independents and Brotherhood members within the party, with 17 Islamist independents resigning from the IAF in protest after failing to win proportionate strength in the party's 120-member consultative assembly.

asked to offer something that will benefit people, not to offer something of no use," he wrote, criticizing that platform's treatment of economic issues "which was satisfied with repeating Arabic rhetoric that means nothing in practice and which has no connection with Islam."[126] The Brotherhood was challenged on the same grounds by independent Islamist Fu'ād Khalīfah who accused it of having failed miserably in parliament in the task of "supervising the government" and maintaining ministerial responsibility. "Islam is not the solution, it is a strategy. It is not a program," he said, pointing to the Brotherhood's failure to address pressing issues such as unemployment.[127] Another critic from a leftist perspective, journalist Sulṭān al-Ḥaṭṭāb, commented:

> They promised many things but they did not deliver very much. The king allowed them to participate in the cabinet to show people what they could do. The king was intelligent to take this step, he showed people they couldn't do anything.[128]

The Muslim Brotherhood was also heavily criticized for cooperating too readily with the regime. Such criticisms came mainly from other Islamists. The Liberation Party claimed that the Brotherhood had deviated from an acceptable Islamic path by recognizing the legitimacy of a monarchy which ruled without an Islamic constitution.[129] Islamist independent Shubaylāt argued that the Brotherhood had only "a rhetoric for change" and did not go far enough within the parliamentary system in challenging the regime. Parliamentary democracy could be acceptable from an Islamic political view but only if the system functioned freely and without the interference of the king. He stated:

> Although I accept the monarchy, I don't want the king to interfere. He interferes more and more. I stuck my neck out too much in parliament, saying this bluntly. . . . I am a critic of the Brotherhood, the Brotherhood made a blunder in their parliamentary behaviour. . . . Unlike the Brotherhood my positions are very close to what I say, and what I promise and I have stood for that. I have a good track record in doing what I believe an Islamist should do—defending everybody, whether Christian, Muslim or communist, defending his rights against the monster which is the government.[130]

---

126 *Al-Ra'y*, October 26, 1989.

127 Khalīfah, interview.

128 Sulṭān al-Ḥaṭṭāb, interview, tape recording, July 22, 1992; Amman, Jordan.

129 Samāra, interview.

130 Shubaylāt, interview.

Criticisms of the Brotherhood's ineffectiveness were reflected in elections. The movement sustained a considerable defeat in the Irbid municipal elections of 1992. The Islamists, who had dominated the municipality for more than a decade, returned only one out of twelve seats with a reform slate winning the remainder. As noted by analyst Rāmī Khūrī in the *Jordan Times*, the Brotherhood's defeat could be attributed in part to decision of the people of Irbid to hold the Islamists accountable as public servants:

> The voters probably decided that the last several councils, dominated by Islamists, did not respond fully to local people's needs. So the Islamists were unceremoniously thrown out of office. Their religious message remains valid, and their emotional appeal strong. But their job rating as public servants appears low. They need to improve their performance as politicians and administrators, not as religious leaders.[131]

The Brotherhood has naturally tried to defend its record in parliament. Members of the movement interviewed by the author in 1992 maintained a philosophical attitude towards their limited achievements in Islamizing reform. They pointed to the youthfulness of the parliament and also to the inexperience and unsuitability of some of their candidates. As Muslim Brotherhood spokesman Abū Ghanīmah stated:

> Frankly speaking I think our Brothers tried their best . . . to achieve our targets in parliament but we can't say they succeeded one hundred per cent and we can't say they failed. One of the reasons is that the new parliament came after twenty years of no parliament. Also, we have to say that some of our Brothers who came to the parliament were not suitable candidates and that made some of our Brothers angry. . . . The first year was a year of training to know the rules of the government.[132]

Other Brothers pointed to the need to take a gradual, long-term approach to Islamic reform. Brotherhood MP ʿAbdallāh ʿUqaylah rated the Brotherhood's performance in parliament as "satisfactory, not very good." But he said:

> We cannot just jump. . . . You cannot come and ask me to reform society in two or three years. Moreover we have a long way to go; We are approaching reform incrementally and we have to build institutions, encourage people to build institutions for Islamic law, social and cultural systems. . . .[133]

---

131 *Jordan Times*, May 19, 1992.

132 Abū Ghanīmah, interview.

133 ʿUqaylah, interview.

House speaker ʿArabiyyāt also stressed the Brotherhood's need of the cooperation of other members of parliament to achieve reform:

> We can only affect issues with cooperation from other MPs. . . . It is not within the plan to apply it directly but to resort to sharīʿah in certain issues. This is a characteristic of the Islamic movement bloc, gradual application of the sharīʿah.[134]

Overall, the Brotherhood maintained that its greatest contribution in the parliament of 1989 was, in the words of brotherhood MP Ḥamzah Manṣūr, "the achievement of the democratic run [sic]" and "support of the parliamentary process".[135] Another Brotherhood observer commented:

> I think their main goal is to maintain democracy as long as possible . . . , participation in the general welfare of the people in the parliamentary process. . . . At least in Jordan the Brotherhood can say something within the framework of a relationship with other groups and parties and the government itself.[136]

There is no doubt that the Brotherhood demonstrated in the 1989 to 1993 period that it was serious about working within the parliamentary system and that it considered liberalization of Jordanian politics to be in its best interests. But criticisms of the Brotherhood's failure to produce concrete solutions to specific problems and issues in Jordanian society are legitimate. The Muslim Brotherhood did not extend its parliamentary agenda much beyond the vaguely-defined principles of its campaign program—"Islam is the solution." The reforms it targeted were confined to anti-corruption legislation and the introduction of sharīʿah in limited areas such as gender segregation.

The Brotherhood's unimpressive record in parliament can be attributed in part to its political inexperience and ideological weakness as well as to the youthfulness of the parliamentary experiment in Jordan. But, to a greater extent, the movement's ineffectiveness is due to the limitations placed on it and on the parliament as a whole by the Jordanian regime. In this regard, a Yarmūk University poll conducted in the spring of 1992 found that disappointment with the Muslim Brotherhood was expressed within the larger scope of general disillusionment with the performance of parliament. Over 80% of people polled were not happy

---

134 ʿArabiyyāt, interview.

135 Manṣūr, interview.

136 Malkāwī, interview.

with the parliament, and nearly three-quarters felt that parliament had become a means for deputies to become cabinet ministers. Two-thirds wanted parliament dissolved and new elections held.[137]

In a sense the Jordanian regime's moves to contain the Muslim Brotherhood in the 1989 to 1993 period were a case in point of what John Esposito has referred in the context of Islamist experiences in Algeria and Tunisia as a policy of "risk-free democracy":

> At best the attitude of many rulers may be characterized, in the words of one Western diplomat, as an openness to "risk-free democracy"! Both the Tunisian and Algerian governments' management of political liberalization reflect this approach. Openness to government-controlled change—yes; openness to a change of government that would bring Islamic activists to power through democratic means—no. Opposition parties and groups are tolerated as long as they remain relatively weak or under government control and do not threaten the ruling party.[138]

Any prospect that the Jordanian regime might relax its position and allow greater freedom for Islamists and other parties was dashed in the period leading up to the elections of 1993. While a detailed analysis of events since 1993 is beyond the scope of this study, it is useful here to make brief mention of the policy pursued by the regime with regard to the elections in as much as it confirms a continuing commitment to containing the Muslim Brotherhood.

The central issue concerning Hussein in the months leading up to the November 1993 elections was that the Islamic Action Front might derive electoral support from opposition to the peace process.[139] As the Front was the only organization publicly opposed to the peace process, it was the political party most likely to garner support in this regard. The signing of the Israeli-Palestinian Declaration of Principles in Washington on September 13, 1993 provoked criticism of Hussein's involvement in the peace process from Transjordanians and Palestinians alike and threatened to deepen conflicts between them:

---

137 *Ittijāh al-Urdunniyyīn naḥwa al-aḥzāb al-siyāsiyyah.* Poll conducted by Dr. Muḥannā Ḥaddād, Department of Sociology, Yarmouk University, Irbid, Jordan, 1992.

138 John Esposito, *The Islamic Threat: Myth or Reality?* (Oxford: Oxford University Press, 1992), 187.

139 For a detailed discussion of Hussein's policy towards the Islamists in the 1993 elections see Frederic Charillon et Alain Mouftard, "Jordanie: les élections du 8 novembre 1993 et le processus de paix," *Maghreb-Machrek* 144 (avril-juin 1994): 40–54.

> Les premiers craignaient que les seconds ne profitent d'une dynamique favorable pour considérer le territoire jordanien comme terre palestinien, les seconds étaient partagés entre les pro-Arafat, accusant déjà le roi Hussein de regretter le succès des negociations, et les radicaux denoncent tout dialogue avec "l'enemi sioniste et americain."[140]

King Hussein took various steps to limit the Islamic Action Front's ability to capitalize on dissatisfaction with the peace talks during the 1993 elections. For example, he banned organized rallies in the weeks leading up to the campaign and forced the transfer of teachers who were members of the party so that they could not campaign in their own districts.[141]

Most significantly though, in August 1993 Hussein, amidst protestations from the Islamic Action Front and several other political parties, dissolved parliament and imposed a royal decree, changing the electoral law.[142] The modifications made to the 1986 law were designed to limit the electability of Islamists and to favor rural over urban representation. A system based on a single member district and the principle of one-person, one-vote replaced the previous system of proportional representation whereby each district elected a number of parliamentary deputies related to the size of the population. The government argued that the new system would be more democratic as it would eliminate unequal representation of the electoral districts and cancel the quota system for minorities.

---

[140] Ibid., 46. A *Jordan Times* headline of September 14, 1992 also declared "Peace Accords Bring Mixed Reaction in Jordan" and riots and demonstrations in support of Ḥamās broke out in Palestinian refugee camps.

[141] Charillon and Mouftard, "Jordanie: les élections," 44. A statement made by a group of 50 political activists following the elections accused the government "in a move reminiscent of the martial law mandate," of resorting to transferring employees from their places of living and work, barring candidates from exercising their legal rights of conducting election campaigns and exploiting the official media and security services which exercised pressure on the public in a bid to influence their voting tendencies. For a text of this statement see *Jordan Times*, November 3, 1993.

[142] *Jordan Times*, August 10, 1993. The dissolution of parliament without any legal justification was widely deplored by an alliance of different interests, headed by the Muslim Brotherhood:

> The coalition of political forces aligned against surrender and capitulation is following with deep concern the implication behind the government's decision to dissolve the Parliament three months before its mandate was due to end according to provisions of the Jordanian constitutions. The decision to dissolve the Lower House of Parliament coincided with a wide scale campaign aimed at paving the ground for a new Election Law and coupled with signs of satisfaction over these developments displayed by certain American circles.

The new electoral law proved, as the government had intended, to be "electorally fatal for the Islamists."[143] The one-person, one-vote system meant that electors could no longer simultaneously select candidates according to tribal/familial and ideological bases. This worked to the detriment of the Islamic Action Front and other ideological candidates who were often passed over in favour of familial ties. As a result the elections of 1993 returned a parliament dominated by Transjordanians, selected primarily on account of their familial or tribal connections and closely tied to the regime.[144] Only 24 of the 80 candidates in the 1989 parliament were reelected. The Islamic Action Front lost 7 of the seats it had held in the 1989 parliament.[145] Through manipulation the regime had succeeded in creating a parliament of Transjordanian loyalists. Palestinian representation on the cabinet was reduced.

In November of 1993 the Jordanian state was dominated by a triumvirate of the palace, the predominantly Transjordanian military and security forces, and the Transjordanian and Jordanized Palestinian business and bureaucratic elite.[146] These groups have dominated Jordan since the Mandate era and were only once seriously threatened, by the National Socialists in 1956.[147] Their durability attests primarily to the cunningness of King Hussein at coopting support through patronage and balancing the interests of competing Palestinian and Transjordanian interests.[148]

But by 1993 Hussein's delicate balancing act was on shaky ground. As discussed in Chapter One, the patronage system was being gradually eroded by the emergence of a new generation of Transjordanians with demands for greater political participation and an economic reward for its high level of education. This is also a generation characterized by "the

[143] Charillon and Mouftard, "Jordanie: les elections," 46.

[144] Charillon and Mouftard, "Jordanie: les elections," 42.

[145] Whereas 14 Islamists represented Amman's 7 districts in 1989, only 7 won in 1993. In Irbid, 5 Islamists won in 1989 and only 3 won in 1993. In Zarqa, an Islamist stronghold, the number of representatives remained the same (4). Karak had 6 Islamist candidates in 1989 and only 3 in 1993, Tafileh had 1 Islamist candidate in 1989 and 2 in 1993, Balqāʾ had 2 in 1989 and 1 in 1993. For a breakdown of the election results see *Jordanian Information Bureau: Election Results of the 12th Jordanian Parliament*, November 8, 1993.

[146] Garfinkle, "Nine Lives," 108.

[147] See the discussion of the situation in Jordan following the 1956 coup attempt, chapter one, 32–33.

[148] This was a style of government inherited from his grandfather ʿAbdallāh, as discussed in Chapter One.

emergence, tentative and almost shy, of a local, purely Jordanian nationalism" which threatens to widen the Jordanian-Palestinian rift in Jordanian society.[149] At the same time, the discrediting of the PLO, the participation of the Jordanian government in peace initiatives with Israel, and the defiant stance of Ḥamās, fuelled the rise of a radical Palestinian nationalism opposed to the Hashemite regime.

The above factors may not bode well for the political stability of Jordan in a post-Hussein era. In speculating about Jordan's future, the fundamental question remains as to what type of political institutions will endure, and both if and how the aspirations of the new Transjordanian and Palestinian generations will be expressed through them.

In 1993 the Muslim Brotherhood remained a growing force in Jordanian society, its popularity fuelled primarily by the economic and political frustrations of the educated new generation of Transjordanians and the hostility of Palestinians to Jordan's peace negotiations with Israel. But by the elections of 1993 it seemed that the Jordanian Muslim Brotherhood's pursuit of a gradualist-reformist agenda and its willingness to abide by the rules of a parliamentary system had not reaped good dividends. The movement was contained and coerced by a regime which realized, as a result of the election of 1989 and the events of 1991–92, that the Brotherhood was too popular to coopt within a free parliamentary democracy. The continued unwillingness of the Jordanian regime to allow the movement more political expression risks forcing the movement into opposition, as has been the case in other Arab states, notably Syria and Algeria. As one Jordanian Brotherhood member warned:

> The Brotherhood has to be understood and allowed to go out in the open. . . . State official institutions should recognize that after a balloon gets inflated it cannot be compressed again. It will only burst."[150]

---

149 Abu Jaber, "1989 Parliamentary Elections," 85.

150 Anonymous Muslim Brotherhood member, in a statement to *Jordan Times*, December 3–4, 1991.

Conclusion

This study has traced the history of the Jordanian Muslim Brotherhood from its founding in 1946 to its experience in the parliament of 1989–1993. In this period the Brotherhood evolved from a loose-knit group of merchants concerned with the jihād in Palestine into a mass-based Islamist party under professional leadership. Overall, this analysis has uncovered three significant trends in the history of the Brotherhood: the evolution of its symbiotic relations with the regime, its willingness to work for reform within a parliamentary system even though its ultimate goal is the creation of a "theo-democracy," and its ability to appeal to a broad sector of the population.

The development of symbiotic relations between the Muslim Brotherhood and the Jordanian monarchy owes much to the circumstances of the movement's founding. Its founder was a merchant of limited political ambitions who sought no confrontation with the regime. King ʿAbdallāh granted the movement legal status as a charitable organization because he wished to avoid the development of an Islamist opposition (as in the Egyptian case) and was eager to encourage Islamic as opposed to secular values and ideologies. The Hashemites' recourse to Islamic legitimacy was an important factor in sustaining cooperative relations with the Muslim Brotherhood. The regime sought to coopt the movement rather than risk an Islamist challenge to its legitimacy.

In the 1950s the symbiotic relations between the movement and the regime were cemented by the Brotherhood's new professional leadership and King Hussein. Two factors helped the regime to continue to coopt the Brotherhood in the 1950s. First, the ideology of the new leadership was reformist, stressing the gradual implementation of sharīʿah. As professionals, the leaders of the movement stressed change through education. They maintained the legitimacy of Hashemite rule. The future Islamic order was ill-defined and the goal of establishing an Islamic state downplayed. The vagueness of aspects of the Brotherhood's ideology reflected the movement's prioritization of action rather than theory. The Muslim Brotherhood has exhibited a strong pragmatic tendency throughout its history, has carefully guarded its legal status, and has avoided openly challenging the regime. Indeed, during the turbulent

1950s the Brotherhood demonstrated its loyalty to the monarchy by standing behind it in the face of the national socialist challenge. Second, Jordan's status as a constitutional monarchy helped the regime to coopt the Brotherhood by allowing it to participate in the parliaments of the 1950s. Although parliamentary life has been curtailed in Jordan, the premise of a pluralist system has never been abandoned by the regime and has provided the framework within which the Muslim Brotherhood evolved its commitment to working with democracy.

As a reward for its cooperation with the monarchy during the 1950s the Brotherhood was allowed to retain its legal status for the next three decades when political parties were outlawed. This legal status gave the movement great advantages. It had the opportunity during the 1960s and 1970s to build a mass support base through the creation of its own institutions and the infiltration of others, including the ministries of education and religious affairs. The Brotherhood also participated in the parliamentary elections of the 1980s as the only legal organization, placing it on higher ground than its fragmented secular opposition. But relations between the Brotherhood and the regime began to sour in the 1980s, as the regime, recognizing the movement's political potential, moved increasingly away from a policy of cooptation to one of containment.

A second, significant aspect of the Muslim Brotherhood's history has been its ability to appeal to a wide range of interests in Jordanian society. In particular, the movement has attracted two forces of support. First, its professional leadership has appealed to students or would-be professionals. Second, the movement's close links with Ḥamās and opposition to a negotiated diplomatic settlement with Israel have also assured it considerable support from Palestinians, especially in the refugee camps. The broad-base of the Muslim Brotherhood's support defies any single universal economic or political explanation. It militates against essentialist or reductionist views of the appeal of Islam. The Brotherhood's vague campaign slogan, "Islam is the solution," held a ring of authenticity for Jordanians (who are 92% Muslim) and captured in its net the economically, politically, socially, and spiritually frustrated. Its demands for political liberalization also considerably enhanced its appeal.

Finally, this study has demonstrated the willingness of the Muslim Brotherhood to work within a parliamentary system in order to achieve Islamizing reform. The Brotherhood's decision to work within parliament can be attributed primarily to practical considerations. This was the best way in which the movement could hope to influence the political system.

However, the Jordanian Muslim Brotherhood has been stymied by the regime in its attempts to work within parliament. As we have seen, the regime has contained the movement in the general context of its desire to suppress opposition forces demanding greater liberalization. But the movement has also been singled out by virtue of its Islamizing agenda which runs counter to the regime's pro-Western stance. In taking this position, the Jordanian monarchy is in the good company of other authoritarian regimes in the Arab world including Tunisia and Algeria, which have tentatively opened the doors to liberalization only to close them in the wake of Islamist successes. We have seen that the argument has been offered by some analysts in defense of these regimes that Islamists should be precluded from participation in parliaments as they do not envisage liberal democracy as their ultimate goal and they only wish to use elections as a stepping stone to authoritarian rule. This analysis confirms the general thesis that many contemporary Islamist movements, regardless of their public agendas, do not seek the creation of liberal democracies. The Jordanian Muslim Brotherhood is a case in point. Yet the movement has made no attempt to "highjack" the state. Instead it has consistently demonstrated throughout its fifty year history a willingness to work with the regime rather than against it. In this light, and in view of its significant support base, it may be a matter of considerable concern for the futures of both the Muslim Brotherhood and Jordan as a whole that the regime has prevented the movement from carrying out its mandate in parliament.

Bibliography

Primary Sources

British Government Documents

United Kingdom Foreign Office, FOR 371 110874. Duke to FO, June 15, 1954. Chancery, Amman to Levant Dept. "Report on a demonstration staged by the Muslim Brotherhood on June 13, in Amman."

United Kingdom Foreign Office, FOR 371.115684. Duke to FO, November 4, 1955.

United Kingdom Foreign Office, FOR 371 121464, Mr. Wikeley, Jerusalem to Foreign Office January 3, 1956 (No. 494).

United Nations Documents

UNESCO. International Yearbook of Education, 1952.

————. International Yearbook on Education, 1962.

————. International Yearbook of Education, 1968.

————. International Yearbook on Education, 1983.

————. UNESCO Statistical Yearbook, 1993.

Hashemite Kingdom of Jordan Documents

H.K.J. Ministry of Information Bureau: Election Results of the 12th Jordanian Parliament, November 8, 1993.

Newspapers

Ākhir Khabar

Christian Science Monitor

al-Dustūr

al-Kifāḥ al-Islāmī

al-Ḥayāt

Jordan Times

al-Raʾy

al-Ribāṭ

Ṣawt al-Shaʿb

Other Media

BBC, Summary of World Broadcasts. ME/0982/7/8; ME/0816/A2.

FBIS Daily Reports, Near East and South Asia, November 1954-December 1993.

Interviews

Abū Ghanīmah, Ziyād. Amman, Jordan, 13 April, 1992.
ʿArabiyyāt, ʿAbd al-Laṭif. Amman, Jordan, 29 June, 1992.
al-Bannā, Muḥammad. Irbid, Jordan, 25 June, 1992.
ʿAzzīzī, ʿIzzāt. Amman, Jordan, 12 November, 1991.
Al-ʿAẓm, Yūsuf. Amman, Jordan, 17 June, 1992.
Farḥān, Isḥāq. Amman, Jordan, February 15, 1993.
Fayyāḍ, Samīrah. Amman, Jordan, 28 March, 1992.
Ghūshah, Ibrāhīm. Amman, Jordan, 6 July, 1992.
Ḥassūnah, Yūsuf. Amman, Jordan, August 23, 1992.
Al-Ḥaṭṭāb, Sulṭān. Amman, Jordan, July 22, 1992.
Khalīfah, Fuʾād. Amman, Jordan, August 27, 1992.
Khalīfah, Muḥammad ʿAbd al-Raḥmān. Amman, Jordan, April 4, 1992.
Malkāwī, Fatḥī. Irbid, Jordan, 22 March, 1992.
Manṣūr, Ḥamzah. Amman, Jordan, June 30, 1992.
Rashīd, Kamāl. Amman, Jordan, April 14, 1992.
Al-Sakīd, Yūsuf. Amman, Jordan, February 21, 1993.
Shubaylāt, Layth. Amman, Jordan, April 29, 1992.
Tārūrī, Fuʾād. Amman, Jordan, 15 April, 1992.
ʿUqaylah, ʿAbdallāh. Amman, Jordan, 28 June, 1992.

Secondary Sources in Arabic

Abū Ghanīmah, Ziyād. *Dirāsah Wathāʾiqiyyah fī Ṣaḥīfat al-Kifāḥ al-Islāmī.* Amman: al-Maktab al-Islāmī, 1991.

al-Ghannūshī, Rashīd. *Ḥarakat al-Ittijāh al-Islāmī.* Kuwait: Dār al-Qalām, 1987.

Hamās. *Mawqifunā min al-taswiyah: bayyān al-Murshid al-ʿĀmm li-al-Ikhwān al-Muslimīn ḥawla uṭrūḥat al-taswiyah li-al-qaḍiyyah al-filasṭīniyyah.* Amman: al-Maktab al-ʿĀmm, 1991.

Ittijāh al-Urdunniyyīn naḥwa al-aḥzāb al-siyāsiyyah. Poll conducted by Dr. Muḥannā Ḥaddād, Department of Sociology, Yarmūk University, Irbid, Jordan, 1992.

Mūsā Zayd al-Kīlānī, al-Ḥarakah al-Islāmiyya fī al-Urdunn. Amman, 1990.

Markaz al-Urdunn al-Jadīd. *Dalīl al-Ḥayāt al-Ḥizbiyyah fī al-Urdunn: Jabha al-ʿAmal al-Islāmī.* Amman: Markaz al-Urdunn al-Jadīd, 1993.

Quṭb, Sayyid. *Maʿālim fī al-Ṭarīq.* Cairo: Dār al-Shurūq, 1980.

al-ʿUbaydī, ʿAwnī. *Jamāʿat al-Ikhwān al-Muslimīn fī al-Urdunn wa Filasṭīn.* Amman: al-Maktab al-Waṭaniyya, 1991.

Secondary Sources in English and French

Andoni, Lamis. "King Hussein Leads Jordan into a New Era," *Middle East International,* 17 November, 1989.

Abd Allah, Umar. *The Islamic Struggle in Syria.* Berkeley: Mizan Press, 1983.

Abed-Kotob, Sana. "The Accommodationists Speak: Goals and Strategies of the Muslim Brotherhood in Egypt." *IJMES* 27 (1995): 321–339.

Abidi, Aqil Hyder Hasan. *Jordan: A Political Study, 1948–1957.* London: Asia Publishing House, 1965.

Abu Amr, Ziyad. *Islamic Fundamentalism in the West Bank and Gaza: Muslim Brotherhood and Islamic Jihad.* Bloomington: Indiana University Press, 1994.

Abu Jaber, Kamel S. "The 1989 Jordanian parliamentary elections." *Orient* 31 (1990): 62–83.

————. "The Legislature in the Hashemite Kingdom of Jordan. A Study in Political Development." *Muslim World* LIX (July-October 1969): 220–231.

Abu Khalil, Asʿad. "The Incoherence of Islamic Fundamentalism: Arab Islamic Thought at the End of the Twentieth Century." *MEJ* 48 (Autumn, 1994): 677–94.

Amawi, Abla. "Democracy Dilemmas in Jordan." *MERIP* 174, (Jan-Feb, 1992): 26–29.

Anderson, Lisa. "Liberalism, Islam and the Arab State." *Dissent* (Fall, 1994): 439–444.

Arjomand, Said. *The Turban for the Crown: The Islamic Revolution in Iran.* New York: Oxford University Press, 1987.

Aruri, Naseer. *Jordan: A Study in Political Development 1921-1965.* The Hague: Martinus Nijhoff, 1972.

Badran, Adnan and Barbara Khader, eds. *The Economic Development of Jordan.* London: Croom Helm, 1987.

Bailey, Clinton. *Jordan's Palestinian Challenge: 1948–1983.* Boulder and London: Westview, 1984.

Al-Bannā, Ḥasān. *Five Tracts of Hasan al-Banna: 1906–1949.* Berkeley: University of California Press, 1978.

Belhassen, Souhayr. "Femmes tunisiennes islamistes." *Annuaire de l'Afrique du Nord, 1979.* Paris: Éditions du Centre National de la Recherche Scientifique, 1980: 138–143.

Bill, James A. and Robert Springborg. *Politics in the Middle East.* New York: Harper and Collins, 1994.

Boulby, Marion. "The Islamic Challenge: Tunisia Since Independence." *Third World Quarterly* 10 (April, 1988): 590–614.

Brynen, Rex. "Economic Crisis and Post-Rentier Democratization in the Arab World: The Case of Jordan." *Canadian Journal of Political Science,* 25 (1992): 624–626.

Calhoun, Craig, ed. *Comparative Social Research: A Research Annual. Religious Institutions.* London: JAI Press, 1991.

Charillon, Frederic et Alain Mouftard. "Jordanie: les élections du 8 novembre 1993 et le processus de paix." *Maghreb-Machrek* 144 (avril-juin, 1994): 40–54.

Cohen, Amnon. *Political Parties in the West Bank Under the Jordanian Regime, 1949–1967.* Ithaca: Cornell, 1982.

Combs-Schilling, Mary E. *Sacred Performances: Islam, Sexuality and Sacrifice.* New York: Columbia University Press, 1989.

Davis, Eric. "The Concept of Revival and the Study of Islam and Politics" in *The Islamic Impulse.* Barbara Stowasser, ed. London: Croom Helm, 1987.

Day, Arthur. *East Bank/West Bank: Jordan and the Prospects for Peace.* USA Council on Foreign Relations: New York, 1986.

Donohue, John and John Esposito, eds. *Islam in Transition.* New York: Oxford University Press, 1982.

Enayat, Hamid. *Modern Islamic Political Thought.* Austin: University of Texas Press, 1982.

Esposito, John. *The Islamic Threat: Myth or Reality?* Oxford: Oxford University Press, 1992.

Esposito, John."Islamic Revivalism," Occasional Paper No 3, *The Muslim World Today*. Washington: American Institute for International Affairs, 1993.

Findlay, Allan and Musa Samha. "Return Migration and Urban Change: A Jordanian Case Study" in *Return Migration and Regional Economic Problems*. Russell King, ed. London: Croom Helm, 1986: 171–184.

Garfinkle, Adam. "The Nine Lives of Hashemite Jordan" in *The Politics of Change in the Middle East*. Robert Satloff, ed. Oxford: Westview, 1993.

Gubser, Peter. *Politics and Change in Al-Karak, Jordan*. London: Oxford University Press, 1973.

————. *Jordan: Crossroads of Middle Eastern Events*. Boulder: Westview, 1983.

Haddad, Yvonne. "Sayyid Qutb: Ideologue of Islamic Revival" in *Voices of Resurgent Islam*. John Esposito, ed. New York: Oxford University Press, 1983: 67–89.

Halliday, Fred and Hamza Alavi, eds. *State and Ideology in the Middle East and Pakistan*. New York: Monthly Review Press, 1988.

Halpern, Manfred. *The Politics of Social Change in the Middle East and North Africa*. Princeton: Princeton University Press, 1963.

Hourani, Albert. *Arabic Thought in the Liberal Age, 1798–1939*. Cambridge: Cambridge University Press, 1962.

Hudson, Michael. "After the Gulf War: Prospects for Democratization in the Arab World." *Middle East Journal* 45 (Summer 1991): 407–421.

Huntington, Samuel P. "Will More Countries Become More Democratic?" *Political Science Quarterly*, 99 (Summer 1984): 193–218.

Husaini, Ishak Musha. *The Moslem Brethren*. Beirut, 1955.

Ibrahim, S. E. "Anatomy of Egypt's militant Islamic groups." *IJMES* 12 (December 1990): 423–453.

————. "Egypt's Islamic activism in the 1980s." *Third World Quarterly* 10 (April, 1988): 632–657.

Jones, L. W. "Demographic Review, Rapid Population Growth in Baghdad and Amman." *Middle East Journal* 23 (Spring, 1969): 209–215.

Kepel, Gilles. *The Prophet and the Pharaoh: Muslim Extremism in Egypt*. London: Al Saqi, 1985.

Kerr, Malcolm. *Islamic Reform: The Political and Legal Theories of Muhammad Abduh and Rashid Rida*. Berkeley: University of California Press, 1966.

Kramer, Gudrun. "Islamist Notions of Democracy." *MERIP* (July-August 1993): 2–8.

Kupferschmidt, Uri. *The Supreme Muslim Council: Islam Under the British Mandate for Palestine*. New York: Leiden, 1987.

Layne, Linda. *Home and Homeland: The Dialogics of Tribal and National Identities in Jordan*. Princeton: Princeton University Press, 1994.

————. *Elections in the Middle East: Implications of Recent Trends*. Boulder, 1987.

Lewis, Bernard. "Islam and Liberal Democracy." *The Atlantic Monthly* (February 1993): 89–98.

Marty, Martin E. and P. Scott Appleby, eds. *Fundamentalisms and the State*. Chicago: University of Chicago Press, 1993.

Mazur, Michael P. *Economic Growth and Development in Jordan*. Boulder: Westview, 1979.

Messara, Antoine. "La régulation étatique de la religion dans le monde arabe: le cas de la Jordanie." *Social Compass* 40 (April 1993): 581–588.

Milton Edwards, Beverley. "A Temporary Alliance with the Crown: The Islamic Response in Jordan" in *Islamic Fundamentalisms and the Gulf Crisis.* James Piscatori, ed. Chicago: American Academy of Arts, 1991.

Mitchell, Richard P. *The Society of the Muslim Brothers.* Oxford: Oxford University Press, 1969.

Moussali, Ahmad. "Hasan al-Turabi's Islamist Discourse on Democracy and Shura." *Middle Eastern Studies* 30 (January 1994): 57–61.

Munson, Henry. *Religion and Power in Morocco.* New Haven: Yale, 1993.

Piscatori, James. "Ideological Politics in Saudi Arabia" in *Islam in the Political Process.* James Piscatori, ed. Cambridge: Cambridge University Press, 1983.

Plascov, Avi. *The Palestinian Refugees in Jordan: 1948–1957.* London: Frank Cass and Co., 1981.

Ramadan, Abdel Aziz. "Fundamentalist Influence in Egypt: The Strategies of the Muslim Brotherhood and the Takfir Groups" in *Fundamentalisms and the State: Remaking Polities, Economics and Militancy.* Martin E. Marty and R. Scott Appleby, eds. Chicago: Chicago University Press, 1993.

Richards, Alan and John Waterbury. *A Political Economy of the Middle East: State, Class and Economic Development.* Boulder: Westview, 1990.

Robins, Phillip J. "Politics and the 1986 electoral law in Jordan," *Politics and the Economy in Jordan,* Rodney Wilson, ed. London: SOAS, 1991: 184–208.

Rogan, Eugene. "Physical Islamization of Amman." *Muslim World* 76 (January, 1986): 24–42.

Satloff, Robert. *From Abdullah to Hussein: Jordan in Transition.* Oxford: Oxford University Press, 1994.

Shadid, Mohammed K. "The Muslim Brotherhood Movement in the West Bank and Gaza." *Third World Quarterly* 10 (April 1988): 664–680.

Sivan, Emmanuel. *Radical Islam: Medieval Theory and Modern Politics.* New Haven: Yale University Press, 1985

Vandewalle, Dirk. "From the New State to the New Era." *Middle East Journal* 42 (Autumn, 1988): 602–620.

Vatikiotis, P. J. *Politics and the Military in Jordan: A Study of the Arab Legion (1921–1957).* New York: Praeger, 1967.

Voll, John Obert. *Islam, Continuity and Change in the Modern World.* Boulder, CO: Westview Press, 1982.

———. "Political Crisis in the Sudan." *Current History* 89, (April 1990): 546.

———. *Sudan, State and Society in Crisis,* Bloomington: Indiana University Press, 1993.

Waltz, Susan. "Islamist Appeal in Tunisia." *MEJ* 40, (Autumn, 1986): 651–670.

Wilson, Mary. *King Abdullah, Britain and the Making of Jordan.* Cambridge: Cambridge University Press, 1987.

Yorke, Valerie. *Domestic Politics and Regional Security: Jordan, Syria and Israel.* Aldershot: Gower, 1988.

———. "Hussein's bid to legitimise Hashemite rule." *Middle East International,* 17 November, 1989.

Zartman, William. "Democracy and Islam: The Cultural Dialectic." *ANNALS, AAPSS* (November 1992): 181–191.

Zghal, Alexander. "Le retour du sacré et la nouvelle demande idéologique des jeunes scolarisés." *Annuaire de l'Afrique du Nord, 1979.* Paris: Éditions du Centre National de la Recherche Scientifique, 1980: 41–64.

Zubaida, Sami. *Islam, the People and the State: Essays on Political Ideas and Movements in the Middle East.* London: Routledge, 1989.

INDEX

al-Saᶜīd, Nūrī, 70
al-Sakīd, Yūsūf, 82
Satloff, Robert, 4
Saᶜūd, (king of Saudi Arabia), 59
ibn Saᶜūd, ᶜAbd al-ᶜAziz, 13
Saudi Arabia, 20, 143, 148
Ṣawt al-Shaᶜb, 129
sharīᶜah, 38, 43, 54-55, 85, 115, 122, 124-26, 128-37, 141, 153-54, 158
Shubaylāt, Laith, 91, 99-100, 108, 142-43, 151-52
al-Sīlāwī, Suᶜād, 122
Springborg, Robert, 50
Sudan, 118, 136; Islamic National Front, 133-35
Suez Canal, 20, 26
Supreme Muslim Council, 40
Syria, 3, 6-7, 10, 13, 18, 20, 40-41, 101; Syrian Arab Independence Party, 7; Syrian Muslim Brotherhood, 49, 101, 106, 138

Ṭalāl (king of Jordan), 17-18
Tunisia, 109; Islamic Tendency Movement, 96-97, 135; al-Nahḍah, 118, 134-35, 137
al-Turābī, Ḥasan, 133-35
Turkey, 52, 144

ᶜUbaydī, Aḥmad, 31, 100
ᶜUlamāʾ, 56-57, 88-89
Union of Soviet Socialist Republics (USSR), 19, 22, 69
United Arab Republic (UAR), 22
United Kingdom, see Great Britain
United Nations, 15
United Nations Special Committee on Palestine (UNSCOP), 48, United Nations Educational, Scientific and Cultural Organization (UNESCO), 80-81
United States of America, 14, 20, 68-69, 120, 145; Point Four program, 64, 67, 84
University of Jordan, 29, 85-88, 90-91, 101
ᶜUqaylah, ᶜAbdallah, 99, 101

Vatikiotis, P. J., 8

Waltz, Susan, 96-97
West Bank: annexation by Abdullah, 5, 13-14, 24, 38, 50-51; Jordanian disengagement in 1988, 32-33, 104
Wilson, Mary, 50
World War II, 9, 11-12, 45, 50-51

Yarmūk University, 29, 99, 153
Yorke, Valerie, 32

abū Zant, ᶜAbd al-Munʾim, 122
Zartman, William, 135
Zghal, Alexander, 109
Zionism, Zionists, 41, 48, 119-20
Zorlu, Gatin, 62
Zubaida, Sami, 128

South Florida Studies in the History of Judaism

240001	Lectures on Judaism in the Academy and in the Humanities	Neusner
240002	Lectures on Judaism in the History of Religion	Neusner
240003	Self-Fulfilling Prophecy: Exile and Return in the History of Judaism	Neusner
240004	The Canonical History of Ideas: The Place of the So-called Tannaite Midrashim, Mekhilta Attributed to R. Ishmael, Sifra, Sifré to Numbers, and Sifré to Deuteronomy	Neusner
240005	Ancient Judaism: Debates and Disputes, Second Series	Neusner
240006	The Hasmoneans and Their Supporters: From Mattathias to the Death of John Hyrcanus I	Sievers
240007	Approaches to Ancient Judaism: New Series, Volume One	Neusner
240008	Judaism in the Matrix of Christianity	Neusner
240009	Tradition as Selectivity: Scripture, Mishnah, Tosefta, and Midrash in the Talmud of Babylonia	Neusner
240010	The Tosefta: Translated from the Hebrew: Sixth Division Tohorot	Neusner
240011	In the Margins of the Midrash: Sifre Ha'azinu Texts, Commentaries and Reflections	Basser
240012	Language as Taxonomy: The Rules for Using Hebrew and Aramaic in the Babylonia Talmud	Neusner
240013	The Rules of Composition of the Talmud of Babylonia: The Cogency of the Bavli's Composite	Neusner
240014	Understanding the Rabbinic Mind: Essays on the Hermeneutic of Max Kadushin	Ochs
240015	Essays in Jewish Historiography	Rapoport-Albert
240016	The Golden Calf and the Origins of the Jewish Controversy	Bori/Ward
240017	Approaches to Ancient Judaism: New Series, Volume Two	Neusner
240018	The Bavli That Might Have Been: The Tosefta's Theory of Mishnah Commentary Compared With the Bavli's	Neusner
240019	The Formation of Judaism: In Retrospect and Prospect	Neusner
240020	Judaism in Society: The Evidence of the Yerushalmi, Toward the Natural History of a Religion	Neusner
240021	The Enchantments of Judaism: Rites of Transformation from Birth Through Death	Neusner
240022	Åbo Addresses	Neusner
240023	The City of God in Judaism and Other Comparative and Methodological Studies	Neusner
240024	The Bavli's One Voice: Types and Forms of Analytical Discourse and their Fixed Order of Appearance	Neusner
240025	The Dura-Europos Synagogue: A Re-evaluation (1932-1992)	Gutmann
240026	Precedent and Judicial Discretion: The Case of Joseph ibn Lev	Morell
240027	Max Weinreich *Geschichte der jiddischen Sprachforschung*	Frakes
240028	Israel: Its Life and Culture, Volume I	Pedersen
240029	Israel: Its Life and Culture, Volume II	Pedersen
240030	The Bavli's One Statement: The Metapropositional Program of Babylonian Talmud Tractate Zebahim Chapters One and Five	Neusner

240031	The Oral Torah: The Sacred Books of Judaism: An Introduction: Second Printing	Neusner
240032	The Twentieth Century Construction of "Judaism:" Essays on the Religion of Torah in the History of Religion	Neusner
240033	How the Talmud Shaped Rabbinic Discourse	Neusner
240034	The Discourse of the Bavli: Language, Literature, and Symbolism: Five Recent Findings	Neusner
240035	The Law Behind the Laws: The Bavli's Essential Discourse	Neusner
240036	Sources and Traditions: Types of Compositions in the Talmud of Babylonia	Neusner
240037	How to Study the Bavli: The Languages, Literatures, and Lessons of the Talmud of Babylonia	Neusner
240038	The Bavli's Primary Discourse: Mishnah Commentary: Its Rhetorical Paradigms and their Theological Implications	Neusner
240039	Midrash Aleph Beth	Sawyer
240040	Jewish Thought in the 20th Century: An Introduction in the Talmud of Babylonia Tractate Moed Qatan	Schweid
240041	Diaspora Jews and Judaism: Essays in Honor of, and in Dialogue with, A. Thomas Kraabel	Overman/MacLennan
240042	The Bavli: An Introduction	Neusner
240043	The Bavli's Massive Miscellanies: The Problem of Agglutinative Discourse in the Talmud of Babylonia	Neusner
240044	The Foundations of the Theology of Judaism: An Anthology Part II: Torah	Neusner
240045	Form-Analytical Comparison in Rabbinic Judaism: Structure and Form in *The Fathers* and *The Fathers According to Rabbi Nathan*	Neusner
240046	Essays on Hebrew	Weinberg
240047	The Tosefta: An Introduction	Neusner
240048	The Foundations of the Theology of Judaism: An Anthology Part III: Israel	Neusner
240049	The Study of Ancient Judaism, Volume I: Mishnah, Midrash, Siddur	Neusner
240050	The Study of Ancient Judaism, Volume II: The Palestinian and Babylonian Talmuds	Neusner
240051	Take Judaism, for Example: Studies toward the Comparison of Religions	Neusner
240052	From Eden to Golgotha: Essays in Biblical Theology	Moberly
240053	The Principal Parts of the Bavli's Discourse: A Preliminary Taxonomy: Mishnah Commentary, Sources, Traditions and Agglutinative Miscellanies	Neusner
240054	Barabbas and Esther and Other Studies in the Judaic Illumination of Earliest Christianity	Aus
240055	Targum Studies, Volume I: Textual and Contextual Studies in the Pentateuchal Targums	Flesher
240056	Approaches to Ancient Judaism: New Series, Volume Three, Historical and Literary Studies	Neusner
240057	The Motherhood of God and Other Studies	Gruber
240058	The Analytic Movement: Hayyim Soloveitchik and his Circle	Solomon
240059	Recovering the Role of Women: Power and Authority in Rabbinic Jewish Society	Haas

240060	The Relation between Herodotus' *History* and Primary History	Mandell/Freedman
240061	The First Seven Days: A Philosophical Commentary on the Creation of Genesis	Samuelson
240062	The Bavli's Intellectual Character: The Generative Problematic: In Bavli Baba Qamma Chapter One And Bavli Shabbat Chapter One	Neusner
240063	The Incarnation of God: The Character of Divinity in Formative Judaism: Second Printing	Neusner
240064	Moses Kimhi: Commentary on the Book of Job	Basser/Walfish
240066	Death and Birth of Judaism: Second Printing	Neusner
240067	Decoding the Talmud's Exegetical Program	Neusner
240068	Sources of the Transformation of Judaism	Neusner
240069	The Torah in the Talmud: A Taxonomy of the Uses of Scripture in the Talmud, Volume I	Neusner
240070	The Torah in the Talmud: A Taxonomy of the Uses of Scripture in the Talmud, Volume II	Neusner
240071	The Bavli's Unique Voice: A Systematic Comparison of the Talmud of Babylonia and the Talmud of the Land of Israel, Volume One	Neusner
240072	The Bavli's Unique Voice: A Systematic Comparison of the Talmud of Babylonia and the Talmud of the Land of Israel, Volume Two	Neusner
240073	The Bavli's Unique Voice: A Systematic Comparison of the Talmud of Babylonia and the Talmud of the Land of Israel, Volume Three	Neusner
240074	Bits of Honey: Essays for Samson H. Levey	Chyet/Ellenson
240075	The Mystical Study of Ruth: *Midrash HaNe'elam* of the Zohar to the Book of Ruth	Englander
240076	The Bavli's Unique Voice: A Systematic Comparison of the Talmud of Babylonia and the Talmud of the Land of Israel, Volume Four	Neusner
240077	The Bavli's Unique Voice: A Systematic Comparison of the Talmud of Babylonia and the Talmud of the Land of Israel, Volume Five	Neusner
240078	The Bavli's Unique Voice: A Systematic Comparison of the Talmud of Babylonia and the Talmud of the Land of Israel, Volume Six	Neusner
240079	The Bavli's Unique Voice: A Systematic Comparison of the Talmud of Babylonia and the Talmud of the Land of Israel, Volume Seven	Neusner
240080	Are There Really Tannaitic Parallels to the Gospels?	Neusner
240081	Approaches to Ancient Judaism: New Series, Volume Four, Religious and Theological Studies	Neusner
240082	Approaches to Ancient Judaism: New Series, Volume Five, Historical, Literary, and Religious Studies	Basser/Fishbane
240083	Ancient Judaism: Debates and Disputes, Third Series	Neusner
240084	Judaic Law from Jesus to the Mishnah	Neusner
240085	Writing with Scripture: Second Printing	Neusner/Green
240086	Foundations of Judaism: Second Printing	Neusner

240087	Judaism and Zoroastrianism at the Dusk of Late Antiquity	Neusner
240088	Judaism States Its Theology	Neusner
240089	The Judaism behind the Texts I.A	Neusner
240090	The Judaism behind the Texts I.B	Neusner
240091	Stranger at Home	Neusner
240092	Pseudo-Rabad: Commentary to Sifre Deuteronomy	Basser
240093	FromText to Historical Context in Rabbinic Judaism	Neusner
240094	Formative Judaism	Neusner
240095	Purity in Rabbinic Judaism	Neusner
240096	Was Jesus of Nazareth the Messiah?	McMichael
240097	The Judaism behind the Texts I.C	Neusner
240098	The Judaism behind the Texts II	Neusner
240099	The Judaism behind the Texts III	Neusner
240100	The Judaism behind the Texts IV	Neusner
240101	The Judaism behind the Texts V	Neusner
240102	The Judaism the Rabbis Take for Granted	Neusner
240103	From Text to Historical Context in Rabbinic Judaism V. II	Neusner
240104	From Text to Historical Context in Rabbinic Judaism V. III	Neusner
240105	Samuel, Saul, and Jesus: Three Early Palestinian Jewish Christian Gospel Haggadoth	Aus
240106	What is Midrash? And a Midrash Reader	Neusner
240107	Rabbinic Judaism: Disputes and Debates	Neusner
240108	Why There Never Was a "Talmud of Caesarea"	Neusner
240109	Judaism after the Death of "The Death of God"	Neusner
240110	Approaches to Ancient Judaism	Neusner
240112	The Judaic Law of Baptism	Neusner
240113	The Documentary Foundation of Rabbinic Culture	Neusner
240114	Understanding Seeking Faith, Volume Four	Neusner
240115	Paul and Judaism: An Anthropological Approach	Laato
240116	Approaches to Ancient Judaism, New Series, Volume Eight	Neusner
240119	Theme and Context in Biblical Lists	Scolnic
240120	Where the Talmud Comes From	Neusner
240121	The Initial Phases of the Talmud, Volume Three: Social Ethics	Neusner
240122	Are the Talmuds Interchangeable? Christine Hayes's Blunder	Neusner
240123	The Initial Phases of the Talmud, Volume One: Exegesis of Scripture	Neusner
240124	The Initial Phases of the Talmud, Volume Two: Exemplary Virtue	Neusner
240125	The Initial Phases of the Talmud, Volume Four: Theology	Neusner
240126	From Agnon to Oz	Bargad
240127	Talmudic Dialectics, Volume I: Tractate Berakhot and the Divisions of Appointed Times and Women	Neusner
240128	Talmudic Dialectics, Volume II: The Divisions of Damages and Holy Things and Tractate Niddah	Neusner
240129	The Talmud: Introduction and Reader	Neusner
240130	*Gesher Vakesher*: Bridges and Bonds The Life of Leon Kronish	Green
240131	Beyond Catastrophe	Neusner

240132	Ancient Judaism, Fourth Series	Neusner
240133	Formative Judaism, New Series: Current Issues and Arguments Volume One	Neusner
240134	Sects and Scrolls	Davies
240135	Religion and Law	Neusner
240136	Approaches to Ancient Judaism, New Series, Volume Nine	Neusner
240137	Uppsala Addresses	Neusner
240138	Jews and Christians in the Life and Thought of Hugh of St. Victor	Moore
240140	Jews, Pagans, and Christians in the Golan Heights	Gregg/Urman
240141	Rosenzweig on Profane/Secular History	Vogel
240142	Approaches to Ancient Judaism, New Series, Volume Ten	Neusner
240143	Archaeology and the Galilee	Edwards/McCullough
240144	Rationality and Structure	Neusner
240145	Formative Judaism, New Series: Current Issues and Arguments Volume Two	Neusner
240146	Ancient Judaism, Religious and Theological Perspectives First Series	Neusner
240147	The Good Creator	Gelander
240148	The Mind of Classical Judaism, Volume IV, The Philosophy and Political Economy of Formative Judaism: The Mishnah's System of the Social Order	Neusner
240149	The Mind of Classical Judaism, Volume I, Modes of Thought:: Making Connections and Drawing Conclusions	Neusner
240150	The Mind of Classical Judaism, Volume II, From Philosophy to Religion	Neusner
241051	The Mind of Classical Judaism, Volume III, What is "Israel"? Social Thought in the Formative Age	Neusner
240152	The Tosefta, Translated from the Hebrew: Fifth Division, Qodoshim, The Order of Holy Things	Neusner
240153	The Theology of Rabbinic Judaism: A Prolegomenon	Neusner
240154	Approaches to Ancient Judaism, New Series, Volume Eleven	Neusner
240155	Pesiqta Rabbati: A Synoptic Edition of Pesiqta Rabbati Based upon all Extant Manuscripts and the Editio Princeps, V. I	Ulmer
240156	The Place of the Tosefta in the Halakhah of Formative Judaism: What Alberdina Houtman Didn't Notice	Neusner
240157	"Caught in the Act," Walking on the Sea, and The Release of Barabbas Revisited	Aus
240158	Approaches to Ancient Judaism, New Series, Volume Twelve	Neusner
240159	The Halakhah of the Oral Torah, A Religious Commentary, Introduction and Volume I, Part One, Between Israel and God	Neusner
240160	Claudian Policymaking and the Early Imperial Repression of Judaism at Rome	Slingerland
240161	Rashi's Commentary on Psalms 1–89 with English Translation, Introducion and Notes	Gruber
240162	Peace, In Deed	Garber/Libowitz
240163	Mediators of the Divine	Berchman
240164	Approaches to Ancient Judaism, New Series, Volume Thirteen	Neusner
240165	Targum Studies, Volume Two: Targum and Peshitta	Flesher
240166	The Text and I: Writings of Samson H. Levey	Chyet

240167	The Documentary Form-History of Rabbinic Literature, I. The Documentary Forms of Mishnah	Neusner
240168	Louis Finkelstein and the Conservative Movement	Greenbaum
240169	Invitation to the Talmud: A Teaching Book	Neusner
240170	Invitation to Midrash: The Workings of Rabbinic Bible Interpretation, A Teaching Book	Neusner
240171	The Documentary Form-History of Rabbinic Literature, II. The Aggadic Sector:Tractate Abot, Abot deRabbi Natan, Sifra, Sifré to Numbers and Sifré to Deuteronomy	Neusner
240172	The Documentary Form-History of Rabbinic Literature, III. The Aggadic Sector: Mekhilta Attributed to R. Ishmael and Genesis Rabbah	Neusner
240173	The Documentary Form-History of Rabbinic Literature, IV. The Aggadic Sector: Leviticus Rabbah and Pesiqta deRab Kahana	Neusner
240174	The Documentary Form-History of Rabbinic Literature, V. The Aggadic Sector: Song of Songs Rabbah, Ruth Rabbah, Lamentations Rabbati, and Esther Rabbah I	Neusner
240175	The Documentary Form-History of Rabbinic Literature, VI. The Halakhic Sector: The Talmud of the Land of Israel A. Tractates Berakhot and Shabbat through Taanit	Neusner
240176	The Documentary Form-History of Rabbinic Literature, VI. The Halakhic Sector: The Talmud of the Land of Israel B. Tractates Megillah through Qiddushin	Neusner
240177	The Documentary Form-History of Rabbinic Literature, VI. The Halakhic Sector: The Talmud of the Land of Israel C. Tractates Sotah through Horayot and Niddah	Neusner
240178	The Documentary Form-History of Rabbinic Literature, VII. The Halakhic Sector: The Talmud of the Land of Israel A. Tractates Berakhot and Shabbat through Pesahim	Neusner
240179	The Documentary Form-History of Rabbinic Literature, VII. The Halakhic Sector: The Talmud of Babylonia B. Tractates Yoma through Ketubot	Neusner
240180	The Documentary Form-History of Rabbinic Literature, VII. The Halakhic Sector: The Talmud of Babylonia C. Tractates Nedarim through Baba Mesia	Neusner
240181	The Documentary Form-History of Rabbinic Literature, VII. The Halakhic Sector: The Talmud of Babylonia D. Tractates Baba Batra through Horayot	Neusner
240182	The Documentary Form-History of Rabbinic Literature, VII. The Halakhic Sector: The Talmud of Babylonia E. Tractates Zebahim through Bekhorot	Neusner
240183	The Documentary Form-History of Rabbinic Literature, VII. The Halakhic Sector: The Talmud of Babylonia F. Tractates Arakhin through Niddah and Conclusions	Neusner
240184	Messages to Moscow: And Other Current Lectures on Learning and Community in Judaism	Neusner
240185	The Economics of the Mishnah	Neusner
240186	Approaches to Ancient Judaism, New Series, Volume Fourteen	Neusner
240187	Jewish Law from Moses to the Mishnah	Neusner
240188	The Language and the Law of God	Calabi

240189	Pseudo-Rabad: Commentary to Sifre Numbers	Basser
240190	How Adin Steinstalz Misrepresents the Talmud	Neusner
240191	How the Rabbis Liberated Women	Neusner
240192	From Scripture to 70	Neusner
240193	The Levites: Their Emergence as a Second-Class Priesthood	Nurmela
240194	Sifra	Ginsberg
240195	Approaches to Ancient Judaism, New Series, Volume Fifteen	Neusner
240196	What, Exactly, Did the Rabbinic Sages Mean by the "Oral Torah"?	Neusner

South Florida Academic Commentary Series

243001	The Talmud of Babylonia, An Academic Commentary, Volume XI, Bavli Tractate Moed Qatan	Neusner
243002	The Talmud of Babylonia, An Academic Commentary, Volume XXXIV, Bavli Tractate Keritot	Neusner
243003	The Talmud of Babylonia, An Academic Commentary, Volume XVII, Bavli Tractate Sotah	Neusner
243004	The Talmud of Babylonia, An Academic Commentary, Volume XXIV, Bavli Tractate Makkot	Neusner
243005	The Talmud of Babylonia, An Academic Commentary, Volume XXXII, Bavli Tractate Arakhin	Neusner
243006	The Talmud of Babylonia, An Academic Commentary, Volume VI, Bavli Tractate Sukkah	Neusner
243007	The Talmud of Babylonia, An Academic Commentary, Volume XII, Bavli Tractate Hagigah	Neusner
243008	The Talmud of Babylonia, An Academic Commentary, Volume XXVI, Bavli Tractate Horayot	Neusner
243009	The Talmud of Babylonia, An Academic Commentary, Volume XXVII, Bavli Tractate Shebuot	Neusner
243010	The Talmud of Babylonia, An Academic Commentary, Volume XXXIII, Bavli Tractate Temurah	Neusner
243011	The Talmud of Babylonia, An Academic Commentary, Volume XXXV, Bavli Tractates Meilah and Tamid	Neusner
243012	The Talmud of Babylonia, An Academic Commentary, Volume VIII, Bavli Tractate Rosh Hashanah	Neusner
243013	The Talmud of Babylonia, An Academic Commentary, Volume V, Bavli Tractate Yoma	Neusner
243014	The Talmud of Babylonia, An Academic Commentary, Volume XXXVI, Bavli Tractate Niddah	Neusner
243015	The Talmud of Babylonia, An Academic Commentary, Volume XX, Bavli Tractate Baba Qamma	Neusner
243016	The Talmud of Babylonia, An Academic Commentary, Volume XXXI, Bavli Tractate Bekhorot	Neusner
243017	The Talmud of Babylonia, An Academic Commentary, Volume XXX, Bavli Tractate Hullin	Neusner
243018	The Talmud of Babylonia, An Academic Commentary, Volume VII, Bavli Tractate Besah	Neusner

243019	The Talmud of Babylonia, An Academic Commentary, Volume X, Bavli Tractate Megillah	Neusner
243020	The Talmud of Babylonia, An Academic Commentary, Volume XXVIII, Bavli Tractate Zebahim A. Chapters I through VII	Neusner
243021	The Talmud of Babylonia, An Academic Commentary, Volume XXI, Bavli Tractate Baba Mesia, A. Chapters I through VI	Neusner
243022	The Talmud of Babylonia, An Academic Commentary, Volume XXII, Bavli Tractate Baba Batra, A. Chapters I through VI	Neusner
243023	The Talmud of Babylonia, An Academic Commentary, Volume XXIX, Bavli Tractate Menahot, A. Chapters I through VI	Neusner
243024	The Talmud of Babylonia, An Academic Commentary, Volume I, Bavli Tractate Berakhot	Neusner
243025	The Talmud of Babylonia, An Academic Commentary, Volume XXV, Bavli Tractate Abodah Zarah	Neusner
243026	The Talmud of Babylonia, An Academic Commentary, Volume XXIII, Bavli Tractate Sanhedrin, A. Chapters I through VII	Neusner
243027	The Talmud of Babylonia, A Complete Outline, Part IV, The Division of Holy Things; A: From Tractate Zabahim through Tractate Hullin	Neusner
243028	The Talmud of Babylonia, An Academic Commentary, Volume XIV, Bavli Tractate Ketubot, A. Chapters I through VI	Neusner
243029	The Talmud of Babylonia, An Academic Commentary, Volume IV, Bavli Tractate Pesahim, A. Chapters I through VII	Neusner
243030	The Talmud of Babylonia, An Academic Commentary, Volume III, Bavli Tractate Erubin, A. ChaptersI through V	Neusner
243031	The Talmud of Babylonia, A Complete Outline, Part III, The Division of Damages; A: From Tractate Baba Qamma through Tractate Baba Batra	Neusner
243032	The Talmud of Babylonia, An Academic Commentary, Volume II, Bavli Tractate Shabbat, Volume A, Chapters One through Twelve	Neusner
243033	The Talmud of Babylonia, An Academic Commentary, Volume II, Bavli Tractate Shabbat, Volume B, Chapters Thirteen through Twenty-four	Neusner
243034	The Talmud of Babylonia, An Academic Commentary, Volume XV, Bavli Tractate Nedarim	Neusner
243035	The Talmud of Babylonia, An Academic Commentary, Volume XVIII, Bavli Tractate Gittin	Neusner
243036	The Talmud of Babylonia, An Academic Commentary, Volume XIX, Bavli Tractate Qiddushin	Neusner
243037	The Talmud of Babylonia, A Complete Outline, Part IV, The Division of Holy Things; B: From Tractate Berakot through Tractate Niddah	Neusner

243038	The Talmud of Babylonia, A Complete Outline, Part III, The Division of Damages; B: From Tractate Sanhedrin through Tractate Shebuot	Neusner
243039	The Talmud of Babylonia, A Complete Outline, Part I, Tractate Berakhot and the Division of Appointed Times A: From Tractate Berakhot through Tractate Pesahim	Neusner
243040	The Talmud of Babylonia, A Complete Outline, Part I, Tractate Berakhot and the Division of Appointed Times B: From Tractate Yoma through Tractate Hagigah	Neusner
243041	The Talmud of Babylonia, A Complete Outline, Part II, The Division of Women; A: From Tractate Yebamot through Tractate Ketubot	Neusner
243042	The Talmud of Babylonia, A Complete Outline, Part II, The Division of Women; B: From Tractate Nedarim through Tractate Qiddushin	Neusner
243043	The Talmud of Babylonia, An Academic Commentary, Volume XIII, Bavli Tractate Yebamot, A. Chapters One through Eight	Neusner
243044	The Talmud of Babylonia, An Academic Commentary, XIII, Bavli Tractate Yebamot, B. Chapters Nine through Seventeen	Neusner
243045	The Talmud of the Land of Israel, A Complete Outline of the Second, Third and Fourth Divisions, Part II, The Division of Women, A. Yebamot to Nedarim	Neusner
243046	The Talmud of the Land of Israel, A Complete Outline of the Second, Third and Fourth Divisions, Part II, The Division of Women, B. Nazir to Sotah	Neusner
243047	The Talmud of the Land of Israel, A Complete Outline of the Second, Third and Fourth Divisions, Part I, The Division of Appointed Times, C. Pesahim and Sukkah	Neusner
243048	The Talmud of the Land of Israel, A Complete Outline of the Second, Third and Fourth Divisions, Part I, The Division of Appointed Times, A. Berakhot, Shabbat	Neusner
243049	The Talmud of the Land of Israel, A Complete Outline of the Second, Third and Fourth Divisions, Part I, The Division of Appointed Times, B. Erubin, Yoma and Besah	Neusner
243050	The Talmud of the Land of Israel, A Complete Outline of the Second, Third and Fourth Divisions, Part I, The Division of Appointed Times, D. Taanit, Megillah, Rosh Hashannah, Hagigah and Moed Qatan	Neusner
243051	The Talmud of the Land of Israel, A Complete Outline of the Second, Third and Fourth Divisions, Part III, The Division of Damages, A. Baba Qamma, Baba Mesia, Baba Batra, Horayot and Niddah	Neusner
243052	The Talmud of the Land of Israel, A Complete Outline of the Second, Third and Fourth Divisions, Part III, The Division of Damages, B. Sanhedrin, Makkot, Shebuot and Abldah Zarah	Neusner
243053	The Two Talmuds Compared, II. The Division of Women in the Talmud of the Land of Israel and the Talmud of Babylonia, Volume A, Tractates Yebamot and Ketubot	Neusner

243054	The Two Talmuds Compared, II. The Division of Women in the Talmud of the Land of Israel and the Talmud of Babylonia, Volume B, Tractates Nedarim, Nazir and Sotah	Neusner
243055	The Two Talmuds Compared, II. The Division of Women in the Talmud of the Land of Israel and the Talmud of Babylonia, Volume C, Tractates Qiddushin and Gittin	Neusner
243056	The Two Talmuds Compared, III. The Division of Damages in the Talmud of the Land of Israel and the Talmud of Babylonia, Volume A, Tractates Baba Qamma and Baba Mesia	Neusner
243057	The Two Talmuds Compared, III. The Division of Damages in the Talmud of the Land of Israel and the Talmud of Babylonia, Volume B, Tractates Baba Batra and Niddah	Neusner
243058	The Two Talmuds Compared, III. The Division of Damages in the Talmud of the Land of Israel and the Talmud of Babylonia, Volume C, Tractates Sanhedrin and Makkot	Neusner
243059	The Two Talmuds Compared, I. Tractate Berakhot and the Division of Appointed Times in the Talmud of the Land of Israel and the Talmud of Babylonia, Volume B, Tractate Shabbat	Neusner
243060	The Two Talmuds Compared, I. Tractate Berakhot and the Division of Appointed Times in the Talmud of the Land of Israel and the Talmud of Babylonia, Volume A, Tractate Berakhot	Neusner
243061	The Two Talmuds Compared, III. The Division of Damages in the Talmud of the Land of Israel and the Talmud of Babylonia, Volume D, Tractates Shebuot, Abodah Zarah and Horayot	Neusner
243062	The Two Talmuds Compared, I. Tractate Berakhot and the Division of Appointed Times in the Talmud of the Land of Israel and the Talmud of Babylonia, Volume C, Tractate Erubin	Neusner
243063	The Two Talmuds Compared, I. Tractate Berakhot and the Division of Appointed Times in the Talmud of the Land of Israel and the Talmud of Babylonia, Volume D, Tractates Yoma and Sukkah	Neusner
243064	The Two Talmuds Compared, I. Tractate Berakhot and the Division of Appointed Times in the Talmud of the Land of Israel and the Talmud of Babylonia, Volume E, Tractate Pesahim	Neusner
243065	The Two Talmuds Compared, I. Tractate Berakhot and the Division of Appointed Times in the Talmud of the Land of Israel and the Talmud of Babylonia, Volume F, Tractates Besah, Taanit and Megillah	Neusner
243066	The Two Talmuds Compared, I. Tractate Berakhot and the Division of Appointed Times in the Talmud of the Land of Israel and the Talmud of Babylonia, Volume G, Tractates Rosh Hashanah and Moed Qatan	Neusner
243067	The Talmud of Babylonia, An Academic Commentary, Volume XXII, Bavli Tractate Baba Batra, B. Chapters VII through XI	Neusner
243068	The Talmud of Babylonia, An Academic Commentary, Volume XXIII, Bavli Tractate Sanhedrin, B. Chapters VIII through XII	Neusner
243069	The Talmud of Babylonia, An Academic Commentary, Volume XIV, Bavli Tractate Ketubot, B. ChaptersVII through XIV	Neusner

243070	The Talmud of Babylonia, An Academic Commentary, Volume IV, Bavli Tractate Pesahim, B. Chapters VIII through XI	Neusner
243071	The Talmud of Babylonia, An Academic Commentary, Volume XXIX, Bavli Tractate Menahot, B. Chapters VII through XIV	Neusner
243072	The Talmud of Babylonia, An Academic Commentary, Volume XXVIII, Bavli Tractate Zebahim B. Chapters VIII through XV	Neusner
243073	The Talmud of Babylonia, An Academic Commentary, Volume XXI, Bavli Tractate Baba Mesia, B. Chapters VIII through XI	Neusner
243074	The Talmud of Babylonia, An Academic Commentary, Volume III, Bavli Tractate Erubin, A. ChaptersVI through XI	Neusner
243075	The Components of the Rabbinic Documents: From the Whole to the Parts, I. Sifra, Part One	Neusner
243076	The Components of the Rabbinic Documents: From the Whole to the Parts, I. Sifra, Part Two	Neusner
243077	The Components of the Rabbinic Documents: From the Whole to the Parts, I. Sifra, Part Three	Neusner
243078	The Components of the Rabbinic Documents: From the Whole to the Parts, I. Sifra, Part Four	Neusner
243079	The Components of the Rabbinic Documents: From the Whole to the Parts, II. Esther Rabbah I	Neusner
243080	The Components of the Rabbinic Documents: From the Whole to the Parts, III. Ruth Rabbah	Neusner
243081	The Components of the Rabbinic Documents: From the Whole to the Parts, IV. Lamemtations Rabbah	Neusner
243082	The Components of the Rabbinic Documents: From the Whole to the Parts, V. Song of Songs Rabbah, Part One	Neusner
243083	The Components of the Rabbinic Documents: From the Whole to the Parts, V. Song of Songs Rabbah, Part Two	Neusner
243084	The Components of the Rabbinic Documents: From the Whole to the Parts, VI. The Fathers According to Rabbi Nathan	Neusner
243085	The Components of the Rabbinic Documents: From the Whole to the Parts, VII. Sifré to Deuteronomy, Part One	Neusner
243086	The Components of the Rabbinic Documents: From the Whole to the Parts, VII. Sifré to Deuteronomy, Part Two	Neusner
243087	The Components of the Rabbinic Documents: From the Whole to the Parts, VII. Sifré to Deuteronomy, Part Three	Neusner
243088	The Components of the Rabbinic Documents: From the Whole to the Parts, VIII. Mekhilta Attributed to Rabbi Ishmael, Part One	Neusner
243089	The Components of the Rabbinic Documents: From the Whole to the Parts, VIII. Mekhilta Attributed to Rabbi Ishmael, Part Two	Neusner
243090	The Components of the Rabbinic Documents: From the Whole to the Parts, VIII. Mekhilta Attributed to Rabbi Ishmael, Part Three	Neusner
243092	The Components of the Rabbinic Documents: From the Whole to the Parts, IX. Genesis Rabbah, Part One, Introduction and Chapters One through Twenty-two	Neusner

243093 The Components of the Rabbinic Documents: From the Whole to the Parts, IX. Genesis Rabbah, Part Two, Chapters Twenty-three through Fifty — Neusner

243094 The Components of the Rabbinic Documents: From the Whole to the Parts, IX. Genesis Rabbah, Part Three, Chapters Fifty-one through Seventy-five — Neusner

243095 The Components of the Rabbinic Documents: From the Whole to the Parts, X. Leviticus Rabbah, Part One , Introduction and Parashiyyot One through Seventeen — Neusner

243096 The Components of the Rabbinic Documents: From the Whole to the Parts, X. Leviticus Rabbah, Part Two, Parashiyyot Eighteen through Thirty-seven — Neusner

243097 The Components of the Rabbinic Documents: From the Whole to the Parts, X. Leviticus Rabbah, Part Three, Topical and Methodical Outline — Neusner

243098 The Components of the Rabbinic Documents: From the Whole to the Parts, XI. Pesiqta deRab Kahana, Part One, Introduction and Pisqaot One through Eleven — Neusner

243099 The Components of the Rabbinic Documents: From the Whole to the Parts, XI. Pesiqta deRab Kahana, Part Two, Pisqaot Twelve through Twenty-eight — Neusner

243100 The Components of the Rabbinic Documents: From the Whole to the Parts, XI. Pesiqta deRab Kahana, Part Three, A Topical and Methodical Outline — Neusner

243101 The Components of the Rabbinic Documents: From the Whole to the Parts, IX. Genesis Rabbah, Part Four, Chapters Seventy-six through One Hundred — Neusner

243102 The Components of the Rabbinic Documents: From the Whole to the Parts, IX. Genesis Rabbah, Part Five, A Methodical and Topical Outline; Bereshit through Vaere, Chapters One through Fifty-seven — Neusner

243103 The Components of the Rabbinic Documents: From the Whole to the Parts, IX. Genesis Rabbah, Part Six, A Methodical and Topical Outline; Hayye Sarah through Miqqes, Chapters Fifty-eight through One Hundred — Neusner

243104 The Components of the Rabbinic Documents: From the Whole to the Parts, XII., Sifré to Numbers, Part One, Introduction and Pisqaot One through Seventy-one — Neusner

243105 The Components of the Rabbinic Documents: From the Whole to the Parts, XII., Sifré to Numbers, Part Two, Pisqaot Seventy-two through One Hundred Twenty-two — Neusner

243106 The Components of the Rabbinic Documents: From the Whole to the Parts, XII., Sifré to Numbers, Part Three, Pisqaot One Hundred Twenty-three through One Hundred Sixty-one — Neusner

243107 The Components of the Rabbinic Documents: From the Whole to the Parts, XII., Sifré to Numbers, Part Four, A Topical and Methodical Outline — Neusner

243108 The Talmud of the Land of Israel: An Academic Commentary of the Second, Third, and Fourth Divisions, I. Yerushalmi Tractate Berakhot (Based on the Translation by Tzvee Zahavy) — Neusner

243109	The Talmud of the Land of Israel: An Academic Commentary of the Second, Third, and Fourth Divisions, II. Yerushalmi Tractate Shabbat. A. Chapters One through Ten	Neusner
243110	The Talmud of the Land of Israel: An Academic Commentary of the Second, Third, and Fourth Divisions, II. Yerushalmi Tractate Shabbat. B. Chapters Eleven through Twenty-Four and The Structure of Yerushalmi Shabbat	Neusner
243111	The Talmud of the Land of Israel: An Academic Commentary of the Second, Third, and Fourth Divisions, III. Yerushalmi Tractate Erubin	Neusner
243112	The Talmud of the Land of Israel: An Academic Commentary of the Second, Third, and Fourth Divisions, IV. Yerushalmi Tractate Yoma	Neusner
243113	The Talmud of the Land of Israel: An Academic Commentary of the Second, Third, and Fourth Divisions, V. Yerushalmi Tractate Pesahim A. Chapters One through Six, Based on the English Translation of Baruch M. Bokser with Lawrence Schiffman	Neusner
243114	The Talmud of the Land of Israel: An Academic Commentary of the Second, Third, and Fourth Divisions, V. Yerushalmi Tractate Pesahim B. Chapters Seven through Ten and The Structure of Yerushalmi Pesahim, Based on the English Translation of Baruch M. Bokser with Lawrence Schiffman	Neusner
243115	The Talmud of the Land of Israel: An Academic Commentary of the Second, Third, and Fourth Divisions, VI. Yerushalmi Tractate Sukkah	Neusner
243116	The Talmud of the Land of Israel: An Academic Commentary of the Second, Third, and Fourth Divisions, VII. Yerushalmi Tractate Besah	Neusner
243117	The Talmud of the Land of Israel: An Academic Commentary of the Second, Third, and Fourth Divisions, VIII. Yerushalmi Tractate Taanit	Neusner
243118	The Talmud of the Land of Israel: An Academic Commentary of the Second, Third, and Fourth Divisions, IX. Yerushalmi Tractate Megillah	Neusner
243119	The Talmud of the Land of Israel: An Academic Commentary of the Second, Third, and Fourth Divisions, X. Yerushalmi Tractate Rosh Hashanah	Neusner
243120	The Talmud of the Land of Israel: An Academic Commentary of the Second, Third, and Fourth Divisions, XI. Yerushalmi Tractate Hagigah	Neusner
243121	The Talmud of the Land of Israel: An Academic Commentary of the Second, Third, and Fourth Divisions, XII. Yerushalmi Tractate Moed Qatan	Neusner
243122	The Talmud of the Land of Israel: An Academic Commentary of the Second, Third, and Fourth Divisions, XIII. Yerushalmi Tractate Yebamot, A. Chapters One through Ten	Neusner
243123	The Talmud of the Land of Israel: An Academic Commentary of the Second, Third, and Fourth Divisions, XIII. Yerushalmi Tractate Yebamot, B. Chapters Eleven through Seventeen	Neusner

243124	The Talmud of the Land of Israel: An Academic Commentary of the Second, Third, and Fourth Divisions, XIV. Yerushalmi Tractate Ketubot	Neusner
243125	The Talmud of the Land of Israel: An Academic Commentary of the Second, Third, and Fourth Divisions, XV. Yerushalmi Tractate Nedarim	Neusner
243126	The Talmud of the Land of Israel: An Academic Commentary of the Second, Third, and Fourth Divisions, XVI. Yerushalmi Tractate Nazir	Neusner
243127	The Talmud of the Land of Israel: An Academic Commentary of the Second, Third, and Fourth Divisions, XVII. Yerushalmi Tractate Gittin	Neusner
243128	The Talmud of the Land of Israel: An Academic Commentary of the Second, Third, and Fourth Divisions, XVIII. Yerushalmi Tractate Qiddushin	Neusner
243129	The Talmud of the Land of Israel: An Academic Commentary of the Second, Third, and Fourth Divisions, XIX. Yerushalmi Tractate Sotah	Neusner
243130	The Talmud of the Land of Israel: An Academic Commentary of the Second, Third, and Fourth Divisions, XX. Yerushalmi Tractate Baba Qamma	Neusner

South Florida-Rochester-Saint Louis Studies on Religion and the Social Order

245001	Faith and Context, Volume 1	Ong
245002	Faith and Context, Volume 2	Ong
245003	Judaism and Civil Religion	Breslauer
245004	The Sociology of Andrew M. Greeley	Greeley
245005	Faith and Context, Volume 3	Ong
245006	The Christ of Michelangelo	Dixon
245007	From Hermeneutics to Ethical Consensus Among Cultures	Bori
245008	Mordecai Kaplan's Thought in a Postmodern Age	Breslauer
245009	No Longer Aliens, No Longer Strangers	Eckardt
245010	Between Tradition and Culture	Ellenson
245011	Religion and the Social Order	Neusner
245012	Christianity and the Stranger	Nichols
245013	The Polish Challenge	Czosnyka
245014	Islam and the Question of Minorities	Sonn
245015	Religion and the Political Order	Neusner
245016	The Ecology of Religion	Neusner
245017	The Shaping of an American Islamic Discourse	Waugh/Denny
245018	The Muslim Brotherhood and the Kings of Jordan, 1945–1993	Boulby
245019	Muslims on the Americanization Path	Esposito/Haddad
245020	Protean Prejudice: Anti-semitism in England's Age of Reason	Glassman
245021	The Study of Religion: In Retrospect and Prospect	Green
245024	Jacques Ellul on Religion, Technology and Politics: Conversations with Patrick Troude-Chastenet	France

South Florida International Studies in Formative Christianity and Judaism

242501	The Earliest Christian Mission to 'All Nations'	La Grand
242502	Judaic Approaches to the Gospels	Chilton
242503	The "Essence of Christianity"	Forni Rosa
242504	The Wicked Tenants and Gethsemane	Aus
242505	A Star Is Rising	Laato
242506	Romans 9–11: A Reader-Response Analysis	Lodge
242507	The Good News of Peter's Denial	Borrell
242509	Romans 8:18–30: "Suffering Does Not Thwart the Future Glory"	Gieniusz